THE FALL OF TOULON

Unusually for one who has spent a lifetime in naval scientific research, Bernard Ireland has maintained a parallel enthusiasm for naval history. Over some thirty years, he has written more than two dozen books on various aspects of naval history and technology, including *Warships of the Age of Sail*. Now retired, he can devote more time to writing and to (too many) other interests. He lives with his wife on the Hampshire coast, pleasurably near to his adult son and daughter.

THE FALL OF
TOULON

*The last opportunity
to defeat the
French Revolution*

BERNARD IRELAND

CASSELL

Cassell Military Paperbacks

Cassell
Wellington House, 125 Strand
London WC2R 0BB

1 3 5 7 9 10 8 6 4 2

Copyright © 2005

First published in 2005
by Weidenfeld & Nicolson
This Cassell Military Paperbacks edition 2006

British Library Cataloguing-in-Publication Data.
A catalogue record for this book is available from the British Library.

ISBN-13 978-0-3043-6726-9
ISBN-10 0-3043-6726-5

Printed and bound in Great Britain by
Cox & Wyman Ltd, Reading, Berkshire

The Orion Publishing Group's policy is to use papers that are natural,
renewable and recyclable products and made from wood grown in sus-
tainable forests. The logging and manufacturing processes are expected
to conform to the environmental regulations of the country of origin.

www.orionbooks.co.uk

Contents

List of Illustrations

EUROPE AT THE END OF THE EIGHTEENTH CENTURY

Atlantic Ocean

NORWAY SWEDEN

Christiania

Gothenburg

Abo
Helsingfors St Petersburg
Stockholm Revel

RUSSIAN EMPIRE

Riga

North Sea

Glasgow
Edinburgh

DENMARK
Copenhagen Malmö

Baltic Sea

Vilna Smolensk

Königsberg Minsk
Danzig

GREAT BRITAIN

Bristol
London

Hamburg
HANOVER
Berlin
Stettin
PRUSSIA

POLAND

Warsaw

Kiev

NETHERLANDS
Antwerp
Austrian Netherlands
Aachen
Frankfurt

SAXONY

Prague

Cracow

Galicia

Vinnitsa

Cherbourg

Brest
Quiberon Orleans
Paris
Metz

BAVARIA
Munich

Vienna

HABSBURG EMPIRE
Buda

Hungary

Jassy

Moldavia

FRANCE

Rochefort
Limoges

Geneva
SWITZERLAND

Transylvania

Wallachia
Bucharest

Lyon
PIEDMONT
Turin
Milan Venice
Genoa
Bordeaux

Nice
Leghorn
(Livorno) Florence
Ravenna

Belgrade
Nish

OTTOMAN EMPIRE

Varna

Constantinople

Toulouse

Marseille
Toulon
TUSCANY
PAPAL STATES
Adriatic Sea
Ragusa

Salonica

SPAIN

Barcelona

Corsica
Ajaccio

Rome

Janina

Aegean Sea
Smyrna

Valencia

Minorca
Mahón

PIEDMONT

Naples Taranto

Patras Athens

Balearic Is.

Cagliari

KINGDOM OF NAPLES
AND SICILY
Palermo

Cartagena

Sicily Catania

Crete

Mediterranean Sea

Algiers

Tunis

Oran

0   400 miles
0   400 km

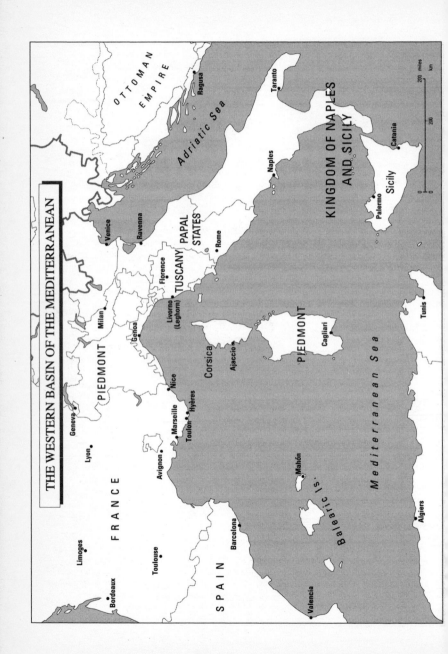

THE WESTERN BASIN OF THE MEDITERRANEAN

OTTOMAN EMPIRE

Ragusa

Adriatic Sea

Taranto

KINGDOM OF NAPLES AND SICILY

Naples

Catania

Sicily

Palermo

Venice
Ravenna

PAPAL STATES

Rome

TUSCANY

Florence

Livorno (Leghorn)

Genoa

Tunis

PIEDMONT

Milan

Geneva

Corsica

Ajaccio

PIEDMONT

Cagliari

FRANCE

Lyon

Nice

Marseille
Toulon Hyères

Avignon

Mediterranean Sea

Mahón

Limoges

Barcelona

Balearic Is.

Toulouse

SPAIN

Algiers

Bordeaux

Valencia

200 miles
200 km

10

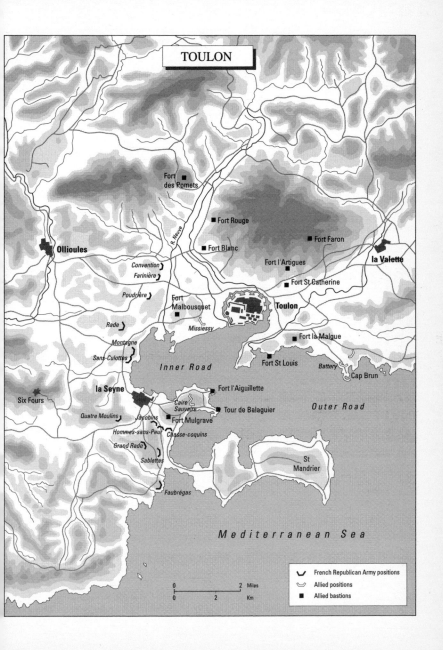

TOULON

Fort
des Pomets

R. Neuve

Fort Rouge

Ollioules

Fort Blanc

Fort Faron

Convention
Farinière
Fort l'Artigues

la Valette

Poudrière

Fort St Catherine

Fort
Malbousquet

Rade

Toulon

Montagne

Missiessy

Sans-Culottes

Fort la Malgue

Inner Road

Fort St Louis

Battery

la Seyne

Cap Brun

Six Fours

Fort l'Aiguillette

Outer Road

Caire
Sauveur

Quatre Moulins

Tour de Balaguier

Jacobins

Fort Mulgrave

Hommes-sans-Peur

Chasse-coquins

Grand Rade

Sablettes

St
Mandrier

Faubrégas

Mediterranean Sea

French Republican Army positions
Allied positions
Allied bastions

0   2 Miles
0   2   Km

11

Foreword

EARLY IN 1793, Revolutionary France declared war on Great Britain and, by so doing, added her to a coalition of enemies. In classic response, the Royal Navy was charged with blockading the French fleet in its various bases. Then, after only six months of hostilities, Vice Admiral Lord Hood, lying off Toulon in the Mediterranean, received a French deputation. It came with the extraordinary offer of delivering up to the British the town, its arsenal and the French Mediterranean fleet that lay within.

The background to this incredible act of treason is complex, the events that followed it heroic and ultimately tragic. Its primary cause was rooted, inevitably, in the tumultuous events of the French Revolution, its extremism and its excesses. To comprehend what happened in Toulon, it is thus necessary to have an insight into an upheaval which, far from unifying the French nation, plunged it into civil war.

A naval squadron and its dockyard are pillars of state authority and hardly likely to be surrendered meekly, without any pretence of opposition. None the less, this happened. To understand why, one needs to look carefully at the French navy of the time. Following a very respectable showing during the American War of Independence, it then withered under the destructive blast of France's own revolution, which reached down into every stratum and facet of society and armed service.

For the complete picture, a brief portrait of the Royal Navy of the period provides not only an interesting counterpoint to that of the French navy, but goes far to explain its general attitudes. The handing over of a considerable portion of France's battle fleet gave the British, gratis, the equivalent of a major naval victory. That they took little advantage of it is one of the most intriguing, and perhaps even now not fully explained, puzzles of naval history.

Like all good stories, therefore, the strange episode of the Royal Navy and the four-month occupation of Toulon has several threads, at first apparently only tenuously connected. Each of these has been pursued in turn in this book, tracing their individual strands until their coming together in the climactic events on the French Mediterranean coast at the end of 1793. In following these separate paths, it is inevitable that there is overlap. Some events may thus be viewed from 'either side of the hill', leading to apparent contradictions in national interpretation. Such is the stuff of history.

If Admiral Hood discovered (to misquote Nelson) that there were no laurels to be garnered at Toulon, the opposite was true for the young Napoleon Buonaparte, for whom the campaign was heaven-sent. Seizing the day, he was able to demonstrate for the first time those qualities that would, so shortly, catapult him to greatness.

Acknowledgements

INDISPENSABLE HELP was given by the staffs at the naval collections and archives in Gosport, Portsmouth (both at the Central Library and in the Dockyard Museum Library), in the British Library at Boston Spa and the London Library in St James's, the National Maritime Museum at Greenwich, the Army Collection and Museum in Aldershot and the Musée de la Marine in both Paris and Toulon.

In particular, however, the author is grateful to the staff at Fareham Public Library, who never failed to track down even the most obscure text or publication. It is reassuring to discover that, despite every government initiative, the national library system remains alive and well.

There is, of course, a huge and varying range of literature dealing with the events of those unstable times. Of all the titles consulted, those that are of most immediate value are listed in the bibliography. To all their various authors, alive or dead, named or anonymous, this author remains indebted.

Finally, as ever, he would like to recognize the support, patience and sheer hard work of his wife, for whom long-established keyboard skills had now to be allied with the mysteries of MS Word 2002.

Bernard Ireland
FAREHAM, MARCH 2005

PART ONE *The Background*

chapter one

Revolution 1789–93

INSURRECTION AND REVOLUTION are conceived on a bed of discontent, for although a people may long endure injustices with little more than complaint, the effect is cumulative. As with steam leaking into a closed vessel, relief is ultimately essential if catastrophe is to be averted.

For ordinary French people in 1789 there were abundant reasons for resentment. And before them, as a perfect model of what could be done about it, stood the recent example of the United States of America. As with the French monarchy and nobility in France itself, the British rulers of colonial America had been extraordinarily unperceptive to legitimate grievances. Many of the colonists were third generation, and a completely new society had developed on the American east coast, a society which considered itself 'American' rather than expatriate British. Government from London was regarded increasingly as out of touch and an interference in local affairs.

Having lost much of their overseas empire to the British in the Seven Years' War (1756–63), the French saw in the American revolt a chance to embarrass their traditional enemy and, possibly, to regain territory. Beginning with shipments of weapons, French intervention extended to a significant naval presence and, ultimately, to a division of troops. For the young marquis de Lafayette, 'to harm England is to serve, dare I say revenge, my country'.

Less defeated than wearily accepting that a continuance of the struggle was simply not worth the candle, Britain agreed to liberal terms at the Peace of Versailles, signed in 1783. Superior regular forces, directed without commitment, had proved impotent in the face of revolutionary fervour.

The American peace commissioners, while acknowledging their fledgling nation's debt to France, were justly wary of the latter's experienced foreign minister, who sought to make French support indispensable to the future of the United States. In reality, the British and the new Americans, despite their differences, were closely bound by family ties, and the commissioners shrewdly laid the foundations of a solid and continuing relationship.

To Great Britain, the political loss of the colonies had been a major blow but, to the poorly informed population at large, it was generally a matter of indifference. To many of those involved at an intermediate level, there was positive relief as the peace resolved a lengthy period of contention.

Driven by the genius of the younger Pitt, Britain sought to repair the financial ravages of the wider conflict, of which the struggle of the American colonies had been but one aspect. Within a decade, the flow of British commerce, including that with the United States, had increased by over 50 per cent. By virtue of a ground-breaking treaty, signed in 1786, this even included trade with the French.

For France, the outcome of the American question was less than fully satisfactory. Not only had poor territorial concessions been written into the peace terms but also, for those with vision, something more dangerous was apparent. France had assisted at the birth of an egalitarian society. In the new United States, where hereditary right to office had been abolished, all that mattered was the ability of the individual. With the abandonment of titles, rich and poor, academic and artisan, co-existed in easy relationship. Comparing this with his own stifled society, the average Frenchman might take pleasure at its harmony, but thinking men were troubled at the effect that such ideas might have should they take root at home. This was, after all, still the Age of Enlightenment. Invention and industry promised a bright future, free from the agrarian grind that was the lot of so many. And above all, it was the age of ideas.

From an absolute monarchy at the top, the French people supported layers of old and new aristocracy, national, regional and local officialdom, trade guilds, restrictive practices and profiteering middlemen. Bribes and preferments were the accepted path to a tolerable life but, for the bulk of ordinary folk, living a hand-to-mouth existence, there could be no stake in this society; they could only endure its iniquities. The Court presided over an effectively bankrupt exchequer yet its excesses, affairs and intrigues provided a major source of popular interest. Of respect and authority, it enjoyed none.

Already straitened by war, French finances were strained further by the need to maintain both the army and navy at a high standard in order to capitalize on possibilities stemming from the recent peace treaty. Too much was wasted, however, through profligacy, graft and incompetence. In addition, a succession of poor harvests had seen the price of grain rocket, arousing a hostile response from the populace at what it perceived as resulting profiteering by the merchants. It was no time for the king, Louis XVI, to be imposing extra taxes.

Needing sound advice, Louis agreed to a suggestion to reconvene the ancient Assembly of Notables. Meeting in February 1787, its 144 members were drawn mainly from the senior aristocracy and clergy, as well as politicians and industrialists. Their brief was uncomplicated: to define the problem, then to agree a solution and its manner of execution. The main difficulty would be in selling the strategy to an alienated public whose popular press depicted the assembly as a gathering of poultry meeting to discover how it was to be plucked and cooked.

The assembly's deliberations were in no way assisted by current events in the nearby Netherlands. Here, too, the populace was bent on the abolition of inherited rights to office and, in its ordered fashion, was pursuing its objective with a maximum of demonstration and a minimum of violence.

During the American Revolution, the rulers of the Netherlands, the Stadholders, had, predictably, supported the British position while public opinion generally sided with that of the colonists. Demands for greater representation of the people were couched in terms that echoed strongly those of the American Declaration of Independence – of liberty being an 'unalienable right' of all citizens, and of the sovereign being no more than 'the vote of the People'.

The Dutch House of Orange had strong marital links with British and Prussian royalty, and there existed a powerful temptation for the French to muddy the waters in order to cause British embarrassment. They held back, however, as their fragile economy was too dependent upon loans raised at favourable rates on the Amsterdam money market.

In May 1787, however, matters in the Netherlands became more heated, skirmishes following when 'patriots' put Princess Wilhelmina under house arrest. As the French postured but took no action due to the potential cost of war, Prussian troops moved in and restored order with little trouble. The patriot leaders were declared ineligible for any public office, although they and their followers had, for the most part, already fled to France where, as refugees, they added to the general air of unrest.

To the Dutch of the United Provinces the situation had not altered and remained ripe for change. For the French, the affair was embarrassing, not least because the chief minister, in vetoing military action on grounds of expense had in effect subsumed the absolute power of the monarch. Implicit was a growing realization that the monarchy could survive only by accepting some form of constitutional restraint, with power exercised through an assembly of representatives.

Following intense debate, the Assembly of Notables concluded that, although the current fiscal climate made heavier tax impositions inevitable, this had to be accompanied by a higher degree of representation on the part of those to be taxed. It also proposed that the income level that determined an individual's right to vote should be reduced to enfranchise a greater number.

Recognizing its own ephemeral status, the assembly also accepted the need for a permanent, parliamentary-style body. The model for this, the Estates General, had last met in 1614. As envisaged, it was calculated that the new assembly could be functioning by 1792 but, in the current highly charged atmosphere, three years or more was a long time.

With a mandate to slash costs, the assembly's representatives closed royal properties and abolished sinecure posts for Court favourites. Hordes of 'pensioners' and minor functionaries were removed from swollen payrolls. As though this was insufficient to alienate a sorely tried monarchy, the first steps were also taken to accept Protestantism as a legitimate religion in France.

The fiasco of French non-involvement in the recent Dutch crisis had brought about the resignation of the army and the navy ministers, both able men. A result was the emergence of the polymath comte de Guibert as *de facto* deputy minister of war. Guibert's vision was to remodel the French army in both its philosophy and its organization. He foresaw that military operations would no longer be centred on set piece battles, fought by regular armies on a limited field and with choreographed manoeuvres. Land war would be more fluid, a mobile affair that would heed the constraints of geography rather than those of national frontiers. He envisaged that conflict would demand a nation's total mobilization, its standing army expanded by a mass of conscripted citizenry.

As the current army list was bloated with time-servers of aristocratic origin, Guibert effected great savings by pensioning them off. He closed the effete central army academy in favour of a number of new schools in the provinces which were intended for candidates from the provincial gentry rather than from the aristocracy. A host of sinecure appointments, created by successive monarchs for favourite courtiers, were declared void on the death of their incumbents. Some of the funds thus saved were devoted to improving the pay and conditions of the ranks. In return, however, they were subjected to a new and more severe code of discipline and punishment.

In the long term, Guibert's convictions would be proved correct but an institution of the size of the French army had huge natural inertia. Forcing it on to a massive change of course required considerable counter energy and the acceptance of widespread discontent at all levels while the reforms took root.

While the Assembly of Notables made some progress in reform, it failed to agree and implement a fair land tax. Its director-general of finance, Charles-Alexandre de Colonne, laid bare the true extent of the national deficit before moving to abolish those abuses 'of the widest extent, [which] enjoy the greatest protection, have the deepest roots and the most spreading branches'. It was, perhaps, inevitable that his progress would be impeded by some powerful members of the assembly itself, who sought to safeguard personal privilege. These had the ear of the king, who exhibited his usual capacity for vacillation before finally bowing to the inevitable. In April 1787, Colonne was dismissed and replaced by Loménie de Brienne, the Archbishop of Toulouse. Having tried and failed to float a less radical agenda, he dissolved the assembly in May.

Laws and royal edicts required the approval of one of the thirteen high courts of *parlement*. Brienne approached that of Paris but here ran into trouble, its senior figures arguing that the opportunity should be taken to challenge the absolute authority of the monarch. Any new plans for taxation, they argued, must be the responsibility of the Estates General, which must include a high proportion of commoners, the so-called Third Estate. Their obstinacy on the issue struck a chord with the populace, which created individual heroes. Pamphlets, posters, the press and street theatre all lampooned authority. This responded with a heavy hand, unsuccessfully seeking to defuse the issue through a physical relocation of the *parlement*.

Emboldened by public acclaim, the Paris *parlement* told the king in April 1788 that his will alone was insufficient to make law, and that the Estates General must be involved. Gravely displeased, Louis's response was to limit the powers and functions of the middle-ranking judiciary that formed the core of the *parlements*.

This was followed, on 6 May, by the arrest of the most influential members of each of these bodies. The courts themselves had been surprised, even dismayed, by the volume of public support that they suddenly attracted as catalysts of a greater process, a growing popular revolt at what was held to be a repressive regime. If anything, feelings ran higher in the provinces than in the capital.

Through the so-called *lits de justice* (literally 'beds of justice'; in reality, a royal hearing), the king possessed the ultimate power to overrule intransigent *parlements* and, days after the arrests, he invoked these to enforce his will. The public mood was now dangerously volatile and, on 7 June, the powder train was ignited when a military detachment was sent to arrest magistrates of the Grenoble *parlement*. Business came to a standstill as townsfolk rallied to prevent the arrests. Insults and scuffles escalated to stone-throwing. Injuries to soldiers led, inevitably, to shots being fired. The reformers had their first martyrs.

Anxious to defuse the situation, the local *intendant* (provincial administrator) and the military governor offered to withdraw the troops on condition that the magistrates volunteered their own arrest. Well aware that matters were getting out of control, the latter were ready to comply but by now the mob was calling the tune. It was the governor who had to leave, his residence then being comprehensively sacked. The triumphant townsfolk then installed what, by this time, must have been thoroughly apprehensive magistrates in their courthouse for a special sitting.

Omens were bad. The events at Grenoble had shown how easily control could break down in the face of mass disobedience, and how little stomach the military had for firing on unarmed civilians. For would-be reformers of the system, they also demonstrated how easily matters could spiral beyond their control.

Tax collection became almost impossible as disobedience and distur-bance became general. Brienne appealed to the clergy for their calming influence, only to be told that they disagreed with government's reforms. In July 1788 he announced that the Estates General would be summoned the following May. He then resigned.

For the interim, the king relented and re-established the *parlements* with full powers. He ran into immediate trouble, however, when the obdurate Paris *parlement* declared that the estates, when they met, must do so in their traditional form. This meant that the three constituent bodies – the nobility, the clergy and the commoners (the Third Estate) – should have equal numbers of representatives. The first two could thus always collude to out-vote the third, maintaining privilege and crushing popular aspirations. This situation could no longer be tolerated, and what had begun as a disagreement between the king and the aristocracy had widened into one setting the privileged against the unprivileged. Fiery public debate demanded that the Third Estate would have to be equal in number to the other two combined and for voting to be by a simple head count as opposed to one vote per grouping. In the framing of the hoped-for new national constitu-tion, the people were insisting on a fair say. By the end of the year the king had acceded to the first demand, although doubts remained as to how the voting itself would be organized. Selection of deputies began early in 1789.

At over 1,200 strong, the Estates General was large. The nobles were not of the Court but were wealthy landowners, mostly conservative, a few liberal. Eighty per cent of the clergy were parish priests, in touch with the congregations that they served but, like the nobility, keen in general to safeguard their existing rights. For the most part, commoners were pro-fessional people of some substance. The Estates General's remit appeared rea-sonable enough, including the retention of the monarchy, albeit one stripped of its absolute authority. There would be an assault on official waste and, importantly, the people would be given a voice in the future framing of its affairs.

During 1788 France had experienced exceptional weather, sufficiently extreme to be a national disaster. Lashing summer hailstorms followed by drought had ruined both vines and grain. Poor harvests had then preceded a particularly severe winter when mills, dependent upon water power but completely frozen, were unable to produce flour. The thaw had then resulted in floods. Inevitably, the price of staples had risen beyond the capacity of working folk to pay. Destitution and debt were followed by mass evictions. The widespread deprivation was also widely blamed on hoarders and speculators withholding stocks until such time as they could be released for maximum profit. General unrest provided a fertile field for agitators of all persuasions.

Wishing to improve matters, the king invited each parish to submit a *cahier* (or register) of grievances upon which the work of the Estates General would be based. Overall, these proved to be remarkably consistent and noble in sentiment. In taxation, all should be treated equally with no exemption due to privilege. All government expenditure should be accountable. Imposition of taxes should be a matter for the Estates General, which should henceforth meet regularly as a national assembly. Land reform and a national education policy also figured largely. But what emerged above all was a desire for freedom of speech, for individuals as much as for the press.

At Versailles on 2 May 1789 the Estates General duly processed before King Louis XVI. The latter began badly by receiving the nobles and the clergy in the prestigious Hall of Mirrors, but the Third Estate (to whom he did not speak) in a neighbouring apartment.

The assembly commenced business against a backdrop of widespread popular dissatisfaction. A volatile populace was played upon by a veritable infestation of hotheads, encouraging them to demonstrate against all manner of targets, from the government to their own employers. Violence was increasing, with bodies such as the City Watch and *Gardes Françaises* frequently having to enlist the assistance of regular forces to restore order. Many of the latter, however, were supportive of the crowds that they had been called in to suppress.

On 17 June, with a Third Estate majority, the Estates General voted to restyle itself the National Assembly, usurping the king's authority in also declaring that all existing taxation was illegal until it reaffirmed and authorized its validity. Louis, grief stricken at the recent death of his 7-year-old son and heir, was not inclined to use force to reimpose his will, deciding instead to declare a *séance royale*, or royal session. Here, all would meet in a forum in which, theoretically at least, any opinion might be freely aired. His intention was to rule illegal the decision to form a National Assembly but to mitigate the inevitable outcry such a decision would provoke by a promise of rapid implementation of agreed reforms.

The usual venue for so formal an occasion had needed to be closed for necessary alteration. Apparently poorly informed, the assembly leaders construed this as some form of lockout and all gathered in a nearby covered tennis court. Having agreed not to push the monarch too far they (with a single exception) then took the famous oath that, before God and the nation, they would not be separated before they had produced 'a solid and equitable constitution' and established it on solid foundation.

The *séance royale* of 23 June 1789 was a tense affair. Louis addressed a silent gathering, the commoners separated from the other two orders. He proposed concessions but hedged them with provisos. All reforms, he declared, must be seen as by royal initiative and not as concessions won by demand. He then commanded the assembly to disperse and to reassemble the following day in their separate chambers. At this, he and his Court withdrew.

After the king's departure, the somewhat chastened gathering was harangued by the imposing person of the comte de Mirabeau. He reminded deputies of their collective oath, that their sovereign had treated them with disdain and that their prerogative was to remain and go about their legislative business. Reminded of the royal command by the Master of Ceremonies, a youthful marquis, Mirabeau asserted that they were assembled by 'the will of the people' and would be dispersed only by bayonets. The supervising dean of debates, the respected academic Jean-Sylvain Bailly, added that 'the assembled nation cannot be given orders'.

The king, still distracted by bereavement, apparently conceded defeat in the face of this defiance, satisfying himself by formally requesting those of the two privileged orders who had not yet aligned themselves to the assembly to do so. His acquiescence, however, may have resulted from rumours that a large throng was preparing to march on Versailles.

To reinforce his remaining authority, Louis began to move army units towards the capital. Regiment by regiment, the troops numbered a reported 20,000 by the end of July. This was increasingly read by Parisians as the means by which the king proposed to suppress the assembly. The popular mood turned ugly and, even as the assembly debated the form of the proposed constitution, supporters of the Third Estate roamed the streets, challenging all who did not overtly declare their loyalties through the wearing of a green favour.

When the king dismissed the increasingly unpopular Calonne, the director-general of finance, the value of money plummeted. This was at that time of the year when, just before the harvest, the price of bread was at its highest. Mobs ransacked shops and suppliers for weapons, prompting the electors (those qualified to select the deputies to serve in the *parlement*) to fund their own militia. Within the city, smaller units of regular troops, many of them foreign mercenaries, were being spontaneously attacked. A half-battalion of the unpopular *Gardes Françaises* defected to join the crowds, precursors of many more. A mass of seditious pamphlets was in circulation, exhorting both the *Gardes* and regular troops to support the popular drive to jettison the old order.

By 12 July, Paris was in disorder. Crowds openly defied troop detachments who, unwilling to use lethal force, were reduced largely to bystanders as stored staples were pillaged. The citizens' militia had reached imposing numbers but was essentially untrained and lacked uniforms. As a distinguishing mark, each member wore a red-white-and-blue favour, comprising the heraldic colours of the city with the white of France. In addition to restoring order, their task was to prevent any repression by the military.

Firearms were in short supply, a situation resolved when a large crowd, more mob than militia, invaded the Invalides. Neither army guards nor resident veterans took any action as the armoury was ransacked for some 30,000 muskets, which were distributed at random. There was, however, virtually no powder. Wisely, this was stored separately but it was known that the bulk, about 15 tons of it, had been removed to the fortress-prison of the Bastille. The general public knew little of the functions of this establishment but its forbidding appearance, coupled with unsubstantiated rumour, made it symbolic of the repressive regime. Those incarcerated there (of whom there were only a handful) were not guilty of crimes against common law but for the most part had been committed under the detested *lettres de cachet*. These were issued by high authority against those who had offended the establishment. There was no trial, no specific sentence.

The Bastille itself was held by a garrison of a hundred or so, the majority pensioners, and, on the morning of 14 July, they looked down on a motley gathering, ten times their number, that had come for the powder. Considerable time was spent parleying with the governor who, without orders, refused to surrender anything.

Upon rumours of a military relief column, the mob forced its way into the undefended outer courtyard. A few desultory shots were fired. Then, defecting *Gardes* aimed two small cannon they had brought at the inner drawbridge. Seeing little future in prolonged resistance, the governor threatened to blow up the entire powder stock if the garrison's safety was not guaranteed. Tempers were high, misunderstandings abounded. As the parley dragged on, the cannon were on the point of being fired when the drawbridge was suddenly dropped and the mob surged in.

Confined for hours in the stifling outer courtyard, they had taken scores of casualties from the muskets of the nervous garrison. Although the latter accordingly found themselves roughly handled, their lives appear to have been spared as the crowd was distracted by the need to remove the powder. This, along with the unfortunate governor and the seven prisoners (all that there were), was brought triumphantly to the Hôtel de Ville. As the powder was distributed the governor was murdered, his head becoming one of the first of thousands to be paraded as trophies on the end of the citizens' pikes.

Long the stuff of legend, the Bastille became an instant attraction as thousands came to probe its supposed horrors. Its significance was immediately apparent to Mirabeau of the Third Estate who, within days, had symbolically knocked out the first stone to signal the process of demolition. It was a metaphor for the whole *ancien régime*.

NO SMALL CONTRIBUTOR to unrest was widespread unemployment. In the engineering and technical sector this had been exacerbated through the contemporary industrial revolution in Great Britain. French trade in general was doing rather well but the trade agreement signed in 1786 had opened the door to the products of British mechanization, and the effects of new processes and volume production were making themselves felt (although, in return, traditional French producers of such goods as wine and silk prospered).

Then, as now, no nation could exist isolated, complete in itself and, contemporary with the upheaval in France, much else was happening in Europe. Events here, it may be argued, might have had very different outcomes had France been actively involved instead of being hobbled by her own internal divisions.

For years, while France and Great Britain had been absorbed in their mutual hostility, Russia had made considerable territorial gains. The no-nonsense Empress Catherine II had dealt with her own domestic revolts and carried through necessary reforms, going on to acquire significant tracts of land in eastern Poland, the Baltic coast in the north and around the Crimea in the south. Russia was thus increasingly able to access the world's oceans not only via the Arctic and Pacific but also through the Baltic and Black Seas.

These developments caused concern in Britain, whose Baltic trade was of great importance. There also appeared every chance that a vigorous, expansionist Russia would push strongly against the flabby Ottoman Empire, driving southward to dominate the Levant and even Egypt, to negotiate porting rights on the Mediterranean and to create a potential barrier across the route to India. Relationships between Great Britain and Russia had cooled by 1785 but there existed a degree of *schadenfreude* with the former with respect to France, which viewed the area as a particular sphere of influence and which was considerably irritated at Russian ambition.

Frequently at war to protect her trade and foreign interests, Britain regularly squabbled with neutral states over her assumed right to stop and search their ships at sea for contraband cargoes. This caused huge resentment and, back in 1780, Russia had enlisted the cooperation of Sweden, Denmark and the Netherlands in forming what was termed the First Armed Neutrality specifically to resist the practice. The alliance directly threatened British Baltic trade, the British also being anxious lest Dutch ports became controlled by overtly hostile forces, which quickly proved to be possible.

The Habsburg powers of Austria and Prussia controlled much of present-day Belgium but then, as now, Dutch Flanders was excluded. As long as this was the case, traffic bound to and from the great port of Antwerp had to pass through Dutch waters in the lower reaches of the Scheldt. However, since the Treaty of Westphalia in 1648, which had ended the Thirty Years' War, the waterway had been effectively closed to international commerce, while the 1713 Treaty of Utrecht had seen the establishment of a line of Dutch-garrisoned 'barrier towns', intended to act as a first line of defence against French adventurism. It was in Britain's interest to maintain this situation.

In 1780, however, Maria Theresa of Austria and Hungary was succeeded by her son, Joseph II. Aggressive by nature, he bundled the Dutch military from the barrier towns and, unhappy at having to use the inconvenient port of Ostend as his nation's main conduit for commerce, made clear his intention to reopen Antwerp for the purpose. But as Austrian forces in this region were isolated, their routes for supply and reinforcement were exposed in flank to action by a hostile, and more powerful, France. A thriving Antwerp might just prove to be too much an attraction for the French. An added complication was the increasingly benign attitude of Russia toward both Austria and France so that, whatever the outcome, she would be guaranteed a friendly port in a generally unfriendly western Europe.

Catherine's new relationships were spelled out when she signed a generous trade agreement with France while pointedly allowing an existing agreement with Britain to lapse. The Dutch, meanwhile, were split into factions variously supported by the British or by the French. With the latter in the ascendancy, Louis XVI warned Joseph that any Austrian move against the Netherlands would be met by force. Support by Prussia, however, looked very likely. Notwithstanding her new-found rapport with France, Russia decided to accept the *fait accompli* of the Austrian occupation. At this, Sweden and Turkey, of which both had lost considerable territory to the Russians, began to mobilize in opposition.

Having thus provoked considerable response, Joseph reconsidered his options, finally losing interest in 1785 when France concluded a treaty with the northern Netherlands, then termed the United Provinces. This served only to inflame the internal factionalism that resulted in the aforementioned state of quasi-civil war of 1787.

In 1786 Prussia's king, Frederick II ('the Great') had died, but his successor, Frederick William II, continued his policies. His intervention during 1787 in support of the Dutch revolutionaries was seen as a means of weakening the Austrian position.

This same year saw Turkey, anticipating a Russian move to seize the Caucasus, launch a pre-emptive attack. As a Russian ally, Austria needed little encouragement to join in, and Turkey was quickly under pressure.

Catherine decided to transfer a Russian battle squadron from the Baltic to the Mediterranean, with an eye to accessing the Black Sea. Along the entire route, however, there existed no base upon which the Russians could rely. Despite her recent rebuffs of British goodwill, the empress none the less approached the prime minister, Pitt. He took restrained pleasure in adopting a strictly neutral, and diplomatically unhelpful, stance, an attitude repeated by the Dutch when they, similarly, were approached. In thus abandoning the project, Catherine reflected upon how valuable would access to the Scheldt have been had Austria established the mastery of it.

To offset spells on half-pay, British naval officers commonly served in the Russian navy. They were much valued but a crisis was sparked through the appointment by the Russians to high command of the American hero John Paul Jones. This renegade son of Cumberland had caused the British much trouble during the American War of Independence a decade earlier. His appearance in Russian uniform led to the threat of mass British resignations and Jones was relegated to a minor command.

Smarting from earlier loss of territory, Sweden took the opportunity to move against Russian Finland. His nation by now in decline, Sweden's Gustav III was chancing his arm, his much-reduced deep-water fleet having been augmented by a specially developed, shallow-water fleet designed for use in the Gulf of Finland. Developed by another son of an English north countryman, Frederik Hendrik af Chapman, its craft were intended for amphibious operations, with priority placed on low draught and manoeuvrability. As Catherine had not been able to transfer the bulk of her Baltic fleet to the Mediterranean as planned, however, it was able to involve the Swedes in a series of fierce engagements. In this war (1788–90) the Swedes had rather the better of the maritime action but the eventual peace benefited neither side.

Denmark, taking advantage of Sweden's preoccupation, tried to settle old differences by invading from its adjacent Norwegian territory. Britain, in a triple alliance with Prussia and the Netherlands, enforced a Danish withdrawal on pain of intervention, and brokered the peace settlement between Sweden and Russia. As the latter had appeared likely winners, the British gained by preventing them securing yet more ground in the Baltic.

Like Turkey, Sweden had a long-standing relationship with France but, with the latter by now so beset with internal problems and without any coherent foreign policy, Britain viewed Russia as the greater potential threat. The Swedish intervention successfully diverted Russian military strength from the Turkish front. As the latter were heading for total defeat and Britain endeavoured to maintain the balance in the north, Russia suddenly concluded a defensive alliance with Austria. Worse, France and Spain, while agreeing to remain neutral in the war against Turkey, pledged to intervene militarily should either Russia or Austria be attacked by a third party.

As this agreement came about at the time of the fall of the Bastille, the French undertaking would, in practice, have had little substance but, for the Triple Alliance, a potentially unfavourable situation was alleviated when, in 1790, Austria's belligerent Joseph II died. Both he and his successor, the more moderate Leopold II, were brothers to the detested French queen, Marie Antoinette.

Leopold feared the Prussians more than he wished to aid Russia, and when the former looked to intervene militarily on the side of the Porte, he moved quickly to negotiate an end to hostilities. The Treaty of Reichenbach saw Austria and Turkey agree to re-adopt their pre-war frontiers, Austria's reward being the return of its territory in Belgian Flanders.

The Triple Alliance attempted similar mediation between Russia and Turkey, but was rebuffed by the strong-willed Catherine. Appalling slaughter on both sides, however, began to dent their enthusiasm for war and when, early in 1791, Britain and Prussia issued an ultimatum, threatening military intervention unless she withdrew from Ottoman territory, Catherine indicated her willingness to cease hostilities in exchange for the retention of ground gained on the north shore of the Black Sea. Fighting ceased in August 1791, although a formal peace had to wait a further year.

Events in the upper Baltic and a dispute with the Spanish over fishing and trading rights on the American Pacific coast (for example, Nootka Sound in 1790), had stimulated the British government to increase the number of fully commissioned ships in the Royal Navy. This force existed as a latent threat behind British diplomacy aimed at achieving favourable balances of power.

IN BRIEFLY REVIEWING EVENTS elsewhere in a restless Europe, we have anticipated somewhat those in France itself. With the carrying of the Bastille on 14 July 1789 public unrest crossed the symbolic line that separated it from outright revolution. On the following day, the reaction of King Louis XVI was wisely conciliatory and unostentatious. He stood down the troops and addressed what was now termed the National Assembly, assuring deputies that he had no designs on its continued existence.

On 17 July the king went to Paris, where his progress was through streets lined with crowds that cheered but carried all varieties of improvised weaponry. His authority, he knew, now lay within the gift of a fickle populace. Arriving at the Hôtel de Ville, he both accepted and wore the red-white-and-blue cockade and, rather ineffectually, addressed a throng described as 'delirious'.

Tempered by a nagging fear of ultimate retribution, the joy of the crowds proved brittle and short-lived. They were hungry. Even the new assembly could not conjure up cheaper bread and grain overnight. In the provinces, increasingly desperate to provide for their dependents, countrymen banded together and rounded on the *seigneurie* on the basis of a false rumour that this action met with the approval of the assembly.

Despite this obvious nonsense, crimes, initially perpetrated against property, soon turned more personal. Central authority quickly broke down and the raising of local militia proved ineffective because, once armed, individuals simply defected to join those with whom their sympathies lay. In the National Assembly, Jean-Sylvain Bailly, the supervisor of debate, noted of the people that now 'all knew how to command but none how to obey'.

Then, on 4 August, came the extraordinary meeting of the assembly, where the two privileged estates, those of the aristocracy and clergy, panicked, believing the public mood indicated that they eventually would lose everything. Hysterically, the members vied to grant the greater concession toward dismantling what was still a largely feudal society. This developed into a mass donation of valuables to assist the depleted national treasury.

Now a notable in the assembly as well as heading the new National Guard, the marquis de Lafayette pressed for a Declaration of the Rights of Man, similar to that adopted by the Americans. The king vetoed the proposal, fearing that he might yet be called to account for agreeing to the erosion of the power of the privileged classes while conferring rights on the citizenry at a time when their parallel obligations as members of society were being conveniently overlooked.

On 5 October 1789, fed by rumours of continuing highlife and excess at Court, an apparently spontaneous gathering of women protesting at the price of bread, the recurrent theme, developed in Paris. Agitators quickly worked them into a powerful anger and, having first invaded the National Assembly, they marched on to Versailles to demand that the king return to Paris. In this they were supported by a powerful contingent of the National Guard, whose discipline had broken down despite Lafayette's personal presence. After some violence, the great procession returned in triumph to the capital with the royal family as trophies. Received with ironic acclaim, Louis was moved into his new quarters. Already the assembly had restyled him as 'King of the French' rather than as 'King of France'.

ALTHOUGH ALL WERE DEDICATED to establishing a new order, the deputies of the National Assembly were divided into all shades of opinion, from the diehard Revolutionaries, through the moderates to the relative conservatives. On the left sat a group of, largely, Bretonnais, who, on the establishment of the assembly, had developed a rhetoric calling for revolution by whatever means necessary. Because they frequently met separately, as a faction, at the convent of the Jacobin friars, they eventually adopted the title of *Societé des Jacobins*, a name that would become synonymous with some of the Revolution's worst excesses.

A great majority of the Jacobins wanted the king deposed and an end to the monarchy. The more moderate element preferred a constitutional monarchy based on that of Britain. This group drifted away from the extremists, forming a faction known generally as the Feuillant Club. As the National Assembly metamorphosed into a constituent, then a legislative, assembly and the early moderates were increasingly displaced by hotheads whose idea of revolution extended to little more than an idealistic dismantling of the established order, the Feuillant group became the only check on the inexorable slide into anarchy. As several of its more influential members hailed from Bordeaux in the Gironde, the faction as a whole became known as the Girondists.

While this group, too, embraced a wide range of opinion, it is generally true to say that they looked for no more than major reform of the existing social system, with monarchy, nobility and clergy stripped of much of the privilege with which they haughtily distanced themselves from the mass.

The Girondists included some of the better brains of the assembly, which enabled their moderating influence to survive as long as it did in the face of opposition from the Left, which had by far the better orators.

The Montagnards (literally, 'mountain men'), formed an inner group of what might be termed the hard Left, taking their name from the raised level of the back benches that they occupied. As the remainder – the undecideds, the fearful and the less committed – occupied the centre of the chamber, between the major groups, they were referred to as the 'plain', or Marais (literally, the 'marshes'). Typical of middle-of-the-roaders, they exerted little influence except when voting was close.

Remorselessly, sector by sector, the assembly assaulted the very fabric of the nation. Hereditary titles were abolished, together with all insignia and trappings that marked a person's elevation above his fellow citizen. Extensive lands and property owned by the church were taken into public ownership against the issue of official bonds. A 'civil constitution' was imposed on the clergy, reducing the number of bishoprics and obliging its members to face election and to distance themselves from Rome. Religious orders, with the exception of those devoted to teaching or charitable work, were abolished.

All clergy were now expected to take a civic oath, a matter of great resentment and outright opposition. In early 1791 came the election of the first bishops of the new constitutional church. Not surprisingly, these procedures were roundly condemned by Rome. The Bourbon rulers of France were devout Roman Catholics and his new obligation to sanction a civic oath so vehemently opposed by the clergy was repugnant to the king.

The first anniversary of the taking of the Bastille was marked by a national *Fête de la Fédération*. In Paris this was an ambitious affair, in the course of which deputies and spectators, representatives of the armed services and militias and, finally, the royal couple themselves pledged to remain faithful to the nation, the new constitution and the law. For Louis, accustomed to absolute power, it must have been a deeply humiliating and depressing experience.

On 2 April 1791 Mirabeau died. He had been increasingly at logger-heads with the Jacobins over their excessive demands. The latest of these was that the *émigrés*, mostly landed gentry terrified by events into retreating to neighbouring states, should be obliged to return on pain of being declared rebels and having their goods and properties forfeit to the state.

Mirabeau had increasingly recognized that it was easier to start a revolution than to control what resulted. Together with other 'founding members' of the revolt he had been a moderating influence against forces demanding 'liberty for all', an ideal apparently synonymous with a total reconstruction of the established order. This went as far as demanding impeachment of the king 'for crimes against the People and the State'. Although the assembly had been issuing and enforcing decrees on the strength of its own authority, Mirabeau's hope had been that the yet-to-be finalized national constitution would somehow still include the monarchy in the decision-making process.

Helped by a good harvest, the mood in Paris was returning to something like normality when the Pope's forthright condemnation of the newly elected clergy triggered a new upsurge of resentment. For months the king had been quietly advised by well-wishers to break free of his virtual confinement and to seek sanctuary across a friendly border, both for his own safety and that of his immediate family, and from where he might then act as a focus for a counter-revolutionary war.

At Easter 1791 the royal family boarded their coach to celebrate Mass at Saint-Cloud. They were confronted by an angry mob, ablaze with Revolutionary fervour, which prevented their vehicle from leaving the Tuileries. It was probably this frightening experience that finally resolved Louis to flee.

On the night of 20 June, with the assistance of loyal friends, the family successfully evaded staff and guards to leave by coach. Progress was slow, however, and the alarm was raised very early next morning. Predictably making for the nearest friendly frontier, they were intercepted at Varennes near the border with the Austrian Netherlands. On the strength of a decree from the assembly, signed by Lafayette, the coach was brought back to Paris, escorted by a motley throng of citizens and National Guardsmen. Paris streets and vantage points were packed by silent crowds, forbidden by edict either to applaud or to insult.

Shortly after the royal return, on the second Bastille anniversary, another extreme faction, the Cordeliers Club, believing that the Revolution was losing its momentum, produced a petition demanding yet more 'Revolutionary democracy'. Invited to the Champ de Mars to sign it, the public arrived in large numbers. As usual, it took little to foment trouble, in this case two perceived miscreants who were summarily hanged. Disturbance quickly spread to the point where Lafayette ordered out the National Guard. As warning volleys were fired into the air, hotheads denounced the actions as the 'people's police' oppressing the people. Order was restored only when a further volley was directed into the crowd. The fifty killed became the new martyrs of the Left and moderates forfeited much of their support.

Across France, many minor clergy remained implacably opposed to the signing of any new code that would loosen their ties with Rome. In this, they very often had the support of the majority in their congregations. Ordinary citizens, who wished nothing more than to stand clear of the problems besetting their nation, were thus now torn between a reluctance to abandon a trusted priest and an official requirement to support a reform that, elsewhere, was widely felt to be necessary.

Recalcitrant priests, together with army officers, had been fleeing in droves and, in neighbouring territories, threats to the Revolution were becoming discernible. European monarchies were interrelated by marriage, and many *émigré* French nobles, in remaining loyal to their king, acted as rallying points for those who detested and feared the course of events in their own country.

The French queen, Marie Antoinette, appealed directly to her brother, Leopold II of Austria. 'Force has overturned everything', she wrote, 'and force alone can rectify the situation.' Despite Austria's fundamental differences with Prussia, therefore, they came together for the sake of the future of European monarchies. In the so-called Declaration of Pillnitz of August 1791 they jointly demanded that Louis XVI's sovereign rights be respected on pain of intervention if (and this was the rub) other European monarchies assisted. Britain, in particular, had no vested interests in being involved.

As the Pillnitz signatories were well aware of this in advance, their declaration was designed only to put heart into the still-sizeable portion of the French population sympathetic to the idea of a constitutional monarchy. It had, however, entirely the wrong result. The assembly's Left saw conspiracies everywhere, at home and abroad. The calls, ever more insistent, were for France to take the initiative and to declare war on those forces that would destroy the Revolution.

In accepting the proposed new constitution in principle, Louis retained his right of veto. He used it to nullify the assembly's decree that *émigrés* be pronounced 'traitors to the Nation', to be condemned *in absentia* to a suitable death and to have their estates declared forfeit. A week later he vetoed a second decree that fought to deprive priests who would not accept the new code of both their living and their pension.

In January 1792, responding to the growing clamour for war, the Legislative Assembly demanded of Austria that it remove the threat implicit in the Pillnitz Declaration. To emphasize the point, the assembly took it upon itself to override any veto from the king. Austria's response was blunt. Feeling confident in the disordered state of France, it demanded not only a full restoration of the monarchy but the restitution of once-Austrian border territory. For good measure, concessions were also to be made to the Pope, slighted by demands on the French clergy. Three weeks later, on 7 February, Austria and Prussia concluded an alliance. As matters approached a climax, there came a complication: the death of Austria's Leopold II. Where he had been viewed as something of a moderate, his son, Francis II, who succeeded him, was much under the influence of advisors and liable to be unpredictable. The resulting increased likelihood of armed intervention from abroad emboldened Louis further.

Austria's unexpectedly belligerent stance took the responsible Feuillant ministers aback. Their confused reaction was seized upon by the more reactionary elements of the Girondins, who were pressing the assembly to charge certain ministers with treason. One, the minister of marine, was a favourite of the king, who responded to the scheme by dismissing one of the instigators, the minister of war. This bold action resulted in a train of ministerial appointments. Reading into this reshuffle preparations for war, the Austrians moved an army to the frontier in Belgium.

Beset by circumstance but, no doubt, with secret hopes for an Austrian success, Louis, loudly cheered by the assembly, declared war on 20 April. In its 'crusade for universal liberty' the French army, fully mobilized, could outnumber the coalition Austro-Prussian forces three to one. It was, however, unfit for war. Many officers, intimidated by the new order, had fled or left the service. Those remaining had little control over their newly enfranchised citizen troops, ever inclined to mutiny and poorly equipped. The first clashes with what might be called the German army were disastrous, even through the French had proven commanders such as Lafayette and Rochambeau. Following one of several reverses, a French general, Theobald Dillon, was actually murdered by his own men.

Louis's recent robust treatment of ministers was used as a pretext for a particularly threatening demonstration on 20 June. An estimated 8,000 workers, skilled and unskilled, mostly armed, invaded the assembly, read a new declaration of rights, sang revolutionary anthems and generally disrupted proceedings. Its more extreme elements probably not uninvolved behind the scenes, the assembly awaited the mob's departure. The mob then marched on the king's quarters at the Tuileries where, bursting in, it subjected the royal family to a humiliating and frightening ordeal. Harangued to his face for his actions, Louis was obliged to toast the nation directly from a bottle while wearing the red Phrygian cap that had become the universal symbol of the Revolution. Louis reacted with what good humour he could muster, maintaining a degree of dignity and even earning some grudging respect. He knew, however, that he retained only as much power as the people were prepared to tolerate.

The quasi-war was still not going in favour of the French army and the assembly anticipated the imminent Bastille anniversary by issuing a proclamation. Entitled *La Patrie en danger,* it was a declaration of a state of emergency, a licence to conscript every able-bodied Frenchman. News spread that the Duke of Brunswick, commanding the coalition army, had threatened the total destruction of Paris if the royal family was harmed or again intimidated.

As armed *Fédéres* swarmed into the capital for its defence, the general mood became ugly, with widespread breakdown in order. The so-called Brunswick Declaration roused tempers everywhere for, if an enemy army was advancing to succour the monarchy, then surely the monarchy must be an enemy of the nation. Neither king nor assembly could withstand the carefully choreographed fury which fuelled the city's militants in their establishment of an Insurrectionary Commune which effectively replaced the council, issuing instructions to the forty-eight regional *sections* where the real authority now lay. The commune demonstrated its power by arresting, executing and replacing the recently appointed head of the National Guard, held to have royalist sympathies.

In the heat of mid August, a crowd estimated at 20,000 marched on the Tuileries, inflamed by street orators denouncing the king as an enemy of the people. To steady the force of National Guardsmen, whose task it was to guard him, Louis held a review. Even as he inspected them, however, groups were defecting to join the general upheaval.

The royal family slipped away in time to take precarious shelter in the Legislative Assembly as the mob burst into the Tuileries with bloody intent. The king's elite Swiss Guard mostly fought to the death to defend first the building, then their lives. Now aroused to a frenzy, crowds surged around the corridors, hunting down the palace staff who, to the last manservant, were clubbed or hacked to death. Some were thrown from windows, others burned. The appalling circumstances of the blood-letting of 10 August became a symbol of the Revolution. The better part of one thousand died on that day, mostly in horrific circumstances. In their shared experience, the Revolutionaries were united in a sort of euphoria, assuming an aura of invincibility. Like mutineers, they now had to succeed or perish.

Astonishingly, the assembly continued its debate throughout this nearby carnage. The royals were given temporary lodging for the night and brought back the following day to hear the deputies, under heavy pressure from the Insurrectionary Commune, approve the king's suspension. All decrees vetoed by him would be reinstated. Rule would be vested temporarily in the Provisional Executive, a council of six ministers, pending the election of a National Convention, whose objective would be universal suffrage. Five of the six caretaker ministers were prominent Girondins. The sixth, ominously occupying the post of minister of justice, was the forbidding lawyer Danton, late of the extreme Cordeliers Club.

There began a round-up of all who could be branded enemies of the Revolution. Old scores, prejudice, envy – all contributed to a mass of detentions so comprehensive that moderate elements of the assembly were moved to query the motives of the commune and its *sections*. This provoked the Montagnards, who included the influential Robespierre and Marat, to charge their colleagues with undermining the Revolution and shielding the guilty. Deterred by the implicit threat of bloody force, the assembly capitulated, agreeing to the formation of a National Convention, selected by a free vote and charged with finalizing a new constitution.

The coalition army, meanwhile, galvanized by the savagery of 10 August, advanced against the fortress town of Verdun. In response and propelled by the fierce energies of Danton, the Provisional Executive raised a force of 30,000 volunteers, who created a powerful new Revolutionary image as they threw up defences on the approaches to the capital.

In the prevailing excited atmosphere, the city's café orators and the pamphleteers then scared the populace into believing that the departure of many of the able-bodied had left in their midst prisons full of traitors and conspirators, the newly incarcerated 'vile slaves of tyranny'. As, somehow, these were claimed to pose an immediate threat from within, there came the unequivocal signal: 'In advancing to meet the common enemy ... leave nothing behind to disquiet us.'

The news, received on 2 September, that Verdun had fallen was sufficient to trigger several days of merciless butchery. First, recalcitrant priests were detained in large numbers in convents. Then, with the complicity of guards, the mob gained access to the city's prisons. Common vagrants, prostitutes, adolescents, imbeciles – none was excepted. In the course of five days of methodical slaughter, perhaps twelve hundred, half of the city's prison population, were murdered. The perpetrators of these, the September massacres, were never brought to book, the commune supporting them with the usual justification that the victims were enemies of the nation. Some shame was evident in that the Girondins, in general, blamed the Jacobins for inciting the killings, but none was free of guilt. Foreign governments reacted with outrage with some, including the British, withdrawing their ambassadors. It was apparent to many that raw violence and terror was becoming the engine that propelled the Revolution forward.

Patriotic fervour reached a new pitch when, on 20 September, the French army engaged the Prussians at Valmy in the Argonne. The Duke of Brunswick's leisurely advance had allowed his opponent, Kellermann, to move his regular troops across the Prussian line of retreat. Both sides were affected greatly by sickness and a paucity of supplies, and the battle itself was a lacklustre affair with Brunswick deciding to disengage rather than risk attacking the superior position of the French, who were using their artillery to demoralizing effect.

In Paris, Valmy was hailed as a victory of a new citizen army over an international league of hostile monarchies. On the same day as the battle the new National Convention met for the first time. Not unlike preceding assemblies in that provincial delegates included a fair proportion of pliant clergy and late nobility who deplored extreme violence for political ends, it was none the less dominated by the representatives from the capital. These, almost to a man, were Jacobins; moderates had been carefully disenfranchised.

One of the Convention's first actions was to abolish the monarchy. It then followed up by declaring that the new French Republic would 'grant fraternity and assistance to all people who wish to recover their liberty'. Through the export of revolution and terror its own sins would, perhaps, be diluted.

Though lacking discipline, the French army was highly motivated. It now saw itself not so much as political instrument as the embodiment of the embattled state itself. On 6 November 1792 it worsted the Austrians at Jemappes, retained its momentum and, within days, had occupied the Austrian Netherlands. Virtually throwing down the gauntlet to the British, the Convention declared free navigation on the Scheldt, quickly underlined by the ostentatious passage to Antwerp of a French naval squadron. By now seriously concerned, the British government stated that it could not tolerate with indifference France creating herself sovereign of the Low Countries 'or the general arbitress of the rights and liberties of Europe'. Uncaring of rumbles abroad, meanwhile, the victorious French army swept eastward to secure all territory to the west of the symbolic barrier of the Rhine. French ambitions were not confined to the north and the centre. In the south, hostilities having commenced against Sardinia, the Revolutionary horde pushed into Savoy and toward the Swiss border and through Nice on the Mediterranean coast.

THE NATIONAL CONVENTION functioned in anything but harmony. With greater diplomacy, the influential Girondins could have emerged dominant. Their attacks on the Jacobins were incessant and immoderate, however, and they did little to appeal to the great number of the citizens of Paris who were appalled and fearful at what was happening around them. They also made no effort to woo the neutral members of the Marais or bring together the capital and the remainder of the nation which increasingly appeared to be separate political entities.

Instead, the militants, ever more heavily criticized, were pushed into acting in a manner even more extreme in order to maintain their position.

The continued presence of the deposed king and his family, under conditions of demeaning house arrest, was a lasting reproach to the Convention and calls for their trial and even execution became more strident. A high proportion of the Convention's members were, however, lawyers by profession. To justify the trial of the monarch and his ultimate punishment a convincing case needed to be made.

Committees created for the purpose satisfied themselves, firstly, that the king could legally be tried by the Convention. As he had been deposed and the Convention had made itself the highest court in the land, there was no impediment. A second committee exhaustively trawled a mass of documentary evidence. It was not difficult to demonstrate that the king had used his extensive connections to explore every means to quell the Revolution and, by definition, to maintain the status quo. His status as an 'enemy of the Nation' was assured.

The trial ran for three weeks and on 16 January 1793 the death sentence was passed by a majority vote. Appeals being dismissed, Louis XVI was executed on the 21st before a crowd of 20,000. The instrument of his death was the recently introduced guillotine, an apparatus which brought new standards of efficiency to judicial murder and which became, in itself, the most powerful icon of the agony of France and the greater frightfulness which was yet to come.

In London, meanwhile, far from the clamour of the mob, diplomatic relations, politely but icily, explored new depths. Reacting to the events of 10 August 1792, the British had withdrawn their ambassador from Paris. With the suspension of the French monarchy, the Foreign Office then deemed the French ambassador in London to be no longer accredited. His own administration was now engaged on more heroic business than to issue any alternative form of credentials and he was, therefore, regarded in London as an unofficial representative of an unrecognized regime.

The reopening of the Scheldt to free navigation had been sufficient in itself to cause the British to consider hostilities but now, in addition, French armies were on the rampage, their weapons a lesser threat than their ideology. During January 1793 British attitudes hardened. An Aliens Act was passed, severely circumscribing the freedoms of foreign nationals in Britain. Deeply concerned at events in France, members rallied to Pitt, who appeared to be ready to oppose Revolutionary principles. With the news of the king's execution, the British government finally expelled the long-suffering French ambassador, an action sufficient for the Convention to declare war on 1 February 1793. For good measure, hostilities were also opened with the Netherlands.

Intoxicated with the sheer momentum of the Revolution, France appeared heedless either of offence being caused or of the number and strength of forces being arrayed against her. A fortnight after declaring war on Britain, France annexed Monaco and, in the following month, opened hostilities with Spain, whose Bourbon monarchy was already planning retribution for the death of Louis. By March 1793, therefore, almost every French border looked on to enemy territory. What developed became known as the War of the First Coalition, although it was a coalition of states with little in common except a repugnance and fear of French Revolutionary fervour.

chapter two

War, Revolution and the French Navy

THIRTY YEARS EARLIER, the Seven Year War had taught France that her ambitions to acquire a major overseas empire were insupportable in the face of hostile British sea power. Her fleet, although large, had not acquitted itself well and, from 1756, over fifty of its fighting ships had been captured by the Royal Navy. Most of these losses had resulted from small-scale encounters, but the main battle fleet had fared no better and was still haunted by the disaster of Quiberon in 1759. Here, in a rising gale, Hawke's ships had risked stranding in their determination to pursue the French fleet under Admiral Conflans into the very estuaries of the Vilaine and the Charente. A huge blow to French morale, the battle was rightly described by Mahan as 'the Trafalgar of the Seven Years' War'.

Sea power underpinned British success from India to Canada, from the West Indies to West Africa. France would probably have lost further foreign possessions had she not made a Bourbon alliance with the Spanish. Their territories, including the veritable eldorado of Havana, proved to be a greater (and less challenging) attraction.

On land, the French, Austrians and Prussians had in total sacrificed half a million men, yet at the peace it suited the politicians to sign away territorial gain and to restore the situation to virtually what it had been at the outbreak of hostilities. From her strong position at the peace table, Britain could, perhaps should, have ensured that France was reined back to being a still-substantial continental European power. Restoration of her overseas interests, however, gave France every reason to revive both trade and fighting fleet. In parallel, there burned a French desire to exact revenge for injuries and humiliations suffered.

Through years of parsimony before the Seven Years' War, the French had allowed their fleet to slide into a state of inferiority and for this the nation had paid dearly. Too late in the day, in 1761, the duc de Choiseul, already minister of war, took over as minister of marine. Defeat for him was bitter, but by 1763 he had already begun the process of reform which the comparatively mild demands of the peace plan permitted him to continue.

The French navy still possessed about forty ships of the line and a dozen frigates. None the less, however powerful a force on paper, individual vessels were in various states of disrepair. As it stood, the naval budget would barely fund the replacement of existing ships as they were condemned; to increase the size of the fleet demanded further measures.

Using his aristocratic connections, Choiseul approached the great provincial councils with a patriotic appeal for assistance. It struck a chord, persuading administrations, municipalities and guilds to fund near a score of new vessels. Many, such as the *Ville de Paris, Commerce de Bordeaux* and *Languedoc,* carried the names of their benefactors. By British rating, the French navy was thus augmented by the addition of one first and one second rate, eight third rates and six fourth rates, besides benefiting from lesser donations to renew the service's decayed infrastructure, including a new base at Lorient. In its heyday, the French East India Company had developed elaborate facilities adjacent to its fortress-headquarters at Port Louis. However, the Seven Years' War had seen the company's fortunes collapse as the British tightened their grip on India and the routes to the east. It was thus obliged to bargain its facilities into official ownership.

Shortly before the war Bigot de Morogues had established a new Marine Academy at Brest. Morogues was an enthusiast for the application of new tactical and signal procedures being proposed by the navy's intellectuals. Choiseul's interest was engaged, ensuring that they were adopted by the French navy at least two decades before similar action by the Royal Navy, which considered intellectual input as slightly effete. French scientific commitment was underlined by the foundation, in 1765, of a Corps of Naval Constructors.

Even after his departure from office, Choiseul's influence continued in such as the establishment of naval medical schools. Their institution was, however, less a sign of concern for the welfare of seamen than a measure to combat the truly horrific mortality rates which, above all on long commissions, greatly reduced fighting efficiency. Choiseul also attacked the navy's great social divisions, principally those between administrators and seagoers, and those separating nobility from commoners in the officer corps. Reform was very necessary, but the minister's own aristocratic background limited his effectiveness. Despite his success in raising private funding to revitalize the fleet, government votes remained insufficient. Much was soaked up in the salaries of over-age senior officers who thickly populated the upper reaches of the Navy List (a problem by no means unique to the French).

Following his replacement as minister of marine by the duc de Praslin in 1766, Choiseul was behind the shrewd French acquisition of Corsica from the tottering Genoese Republic in 1768. The transfer made strategic sense in that British interest in the island as a forward naval base was well appreciated. Its population was rebellious and, effectively, only the major centres of population ever came under French control.

French Court intrigues resulted in 1768 in the abrupt dismissal of both Choiseul (as minister of war) and Praslin. Continuing the former's policies, Praslin had overseen fleet expansion to about sixty ships of the line and some fifty frigates and minor warships. A specialist corps of gunners had also been established to overcome the particular problems posed by firing from a moving deck. At the same time, measures were already in hand to introduce an *escadre d'essai* ('squadron of evolution') to develop new procedures in the handling and manoeuvring of ships in company and to evaluate promising technical innovation. This concept pre-dated British ideas on 'experimental sailing' by about twenty-five years.

Fleet renewal then began to falter until the accession of Louis XVI in 1774. His first minister of marine, Sartine, had a short career but benefited from the king's interest in the service. Once again, France was buzzing with the prospect of war against Britain, and ship construction proceeded apace.

An opportunity for revenge had arisen with the revolt by the American colonies against British rule in 1775. Assistance to the rebels had the prospect of not only embarrassing the old enemy but re-establishing lost French influence in North America. The innate Anglophobia of Louis's foreign minister, the comte de Vergennes, was further influenced by the young marquis de Lafayette, who had committed himself totally to the American cause and who, having shared the tribulations of General Washington's hard-pressed troops at Valley Forge in the harsh winter of 1777–8, had Washington's full confidence.

Lafayette's involvement to date had been voluntary, and the French government bided its time until it was convinced about the rebels' ultimate chance of success. This came with General Burgoyne's capitulation at Saratoga in 1777 and, satisfied that it was backing a winner, France concluded a treaty of alliance with the American revolutionaries just five months later.

Such overt meddling resulted in the withdrawal of the British ambassador from Paris which event, far from prompting any explanation or apology, was met with reciprocal action. A formal declaration of war followed in July 1778. Seeking restitution from the British for what they saw as the humiliation of the peace settlement of 1763, the French again played the Bourbon family card to gain Spain as an ally, for she too had gained little from the 1763 treaty.

For the French navy, the renewal of hostilities promised much, for the new United States lay beyond 2,500 miles of ocean. The naval dimension to the conflict would necessarily prove crucial. A force of twelve ships of the line and five frigates was assembled at Toulon. Commanded by soldier-turned-sailor the comte d'Estaing, the squadron sailed before war was declared. Its orders were to land a spearhead French military force in America and then to support Washington's army as required. With the onset of winter, d'Estaing was to make for the West Indies. Here he was to cause a general nuisance threatening, and if possible taking, British island possessions and disrupting trade. All such action would oblige the Royal Navy to commit more vessels to the American station and to dissipate its strength further.

It has been noted by others that the British failure to retain the American colonies hinged on the surrender of two armies, each event being preceded by a naval operation. Neither involved d'Estaing. The surrender at Saratoga, which enticed France into the war, had resulted when Burgoyne's colleague, General Howe, failed to advance to link with him. Instead, he preferred to sail his army around to the Chesapeake in order to take Philadelphia. Tactically, the operation was a success. Strategically, it proved a disaster, well illustrating the weakness of divided command.

Having sailed before war began in July 1778, d'Estaing was on the American seaboard promptly, but he failed to impress. Unable to goad an inferior British squadron to action near New York, he moved on to the British base at Newport, Rhode Island. Here, cooperation with the American revolutionaries was poor and, while he marked time, cruising off and on, d'Estaing was concerned at the arrival of a smaller British squadron. Too weak to attack the French, this force stimulated days of indecisive manoeuvring which were terminated by a great gale that inflicted significant damage to both sides. This was sufficient to make d'Estaing sail for Boston to effect repairs. Then, having failed to render 'positive assistance' to the Americans, he left for the Caribbean.

Once in the West Indies, d'Estaing awaited reinforcement before making a move against the poorly defended island of St Vincent, which he took in June 1779. When unfavourable winds frustrated an attempt to take Barbados, the French seized Grenada instead. Here, d'Estaing was attacked by a slightly inferior British squadron. A hard-fought action resulted in no ships being lost but several British vessels being so damaged that they could well have been taken had the French so chosen. Instead, d'Estaing strictly observed his principal task of covering the military force that he had landed. Having been at sea for a creditable twenty months, d'Estaing then returned with a convoy and the ships of the original Toulon squadron, leaving the later arrivals to the new commander-in-chief, the comte de Grasse.

General Washington, already less than impressed by d'Estaing's assistance, was reinforced in the summer of 1780 by the landing of the comte de Rochambeau with 4,000 troops. These, too, showed no initial propensity for activity.

Following a protracted campaign in the southern states, and having incurred considerable loss, the British general, Cornwallis, concentrated his army at Yorktown, Virginia, early in 1781. Located on a peninsula, Cornwallis's position was strong as long as it could be maintained by sea. His route inland was blocked by Lafayette, who had a force sufficient to contain the British but not to defeat them. Lafayette was awaiting the arrival in September of de Grasse, with reinforcements from the West Indies.

Alive to the French naval activities, the newly promoted Rear Admiral Samuel Hood contrived to prevent de Grasse landing but, arriving first and finding that all was quiet, he moved on to join his senior officer, Rear

Admiral Graves, at New York. Shortly after, de Grasse was thus able to land his force undisturbed. He then remained in position so that, when Graves returned with a convoy of vital stores and reinforcements, he was unable to put them ashore. De Grasse conducted a skilful battle of manoeuvre to keep Graves (who seemed not to appreciate the implications of the situation ashore) at a distance. For imminent want of relief, Cornwallis was obliged to surrender.

Although the struggle for the American colonies was not yet over, the issue was no longer in doubt. De Grasse departed for the West Indies, where he discovered his British opponents to be tactical equals. When, in January 1782, the French overran the island of St Kitts, Hood arrived with a force too small to influence events ashore. Threatened by de Grasse's larger covering force, Hood anchored in tight line across a small bay and resisted every effort to dislodge him.

Three months later, Hood was second-in-command to Admiral Rodney when, near Dominica, the latter broke de Grasse's line of battle into three disordered groups. In this, the Battle of the Saintes, de Grasse was captured and only the aged Rodney's reluctance to pursue saved the French from major defeat.

It was not only in America that British and French naval forces clashed. Control of Ceylon and the east coast of India was still a matter of dispute between the two countries and, for two years, opposing squadrons under Commodore Suffren and Rear Admiral Hughes battled for supremacy. Unsupported by bases, the French commander had to rely greatly on captured materials and supplies. Between February 1782 and June 1783 the two groups fought five actions, mostly in support of operations ashore. Neither commander could afford to take an all-out risk, so neither achieved a clear-cut victory. Suffren, however, had proved a resourceful leader, albeit fortunate that the British Admiralty did not have the resources to reinforce Hughes to decisive strength.

When en route to the Indian Ocean in April 1781, Suffren had departed from the usual French 'mission-first' philosophy by surprising and attacking a British force at Porto Praya in the Cape Verdes. Caught at anchor, the British rallied and inflicted the higher casualty toll. They had, however, been en route to seize the Dutch colony at the Cape, and the damage they received at Porto Praya delayed them sufficiently to allow Suffren to arrive first to reinforce the Dutch garrison. The outpost remained Dutch for the duration of the war.

Two of Suffren's captains were killed at Porto Praya and the commodore replaced that of the *Annibal* 74 with her promising first lieutenant, one Morard de Galles. Being junior to others, his election caused some rancour and he was moved to a frigate command. He continued to discharge himself well, however, and we will meet him again (as, indeed, we will Rear Admiral Samuel Hood).

The continuing policy of Vergennes, the French foreign minister, was to seize British colonies wherever and whenever possible. As this required local naval superiority, it was essential for the French to ensure that the main strength of the British battle fleet remained tied to home waters, a course of action only possible if France could maintain a credible threat of an invasion of Britain. Vergennes feared, however, that any such enterprise if actually undertaken would bring about a coalition of states in Britain's defence which would overpower France. The comparatively leisurely British response to the French threat suggested the British were aware that the prospect of a cross-Channel invasion was more apparent than real, even if the Admiralty could not afford to ignore it entirely.

But that the broader French aim of stretching British naval capabilities to the limit was successful elsewhere was highlighted in America. Frustrated by the continuing French naval intervention there, the British aimed to bring Washington's army to decisive action. In refusing to be so drawn, the American general bought time that diluted and exhausted British resources and, increasingly, encouraged British conciliation.

In home waters, Britain's first line of defence was the Channel fleet, commanded by Admiral Augustus Keppel. Initially inferior in strength to the comte d'Orvilliers' Brest squadron, it was quickly reinforced to a similar strength of thirty ships of the line.

An experienced but cautious 68-year-old, d'Orvilliers was fortunate in having talented subordinate commanders such as Guichen, la Motte-Piquet, du Chaffault and, for a period, de Grasse. Indeed, the admiral was exhorted by Sartine, the minister of marine, to expunge past shortcomings through the élan of his younger divisional commanders. However, although told that 'the eyes of Europe would be upon [him]', he was also warned of the importance of preserving his fleet as a threat 'in being', and that royal opprobrium would attend the loss or capture of any of his ships. Such conflicting advice was not calculated to generate bold action from an elderly commander-in-chief.

Both fleets were quickly at sea, however, and in December 1781 clashed at what became known as the Battle of Ushant. As, after a period of peace, each admiral was again accustoming himself to action and neither wished to make an error which would leave the other undisputed master of the Channel, the action became one of manoeuvre. At this, the French held the stronger hand and their gunnery damaged British rigging to the extent that it caused some disorder. Being numerically inferior, d'Orvilliers was content and did not press home his advantage.

Ushant was a drawn battle, with the British suffering more damage and casualties. This unsatisfactory outcome resulted in a major public quarrel between Keppel and his second-in-command, Palliser. Political opponents in their extra-service alter egos, they blamed each other for what was seen as a failure. Both were exonerated by relevant inquiries, but criticized. The seagoing career of neither progressed further, but the real culprit was the tactics of the time.

Unable to establish ascendancy in the English Channel while acting alone, the Brest squadron remained out of it until French diplomacy was finally successful in securing the Spanish as allies. From July 1779, therefore, the British Channel fleet faced potential combined odds of about seventy to forty.

Spain's ambition was to recover lost territories but, being unable to afford a long war, insisted that France prepare and lead a cross-Channel invasion. Two armies, each of 20,000, were thus assembled in western France, together with the necessary transports. The initial plan was to seize the Isle of Wight, from which Portsmouth could be neutralized. To contain the Royal Navy would require fifty of the combined ships of the line. The remaining sixteen would act as escorts during the short Channel crossing.

Having clearly read the developing threat, the British made preliminary moves. Fearing that he would be blockaded in Brest, in early June d'Orvilliers hurried to sea, not waiting to complete with sufficient stores for an extended operation. Following a week on passage, the French then had to mark time off Vigo for a further six weeks until, on 23 July, the Spanish finally emerged.

Despite earlier high-level liaison, signals and procedures between the two fleets had not been harmonized. Flouting agreement, the Spanish also refused to operate under French command, their contribution being thirty-six ships to the French thirty. Already low on provisions, the French contingent was then ravaged by smallpox. D'Orvilliers' only son was an officer aboard the flagship and the admiral helplessly watched him die, as so many others had already. The old man was devastated by his loss which, without doubt, affected his resolve.

Unaware of their enemies' difficulties, the British were concerned. At best, only forty-two ships could be mustered for the Channel fleet. Politics had so divided the senior ranks of the Royal Navy that an apolitical commander-in-chief had to be appointed. The best available was Admiral Sir Charles Hardy, who had last seen sea service some twenty years previously and who had already been given the pre-retirement sinecure of governor of Greenwich Hospital. Fortunately he had in Kempenfelt an able flag captain. Neither side, therefore, looked set to exhibit any high degree of operational brilliance. Nor did they.

At last, in August, the combined fleets entered the English Channel, only to encounter strong and persistent easterlies. Unable to beat up-Channel, short of every necessity and with his sick and dying multiplying by the day, d'Orvilliers conveyed his despair to his superiors, who accordingly ordered him to invade the Cornish coast. Fortunately for the French, this preposterous idea was not put to the test for, as he looked increasingly unable to contain British naval activity, the admiral was then ordered to bring the British fleet quickly to decisive battle. In Hardy, however, the Admiralty had chosen well for, in resolutely seeking to avoid an engagement, he seized the weather gauge and hovered enticingly out of reach. On 3 September, d'Orvilliers gratefully received orders to return to Brest, ostensibly for rest and recuperation pending a further attempt. The 8,000 sick that he put ashore, however, convinced the administration that the attempt was over.

From this sorry episode, neither side emerged with credit. Britain had suffered a major invasion scare that could readily have been avoided. Historically, any Franco-Spanish alliance spelt the possibility of their two fleets combining to outnumber that of the British and thus to threaten invasion. The traditional response had been to watch and, if necessary, blockade

Brest to prevent any such junction. Not only was Brest not so watched from the April, when the alliance was concluded, but when d'Orvilliers was later waiting off the Spanish coast for six weeks he was not hunted down by Hardy, whose fleet was superior in strength to the French alone.

The French, for their part, were cruising within easy range of their coasts. Why were their ships not rotated to complete with stores and crew replacements? And, with the French condition degenerating so obviously, why had their ally not then assumed the lead role to maintain the operation's momentum? The intention to invade has to be seen as lukewarm at best, while Spanish interest lay less in crushing Britain than in the recovery of Gibraltar and Minorca.

For both latter enterprises the French cooperated willingly, even to the extent of placing naval units under Spanish command. With the Royal Navy's presence in the Mediterranean reduced to a few cruising ships, it proved an easy task to land a military force on Minorca during the summer of 1781. Following a successful, six-month siege of the British base at Port Mahon, the island was again in Spanish hands.

Gibraltar proved an altogether tougher objective. Climaxing months of siege, an all-out Franco-Spanish assault was launched from across the bay in September 1782. It was repulsed with heavy loss and, one month later, Admiral Howe effectively lifted the siege by outwitting the combined fleets with an inferior force and running in a timely convoy of upwards of 150 sail.

Back in January 1780, Admiral Rodney had already rudely exposed the inadequacies of the Spanish fleet. En route to the Leeward Islands station, he escorted a supply convoy for Gibraltar and Minorca. Accompanied by a detachment from the Channel fleet, Rodney was in considerable strength. This he used off Cape Finisterre, rounding up a complete Spanish convoy and escort, the latter comprising a 64 and six frigates. Nine days later, near Cape St Vincent, he surprised a powerful Spanish squadron of eleven ships of the line and two frigates under the flag of Admiral Don Juan de Langara. In the course of a ten-hour pursuit, much of it at night, the British captured six ships of the line and sank a seventh. (Langara, who we will meet again, was considered by the British to be one of the better Spanish admirals.) Meanwhile, Rodney departed for the West Indies there, with Hood as his second-in-command, to crush de Grasse at the Saintes.

The French had a poor opinion of the sailing qualities of Spanish warships yet, so short were the British of fighting vessels, that all of Rodney's captures that were still serviceable were taken into naval service. Throughout the war the Royal Navy was shuffling its strength in order to maintain superiority where required.

Not the least problem centred on the controversial figure of Augustus Keppel as First Lord of the Admiralty. His appointment followed the change of administration caused by Lord North's downfall in March 1782. Keppel had previously refused any appointment that would have obliged him to fight Americans in what he considered an unjust war and, while he was considered to have insufficient breadth of vision to run a navy engaged on a global scale, he was the best that there was.

North, who had governed with assurance, had been a casualty of war. He knew that total victory meant large-scale borrowing and consequent increases in taxation. An unsatisfactory peace, however, would attract political opprobrium. Relentless increase in the national debt ran parallel with reverses in America and problems in the governance of British India.

Ireland also continued to be a major source of discontent and was another contributory factor in North's downfall. Its impoverished peasantry had no love for the English yet depended upon them. One of their greatest sources of revenue, the thriving wool trade with America and France, had been made illegal by war. Unemployment forced many Irishmen into the ranks of the British army, while home defence depended increasingly upon locally raised militias with close ties to their local communities. Even the least intelligent of politicians could appreciate parallels between Ireland and the lost American colonies. Seeing the Americans gain concessions on trade by taking a firm line with London, the Irish, headed by non-absentee landowners, did likewise. Parliament, concerned that the French might exploit the situation with an invasion of Ireland, had to buy off the agitators.

North's darkest political hour came in 1779 when the combined enemy fleets cruised the Western Channel with impunity, watched from a safe distance by a British Channel fleet of barely half its size and commanded by an elderly admiral who was also Member of Parliament for Portsmouth. Alarmed, the British public asked pointedly about the state of the Royal Navy.

It continued to do so as Gibraltar, notwithstanding its surviving a long siege, was also largely neutralized by it. Minorca fell to an operation mounted by the same combined fleets which then again came to cruise the Channel.

No longer able to hack his way through the thicket of problems that beset him, in early 1782 North resigned, yielding to an administration, headed by Lord Rockingham, riven by factionalism but anxious to end the war. In this, it ran counter to the instincts of the king. The canny George knew that the war, while expensive for Britain, was ruining France. To keep fighting the French would be to bankrupt them, while to appease the Americans would only encourage similar demands from the Irish. Above all, the king feared for Britain in the general spirit of revolution that heeded no national frontiers. But, as both his government and his people demanded peace, peace it had to be.

Given which, British policy could hope only that the new United States, in flourishing, would do so with Britain as a natural and influential partner and mentor, acting as a conduit to the world. For the French, the peace was unsatisfactory. Even as George III suspected, France had expended the bulk of her wealth in what Vergennes had hoped would prove an investment. Revenge on Britain was, indeed, a bonus but, being instrumental in gaining independence for the Americans, the French foreign minister felt entitled to better reward. As it was, Britain had yielded to the United States more than sufficient territory to satisfy the one-time colonials, leaving them with no grievance that the French could exploit. In being generous at the peace the British, rather than the French, appeared the benefactors; further, Britain retained the enormous tracts of land that were eastern Canada and Newfoundland as well as title to the rich Atlantic fishing grounds. In the West Indies, where she had hoped for major gain, France was required by the peace to restore most of what territory she had taken, while in India her remaining influence was negligible.

As a further irritation to the French, the Spanish, having contributed less to the great effort, appeared to have gained more. Their claims had been shrill and extensive and, having tried in vain for three years to take Gibraltar, they were now offered the fortress in return for concessions in America. Spain refused, preferring to retain her holdings in Florida. As the territory bordered that of the southern United States, Britain could foresee future complications and did not press the point. In agreeing to drop any further claim to Minorca, Britain also acknowledged no current interest in control of the western Mediterranean.

Lord Rockingham had died just months into his new ministry and it is to his successor, Lord Shelburne, that credit should be given for the sound common sense that pervaded the peace negotiations. He recognized that, militarily, Britain was exhausted and that concessions, if not offered, would quite likely have been wrung from him. By appearing generous through the concealment of weakness, he made considerable gains. However, because he could not reveal the underlying weakness of his negotiating position, he acquired a reputation of being a political schemer. For this he paid the political price, resigning in February 1783 following defeats in Parliament.

It remains a matter of debate whether political disunity at home affected the direction of the war to a greater extent than the greatly diverse war objectives caused political upheaval.

If France herself considered that she had gained something of a Pyrrhic victory after 1783, she could derive some satisfaction that her navy had acquitted itself well. Its revival had begun under Choiseul and continued under Sartine and, after October 1780, Castries. All shared the burning resolve of Vergennes to exact retribution on Britain. Castries, more than Sartine (and certainly more than his British equivalent, Keppel), thought in global terms, which maximized the flexibility of sea power. Reacting quickly to events or to perceived future advantage, it was Castries who had placed de Grasse in a position to intervene decisively prior to Yorktown and who had directed Suffren to cause a nuisance in the Indian Ocean. As both fleets were being operated to the limits of their resources, however, neither could strike a decisive blow.

The French took a pragmatic view of the performance of their fleet. Defeat and setback were accepted as necessary features of a grand strategy whose only important result was the final one. Drawn or indecisive engagements were not generally a matter of argument and recrimination, as they were with the British, but were gauged against their success in impeding the enemy's strategic aims.

During the War of American Independence the fundamental problem for the French was simply that the British were numerically superior in warships and had not neglected their supporting infrastructure. Only through alliance with Spain could the French achieve local superiority and cause the Royal Navy to be stretched to a dangerous extent. To win a war against the British, a powerful fleet was essential while France, unlike Britain, could afford the loss of such a fleet without facing defeat.

That their assistance to the Americans cost the French dearly is evident from the correspondence of Washington to French ministers, correspondence that reveals his own anxieties about an ultimate outcome which could be decided only through military reinforcement, naval superiority and, above all, money. 'Next to a loan of money, a constant naval superiority upon these coasts is the object most interesting.' And:

> If France delays a timely and powerful aid in this critical posture of our affairs, it will avail us nothing should she attempt it hereafter ... We are at the end of our tether, and that now or never deliverance must come [through maintaining] a superior fleet always in these seas, and France [putting] us in condition to be active by advancing us money.

Despite the formal ending of the war with the Treaty of Versailles of September 1783, Castries believed that peace would not last and moved successfully to increase the fleet strength from its current establishment of sixty to eighty. Considerable economies resulted from building to standard designs but the cost of fleet renewal and expansion proved punitive, not least because many materials needed to be sourced from abroad. Following a series of disputes with the controller-general of finance, Calonne, Castries resigned in 1787 but his successor, the less able comte de Luzerne, continued his policies.

The French navy's own administration was headed by the minister of marine who, like the First Lord of the Admiralty, was a political appointee. As the First Lord was not a member of the Cabinet so the minister of marine was not one of the King's Council of State, despite his title of secretary of state. Only after 1788 did the French institute a system which approximated to the British Board of Admiralty. This, the *Conseil de Marine*, was again headed by the minister, but included seaman officers, administrators and, when required, technical experts.

The ministry comprised four separate departments, having responsibility for ports and arsenals, finance, recruitment and, surprisingly, colonial affairs. Day-to-day operation of the fleet was the function of the first. It supervised subsidiary organizations at the major *arsenaux* (arsenals) of Brest, Rochefort and Toulon, with lesser administrations at Dunkirk, Le

Havre, Lorient, Bordeaux, Bayonne and Marseille. Of the latter group Lorient, recently acquired from the bankrupt East India Company, was so well equipped that it, too, attained arsenal status during the forthcoming French Revolutionary War.

It will be noted that there were only minor naval facilities facing the major enemy across the English Channel. Work had begun in 1783 on the construction of a deep-water roadstead at Cherbourg. Because of the depth of water the enclosing moles were to be based on about ninety enormous conical structures, built ship-fashion, ballasted with rock, towed to the appropriate site, moored and sunk in position through the introduction of further rock through numerous apertures. For the age, it was engineering on a bold scale, demanding vast quantities of timber, ballast and skilled manpower. Great prestige surrounded the project through the close attention paid it by the king, who was greatly interested in his navy and its activities. The local economy boomed and, at least in Normandy, Louis enjoyed a considerable boost to his popularity.

Again, however, the expense was crippling and, by 1786, Calonne, who had spent enthusiastically on both navy and military, had to pronounce the financial cupboard bare. As funds petered out, the Cherbourg project came to a halt, to be abandoned totally in 1789 as Revolution gripped the nation.

The organization of the country's naval ports could almost have been designed to promote factionalism, a failing that in fact permeated the entire service. Louis XIV's great minister, Colbert, had established the caste of *intendants* who, across the land, took instruction directly from the Royal Council of State to initiate and oversee required action. Incumbents acquired considerable status and power, usually reflected in their manner.

Until 1776, an *intendant* represented supreme authority in each naval arsenal. In that year they were subordinated to the *commandant de la marine*, a serving flag officer. Three separate departments, each headed by a director, reported through a director-general to the commandant. Each director was a serving seaman officer and their responsibilities were for shipbuilding, ordnance and port operation. There were also five administrative bureaux: for shipyards and workshops; central stores; ships' stores and victualling; hospitals and labour; and pay and establishment. Each bureau was headed by a commissioner reporting through a commissioner-general to the *intendant* and, thence to the commandant. Every fortnight the commandant chaired a meeting of a local *Conseil de Marine*, comprising the *intendant*, the director-general and commissioner-general and their aides, and the secretary to the committee.

Although civilians, the administrators were members of a corps. Responsible to an *intendant* and thus, until recently, directly to the highest levels of government, the corps had its own structure, uniform and powerful sense of group identity. It greatly resented losing overall authority and its opinion of naval officers was that, in general, they were incompetent.

For their part, the naval officer class, much of it from aristocratic background, regarded the administrators simply as social inferiors, and to be treated as such. Not surprisingly, therefore, the commandant and the *intendant*, as leaders of disparate groups, did not usually enjoy the smoothest of relationships.

French naval officers were recruited rather differently to their British counterparts. They fell into two distinct categories, an arrangement which again encouraged divisions. The upper tier was termed the *Grand Corps*, an officer of which could command a king's ship and progress upward in rank without any artificial bar. Entry qualification included the mandatory noble birth and, further, a family prepared to meet the considerable bill for incidentals attached to training. Once accepted, a boy was rated as a *garde*, the process of social subdivision beginning immediately through his being attached to either the *Compagnie des Gardes de la Marine* or to the more exclusive company of the *Gardes du Pavillon Amiral,* from which were recruited aides to senior personnel.

Officers of the *Grand Corps*, by virtue of that colour's inclusion in their uniform, were known colloquially as *Rouges*. All other than their own were treated with the disdain then common to all aristocrats. A debilitating feature was the assumption that social superiority counted for as much as rank. As members of an exclusive club, all ranks in the *Grand Corps* mixed freely and with considerable informality. An order received by a junior rank might well be a matter of discussion before it was executed. Their studied arrogance guaranteed continual friction with all other grades. The practical arts of seamanship and gunnery, so much a part of the British officer's experience from the outset, were inclined to be regarded as the province of others, the preferred education being theoretical.

Serving alongside the *Rouges* were officers of the so-called *Petit Corps*, whose plainer uniforms led to their being termed *officiers bleus* or, simply, *Bleus*. This term itself carried pejorative overtones as it referred to officers recruited from the lower social strata that, being of other than the nobility, barred them from command of a royal warship. Paradoxically, as *Bleus* tended to be drawn from the merchant service, or promoted from the navy's own lower orders, they tended to have a superior grounding in the more practical requirements of their calling, together with a better understanding of, and relationship with, the lower deck. The relative importance of the *Bleus* reflected the state of the service at any time for, in emergency, their numbers could be expended fairly rapidly while those of the *Rouges* could not. The latter thus viewed them as a potential threat to their own privileges, not least with respect to the command of smaller regular warships.

The manner in which the *Rouges* distanced themselves not only generated a considerable fund of hostility but also concealed a goodly proportion of incompetent officers, who rose to considerable seniority by virtue of birth rather than ability. Although the Royal Navy was not above criticism in this respect, its wider emphasis on practical seamanship and the sea time in which to practise it tended to identify and weed out the poorer material.

A further unhealthy trend, again not unique to France, was for a large number of aged senior officers to crowd the upper reaches of the navy list, blocking the advancement of the younger and more able. Efforts to introduce change had, to date, proved ineffective until the marquis de Castries became minister of marine in 1780.

Following the end of the American War, Castries introduced a series of reforms to redress the more obvious failings of the service. Boys would now be recruited for officer training from a wider social background, being allocated to one of two new naval colleges. The *Garde* was no more, being replaced by a new *élève-aspirant* who was, however, still to be drawn from the nobility. Those from the more impoverished end of the aristocratic scale could now be supported by the state if they possessed genuine academic ability.

Those from the very fringe of aristocracy could join as *volontaires*, in company with those from non-aristocratic but respectable background and selected merchant navy officers. Although the term echoed that of the British system, there existed no similarity: although such entrants might serve with considerable distinction and gain promotion, it was only rarely to the ranks of the *Grand Corps*.

Castries's intention was that the *aspirants* of lesser social standing, primarily the *volontaires*, should graduate to a new grade of junior officer known as a *sous-lieutenant de vaisseau*. These would considerably out-number the still-exclusive *élèves*, and would constitute a pool of trained professionals for times of emergency. In peacetime, they would be allowed command of minor, i.e. non-line, warships. Failing such a posting, a graduate would be put on half-pay but remain free to take a mercantile position to maintain and extend his skills. Exceptional *sous-lieutenants* could be promoted to lieutenant, thus joining the *Grand Corps*, but this was rare.

Although social distinctions were still being observed, therefore, the process of merging the *Rouges* and *Bleus* had begun. In fairness, it should be stated that the aristocracy were nothing if not well-educated and many accepted the reforms as a force for good. Some, indeed, were known to support the principles of emancipation and individual rights enunciated by the new Americans as justification for revolution.

Castries's reforms affected all departments of the navy. It was he who introduced the new grade of seaman-gunner, controversially recruited from the ranks of army artillerymen and retrained as naval specialist gunners. Important technical matters, such as ship construction within the arsenals, ordnance and port movements, he allotted to new port officers who, although serving ashore, were drawn from the naval officer corps rather than from the administrators.

There was still little done to improve the lot of the average seaman, however. As in the Royal Navy, budget shortfalls usually translated into his pay falling into arrears, a cause of widespread discontent. With a smaller base of commercial shipping and fishing than was available to the British, the French had greater difficulty in raising the requisite number of men to crew their steadily growing fleet. Despite this, they did not resort to the impress-ment of landmen. Instead, all males of active age resident in coastal districts were required to register for a form of conscription. Each was called to the colours for spells which could be years apart and which varied in length according to urgency. In return for this somewhat irregular upheaval the government granted them exemption from certain taxes or commitments and, theoretically at least, compensated the severely injured or the families of those lost at sea.

Poor pay, or even, on occasion, no pay, spelt shortage or even destitution for a sailor's family, so evasion of call-up and desertion were common. A deserter in the Royal Navy could usually expect to be summarily executed if apprehended and this, too, was the ultimate theoretical punishment for his French counterpart. A degree of official pragmatism, however, saw such a sentence rarely applied. After all, if the navy was already short of personnel, what purpose would be served by killing those it did have? Savage physical punishment was an alternative but, again, was less often applied than stoppage of pay and privileges, such as they were. Persistent offenders were made to serve longer spells, even a lifetime, in the service. Small wonder that serving the nation was, itself, seen as a form of prison sentence. Disobedience, mutiny or incitement to mutiny were most likely to attract capital or severe punishment, the latter including service in the galley squadron still maintained in the Mediterranean.

TOULON WAS AN EXAMPLE of what would later be called a 'company town', being dependent for employment, directly or indirectly, on the arsenal. French royal yards, like their British equivalents, tended to be overmanned in order to guarantee sufficient skilled labour in time of emergency. The average *ouvrier* therefore enjoyed the comparative luxury of protected employment and, at least in peacetime, a leisurely pace of work, free health care and a contributory pension scheme. In return, his rate of pay was somewhat less than that to be expected in private yards.

However, the American War had so depleted the national wealth that economies were necessary across the board, dockyards being no exception. Following what was already common commercial practice, therefore, the labour force was reduced by about two-thirds and naval work put out to competitive tender. As most of the workers 'released' by the yard found re-employment in new private enterprises established to take advantage of the revised system, there existed a powerful solidarity between workers within and without.

A typically French paternalism was evident as groups of workers were gradually driven to tendering for work at entirely unrealistic low prices in order to remain employed. The then *intendant* of Toulon, Pierre-Victor Malouet, believed that society had a duty to support all its members and found means to pay small retainers to key workers and to subsidize contractors for the training of apprentices.

As the l780s progressed, however, state funding was steadily reduced and paid irregularly. By 1788 contractors were being paid over four months in arrears, individuals three. Official reports spoke of 'a spirit of rebellion' about which authority could do nothing. Genuine hardship was evident across the town, accompanied by a natural sense of grievance. Hope that action was being taken was engendered by the compilation of the *cahiers de doléances* and the reactivation in 1787 of the ancient Estates General for all that it would be dominated by the landowning nobility.

Shortfalls in production ensured that the cost of grain, cooking oil and meat, all staples, rose inexorably. In past times, more severe increases had occurred without causing unrest but in the particularly straitened circumstances in which Toulon found itself demonstrations began, initially directed at property. Punishments meted out by the courts failed to prevent their proliferation.

The commandant of the arsenal was d'Albert de Rions, a 61-year-old veteran of proven ability who had served with de Grasse and Suffren. He was determined to maintain order, seeing this to be the only way in which the naval base could continue to function. In law and order he saw security for his workers and the populace at large, together with a continuing respect for individual rights. D'Albert pleaded with the minister of marine for funds with which to pay arrears in wages and to keep the yard working full time. He resolutely opposed the increasingly arrogant behaviour of the militia, now known as the *Milice Nationale*, and endeavoured to prevent dockyard workers from joining. To the commune of Toulon he was 'deeply imbued with aristocratic prejudices'.

In the midst of social upheaval the arsenal succeeded for a while in remaining detached. A first clash arose over what should have been the trivial matter of wearing cockades, or favours, either the tricolour of the Revolution or the black Austrian symbol of royalist sympathy. The *milice* attracted a considerable element of troublemakers and in November 1789 one patrol arrested an officer who was sporting a black favour. Strong representations to the municipal leaders gained his release, the military authorities demanding, though not receiving, an apology.

As was the way during the Revolution, the civic Permanent Committee complained directly to the National Assembly in Paris. This produced no direct result from an organization which already had more than enough with which to concern itself, but the commandant's own impulsiveness then inflamed the situation further.

Accusing them of troublemaking, d'Albert dismissed two employees of the arsenal. As they were also members of the *milice*, however, this action was popularly denounced as victimization. D'Albert was entreated by the civic authorities to reinstate them but refused, regarding this as a sign of weakness. The pair were promptly elevated to the status of martyrs and the following morning a large proportion of the workforce refused to work, appearing instead outside d'Albert's official residence, where he was meeting with a deputation from the Permanent Committee in an effort to take action against the mob; deprived of his most obvious symbol of authority, the commandant belatedly acceded to the committee's demands. Enraged by rumours that the marines had been ordered to fire on civilians, however, the mob overran the building, seized d'Albert and several of his staff and consigned them to cells as common prisoners.

Proceedings at Toulon considerably alarmed the National Assembly, which was reminded by the minister of marine that a quarter of the nation's naval strength was here hostage to events. Debate aired the usual polarized points of view: whether ultimate authority rested with the National Assembly or with the crown and its representatives; whether serving naval officers should be dismissed *en masse* and be replaced by men 'not suspected by the people'.

Released by order of the assembly, d'Albert was none the less refused permission to plead his case before it. Although he and his staff were now cast in the role of counter-Revolutionaries defying the 'people's will', he was fortunate in that, for once, the assembly agreed a moderate outcome. Despite a plea from no less an orator than Robespierre, that he feared that the assembly would be seen as encouraging the 'enemies of liberty' above 'patriotism', the verdict was that both sides had acted in what they considered the nation's best interests.

Ominously, the prisoners were finally released, early in 1790, by order of the National Assembly, a demand from the king's minister having been ignored. The refusal of the assembly to consider prosecuting the municipal leaders gravely undermined the authority of the navy. Pointing out the imminent danger of a total collapse in discipline if the National Guardsmen concerned were to go unpunished, every available officer at Toulon signed a petition, which was sent to the assembly. The response was an anodyne statement from the minister of marine adjuring d'Albert's successor to act with circumspection and to avoid any action that might inflame the situation. It was clear that final authority no longer rested with the minister. The civic authorities, meanwhile, extended membership of the militia to a total of 4,000, a considerable proportion of the town's eligible male population.

As a royal government could no longer support naval officers in the maintenance of discipline, and the National Assembly favoured interference by the civic authorities 'in the name of the people', the immediate future looked bleak. One French commentator noted that naval officers had become outlaws: 'Anyone sanguine or patriotic enough to remain at his post would come, by virtue of his origin, and without further enquiry, to the prison or to the scaffold.' Matters had not yet quite degenerated to that extent but the prophecy would prove to be accurate enough.

IN OCTOBER 1789, while Commandant d'Albert de Rions was still struggling to keep the Toulon arsenal functioning in the face of a growing tide of dissent and disobedience, the National Assembly took a fundamental step in reshaping the French navy according to Revolutionary ideals. A twelve-man Marine Committee was formed with the broad brief of looking in depth at the current structure and administration of the service, to evaluate similar foreign institutions and to recommend the size and form of an affordable fleet, 'founded on reason' and best suited to the nation's needs.

To undertake this very necessary review were appointed initially, and very liberally, six of the nobility and six of the Third Estate. Of the former group, five were officers from the navy, one from the army. Of the latter, four were drawn from the world of commerce and the merchant marine, one was a lawyer and the other the late *intendant* at the Toulon yard. Here were a dozen eminently sensible men, well qualified to carry out what was required of them. Already, however, the contagion of social division had taken hold to the extent that men of like professional opinion and training were irrevocably divided by their origins. To stoke the fires of controversy further, six more members were added to the committee in the following June. Of these, only one was a naval officer of the *Grand Corps*.

Despite time-consuming wrangling, the committee did a thorough job. Ironically, however, its main findings resulted in decrees which caused upheaval in the service at precisely the wrong time. Its prime target, naturally, was the unpopular *Grand Corps* and the whole procedure for selecting naval officers. The nationwide collection of complaint and injustice contained in the *cahiers* of 1789 included much criticism that capable men from the merchant service and experienced non-commissioned officers were unable to advance their careers in the face of what was effectively a closed shop populated exclusively by the nobility.

A first objective, then, was to abandon privilege and to promote equality, the noble ideal of the Revolution. The king would still be recognized as the supreme commander of the service but appointments within its officer corps would now be a matter for the body appointed by the assembly. The assembly would also vote annual budgets.

More idealism, and the opinions of the commercial element of the Marine Committee, was evident in the fleet now being dedicated primarily to the protection of French commerce and the colonies which stimulated it. Emphasis on the use of the navy as an instrument of national policy was played down, interestingly inasmuch as the assembly was careering down a path that would shortly lead to war with half of Europe.

The new scheme for the provision of officers would favour a core of professionals who would join the service at the age of 15. As *aspirants* they would spend five years under training. Men between the ages of 18 and 30 could also be recruited to the lowest grade of officer, the *enseigne*. This required four years' sea time and the passing of an examination and, while being fully open to men of the merchant service, was the obvious next step for the *aspirant*, who would have more knowledge of the specialist skills required by the regular navy.

Beyond the age of 24, a suitable *enseigne* could hold a minor command, which commission entitled him to be classed *entretenu*, or salaried. The remainder, or *non-entretenu,* had no naval pay or rights and formed a qualified reserve pool within the merchant service.

Switching from one service to the other appears to have been regarded as perfectly in order up to the age of 40, by which time *enseignes* were expected to have passed for lieutenant. By this age, of course, a man would have had his best years and, as Mahan has pointed out, a period of commercial prosperity would be sufficient to rob the regular navy of its best men.

For the moment, the assembly had to recognize the existing situation and, while it could abolish the whole officer corps by decree, its initial selection of replacements would necessarily be from its ranks. Those not selected were treated generously, their basic entitlement on retirement being 'at least' two-thirds of their then-current pay. Any that had served a minimum of ten years in the rank that he was then holding would be retired in the next higher.

We have already seen how recruitment for the lower deck was through obligation placed upon able-bodied men in coastal communities. Personnel from this service were made eligible for service in groups, or *classes*. Administering the system in each area were retired naval officers, themselves responsible to an *intendant-général*.

To the extent that an individual, beyond his liability for service, was free to pursue his chosen occupation, the *classe* system appealed to the Marine Committee. Although the system was therefore to remain, its method of supervision had to change, for a majority on the committee maintained that a seaman before his actual mobilization was a 'citizen of the State' and as such was entitled to be directed by an elected representative rather than a member, retired or otherwise, of the military. In imposing this change the committee effectively removed the responsibility of manning the fleet from central authority to virtually unregulated local democracy.

Nor did the Marine Committee approve of the system in the dockyards, whereby the naval commandant exercised authority over the administrative *intendant*. Here again, by virtue of his connection with the *Grand Corps*, a commandant was inevitably seen as an agent of royal executive power. Rather than return to the earlier arrangement, where the *intendant* possessed the greater authority, the committee decided to add yet another level of management by creating the post of overall director, to be known as the *ordonnateur civil*.

IN SEPTEMBER 1790 the great arsenal of Brest followed Toulon into mutinous chaos. A new naval penal code had been approved by the Constituent National Assembly with the laudable aim of removing the arbitrary nature of punishment through the institution of a standard tariff. Rather unfortunately, the ex-commandant of the Toulon arsenal, d'Albert de Rions, had been posted to Brest as squadron commander. It was among the crews of his ships that disaffection arose, triggered by provisions in the penal code to which they took exception.

Still wearied with his recent experiences, d'Albert pleaded to the minister of marine that either the affected crews be broken up or that commissioners be appointed to restore order. Now effectively powerless, the minister, the comte de Luzerne, could only refer the matter to the assembly, which took no action. Their demands disregarded, the seamen responded by refusing to allow a small squadron to sail for the West Indies as ordered.

For over a year Brest had been administered by a body which styled itself the General Council of the Commune. This had insisted upon, and received, expressions of loyalty from the commandant of the arsenal and the senior officer of the army garrison. Despite this, both officers were still regarded with some suspicion, a suspicion that became outright hostility with the establishment in the city of an extreme Jacobin Club.

The civic authorities made continuous efforts to increase their control of the military, mainly through endlessly eroding the authority of its officers. Appeals by the latter to their relevant ministers had no effect and the council succeeded in gradually alienating the ratings and their officers, groups that had previously harboured no particular animosity toward each other.

Matters deteriorated suddenly when, on 14 September, the *Léopard* 74 arrived alone. Her crew had mutinied during the previous month while off San Domingo (now the Dominican Republic), had sent their captain and most of his officers ashore and had then embarked the colony's rebel assembly and a regiment of mutinous troops. Upon arrival at Brest, the self-appointed commanding officer reported directly to the municipality rather than to the naval authorities. He and the crew were fêted by the city as Revolutionary patriots.

The arrival of the *Léopard* incited mutiny aboard other ships in port. Their commanding officers appealed to their admiral to restore order but d'Albert, his authority already undermined by experience at Toulon, was ignored. Unable to continue, he resigned his commission.

A number of junior officers then made a general appeal to the rebel crews in an effort to persuade them that their officers were being unfairly branded as counter-revolutionaries. They were met with a mixture of indifference and outright hostility, although, in some ships, relationships between crew and officers remained normal.

In Paris, the assembly was well aware that the current troubles with the navy were not in the national interest. The national reputation had taken a knock due to the inability to stage a naval show of strength either to support Spanish allies during the Nootka Sound affair or, in India, to back the activities of the rebel Tippu Sultan.

Interestingly, therefore, the assembly invoked the king's authority to despatch two special commissioners to Brest. Arriving at the end of September, these joined with two municipal officials successfully to enlist the assistance of the Jacobins to restore order. This, however, remained on condition that the assembly modify the penal code.

The commissioners' report none the less undermined further the waning authority of ships' officers in praising the 'patriotism' of the mutineers, the citizens and the civil authorities of Brest, while commenting that they, the commissioners, were 'well persuaded' that the officers would put every effort into consolidating the work of 'the Friends of the [new] Constitution'.

On 19 October the Constituent Assembly received the final report on the situation in Brest. Concerned at the state to which affairs had degenerated, it proposed to censure the municipality for exceeding its authority. Moderates, in fact, demanded that curbs be applied to the new 'aristocracy of the municipalities'. The penal code, in addition, would stand unaltered. Once again, however, it proved all too easy for the assembly's extremists to reverse such intentions by playing on the universal distaste for the monarchy and by denouncing ministers as being the instruments of its power. Breakdown of discipline in the fleet, it was claimed, had stemmed from the incompetence of the minister of marine.

Spirited debate resulted again in a public expression of the assembly's gratitude to the commissioners and the citizens of Brest. The penal code would, after all be modified and, as a gesture to the Revolution, the pure white national ensign, as worn by the fleet, would be defaced by the addition of the new tricolour in its upper hoist.

An immediate result was the resignation of de Luzerne, the minister of marine. While not the most effective, he had been the latest in a series of ministers to devote honest effort to strengthening the service. On his departure, he noted with disillusion that while 'the fleets of other nations cover the seas ... our naval forces [are] condemned to inaction and inertia by ... indiscipline'.

Not surprisingly, there was a general exodus of experienced naval officers, stimulated by a combination of hostility shown them and the generous retirement terms agreed by the Marine Committee. Convinced that France was descending into anarchy, many went abroad. It was the task of the committee (itself considerably affected by change and resignation) to define the form of a new and acceptable officer corps to the provision and maintenance of which the Constituent Assembly could give its approval.

The way ahead, agreed in April 1791, was that the standing strength of the French fleet should first be defined and, based on this strength, that of the permanent corps of officers with which to man it. All permanent naval officers would be recruited as *aspirants*, who would be required to make an early career commitment. In addition there would be a body of officers, serving in the merchant marine, who would be accepted as *enseignes non-entretenus* and who, in times of fleet expansion, could be commissioned as lieutenants. On the basis of this proposal the assembly formally dismissed the whole officer corps on 1 May 1791. Those who were not then retired were reappointed a fortnight later to the revised structure.

The navy reflected the condition of the nation itself in that the Constituent Assembly discovered that widespread dissent was easier to foment than it was to halt. Having been fulsomely congratulated on the outcome of the damaging Brest mutiny, the various parties involved were made quickly aware that the general outrage had been damped down but was far from extinguished. On the American station, French crews were in open revolt, refusing orders on the specious grounds that the only will that mattered was 'the Will of the People', i.e. themselves. This distorted logic soon escaped ashore, first to the European population, then to the native. Military authority had imposed unpopular colonial rule; its weakening revealed both its fragility and the true extent of popular resentment. As an awful warning to France herself, her richest colony, San Domingo, fell prey to total and bloody insurrection, leading to its eventual loss.

In an effort to placate the rumblings at Brest, the new minister of marine, the transient comte de Fleurieu, made what he assumed to be a popular appointment to replace the unfortunate d'Albert. The comte de Bougainville was already a notable figure – scientist, explorer and naval commander of proven ability. Of the nobility, yet a known opponent of privilege, he was still obliged to meet the mutineers head-on. He published and distributed a general call to reason but, having had it disregarded, he made examples of some ringleaders by having their names removed from the register of seamen. This, with the current arrangements, meant that they could not seek alternative employment in commerce or in fishing. Like his predecessor, Bougainville was unable to convince his men that he embodied 'the Will of the State' or that, as the state was now personified in the elected Constituent Assembly rather than in the sovereign, his orders represented 'the Will of the People'.

A diplomatic solution between Britain and Spain fortunately solved the Nootka Sound crisis and the French navy could be stood down from its embarrassingly unsuccessful attempt at mobilization. Aware that it had been only with the greatest difficulty that he had mustered a reliable squadron for despatch to the West Indies, the distinguished Bougainville ended his career by resigning in disgust, fulminating at 'perverse men, deaf to the voice of reason'.

By mid 1791, the flow of officers deserting the service had become a flood. Traditional hierarchical discipline had disintegrated. Naval authority, centrally exercised through the Ministry of Marine, was subordinated to that of local municipalities. Insubordination and outright mutiny were rife. In the name of the 'People's Will', neither was corrected by the Constituent Assembly.

Reduced to a figurehead, the minister of marine had little more function than to legitimize the assembly's demands. In an attempt to define the structure of the new officer corps, he published in May 1791 a list justifying a core strength of 9 vice admirals, 18 rear admirals (*contre-amiraux*), 170 captains and 530 lieutenants. This cadre would be expanded from the reserve in time of general mobilization.

In the following October yet another minister, Bertrand de Moleville, took over the increasingly thankless task of directing naval affairs. In February 1792 the assembly charged him with creating a register of available officers. Each electing to serve had then to provide evidence of domicile in France and to swear a civic oath. Yet more were alienated and the haemorrhage continued. Published in March 1792, the list comprised just 2 vice admirals, 3 rear admirals, 42 captains and 356 lieutenants. Even this total was diminishing daily.

From the Atlantic ports to the Caribbean, from the Mediterranean to

India, the French navy was now afflicted by revolt. The colonies themselves were in a ferment but crews of French warships obliged their commanding officers to return home rather than take action against their 'brothers' ashore, action for which they claimed they would be 'reproached and denounced' by authorities at home.

Increasingly politicized, crews saw themselves as an integral part of the Revolutionary movement. Experienced officers noted that their attitudes had little or nothing to do with poor conditions, rations or pay, or even with the customary level of distaste shown by the lower deck for its officers. Rather, the latter were viewed as counter-revolutionaries to be watched, reported upon and if necessary denounced. Those who orchestrated this breakdown in relationship were fully protected in their activities, being granted absolution through the Constituent Assembly's general amnesty for 'political' action, declared in September 1791.

A new and more sinister turn of events occurred when a newly appointed commanding officer was attacked in Brest by an armed group unknown to him but who obviously targeted him. He escaped with his life only through fortuitous intervention by members of the National Guard. The municipal authorities, far from condemning the act, or seeking out the perpetrators, declared that the officer concerned was known to have quelled trouble in San Domingo. In the current hothouse atmosphere of France, this translated as 'oppression of patriots' and, therefore, the officer should be debarred from returning in a new command.

Pressing home their attack, the civic authorities blamed the minister of marine for provoking trouble through his unsuitable selection, i.e. poor judgement. As similar accusations could be levelled at many commanding officers, a significant number were sufficiently alarmed to refuse offered commands.

This only added to the general problem of the disintegration of the officer corps. As shortfalls increased, procedures were tightened, preventing many from leaving the service by request. The result was that officers simply deserted, sufficiently alarmed to abandon career and pension. As they would be damned if they stayed or damned if they left, it is not surprising that many became *émigrés*.

Individual decisions taken by officers could not help but have been influenced by the abortive flight of the king and his family in June 1791.

Their apprehension at Varennes, ignominious return to the capital and subsequent house arrest could only have been deeply unsettling. The monarch was the embodiment of the state to which they had pledged their oaths of loyalty. That state was visibly disintegrating, its figurehead reduced to a puppet. With their customary authority no longer enforceable, all that awaited them was what one termed 'a continual source of grief, perhaps of disgrace and humiliation'.

De Moleville articulated a royal appeal to officers who were considering desertion and, indeed, to those who had already gone abroad, through a letter to all port commandants. In its emphasis on loyalty, honour and duty, however, it served only to inflame the temper of the Left of what was, by now, the Legislative Assembly. This body, in November 1791, went on to decree that all *émigrés* were suspected of conspiracy and that all those who did not return by 1 January 1792 to explain themselves would be condemned, *in absentia*, to capital punishment. The king still retained sufficient authority to veto this monstrous proposal, but the minister of marine's further attempts to defend and to appeal to the officer corps only drew upon himself the full fire of the assembly.

Accused of entirely misrepresenting the state of the navy and conniving with its officers to facilitate their desertion, the minister attracted a stinging vote of no confidence from the Marine Committee. As ministers were appointed by the crown rather than by the assembly, this did not mean that de Moleville was obliged to resign. With some courage he stuck to his post, but the wilder elements of the assembly continued their personal attack, seeking no less than his impeachment for treason. Pushed to the limit, the assembly finally ran into the question that none wished to answer: what if the king, informed that his minister had lost the confidence of the assembly, replied that he retained every confidence? In the face of this constitutional issue the assembly recoiled, voting by a slender majority to reject the demands for the minister's impeachment. The resulting implication was important inasmuch as the supremacy of royal executive power had been reaffirmed. This was, however, not an end to the matter as the Legislative Assembly was by now divided hopelessly into small factions that could not be categorized as simply Left or Right but which pursued their own shrill agendas.

De Moleville had disagreed with the comte de Narbonne-Lara, the minister of war, who believed that the concept of constitutional monarchy would best be served through the various ministers giving their whole-hearted support to the assembly. Narbonne, however, was all for war against the *émigré* forces that were gathering beyond the frontiers of France, although the robust response from Austria and Prussia early in 1792 had thrown the assembly into confusion. Charges and counter-charges of treason were bandied, the king dismissing Narbonne, who was also associated with the now-disgraced Lafayette, on 9 March.

The position of the minister of marine was now intolerable but rather than step down because of public opinion, and thus appear to accept the accusations levelled at him, he agreed to go a week later, which date coincided with the review of the revised officer corps. Implicit in his res-ignation, rather than impeachment, was that the constitutional monarchy remained the absolute authority in the state and, by extension, in the navy, despite the actions of Revolutionary civic communes.

In handing over to his successor, the ineffective Lacoste, de Moleville left a government headed by a king who was now completely a prisoner of the situation in which he found himself. A major crisis could only be a matter of time.

EVEN DURING THE American War of Independence the French navy had suffered a shortage of experienced officers. Measures taken to reform the system and to expand the Navy List had had too little time to take real effect before Revolution saw the near dissolution of the officer corps. By mid 1792 it was acknowledged that, in the event of a general mobilization, there would be too few commanding officers and lieutenants to man even existing numbers of ships.

Deputations of merchant marine officers had been lobbying hard at the assembly, their workaday image creating a favourable impression. Opportunities for rapid career advancement were obvious and numbers were so short that the acceptance of those eligible was inevitable.

In September 1792 the Legislative Assembly declared France a republic. With the monarchy thus suspended, other European monarchies evinced varying degrees of hostility. War became a growing possibility and one involving the British would again hinge upon sea control. Urgent action was necessary, the assembly's Marine Committee having to lower its preferred standard of qualification in order to attract sufficient entrants. Any regular naval captain with just one month's experience now found himself eligible to be considered for promotion to rear admiral. Masters from the merchant marine who could demonstrate a minimum of five years in the foreign trade could be made post captain with immediate effect. Five years of sea service of any kind qualified a mate to be made a regular lieutenant.

As so few of the *Rouges* remained, it might be assumed that class tensions had relaxed. Class may, indeed, have diminished as the primary cause of trouble, but it had now been replaced by a deep-felt sense of inequality. The *Bleus*, having endured the attitudes of the *aristos* for so long, felt strongly that they should fill the greater part of the vacuum now created among senior ranks only to find themselves competing with a flood of entrants from the merchant marine, men who had never trod the decks of a warship but who were being fraternally embraced by the now all-powerful civic authorities.

Purged of 'counter-revolutionaries', the officer corps was increasingly cooperative with local communes. New-style oaths were taken under the latter's auspices, swearing loyalty to the state, no longer to the crown. These were but a contribution to a wider ceremony, a *jour de fête* to emphasize the new-found solidarity between the local populace ('the People') and the service. The few remaining *Rouges* had by now adopted a pragmatic approach, accepting the situation in return for keeping their posts. Otherwise the readiness with which the corps exhibited its fealty reflected its vastly altered composition.

In a spirit of fraternity, each ship received a large representation of the Phrygian cap, the red cap of Revolution sported by activists nationwide and now to be secured at the masthead.

IN THE FRENCH FLEET'S *ports de l'océan*, naval authorities succeeded in maintaining some sense of order and discipline despite municipal interference and the occasional lapse into mutiny, but at Toulon the situation was intractable.

Superficially, the problems faced by the city were no different from those affecting many others. Established authority had been overthrown in a sincere desire by all to achieve an eventual goal of a stable and equitable society based on a revised and fair constitution. Class divisions ran deep, however, and city populations were every bit as stratified as the navy. National movement toward a new society involved many a contest, no less bruising, between professionals and artisans to exercise power on a local scale. As matters developed, it was apparent that unrest, due initially to social problems and injustices, had also acquired a political dimension. The general foment suited the purposes of local activists, who tended inevitably to gravitate toward membership of the nearest Jacobin Club.

Lack of central funding had obliged the commandant of the Toulon arsenal first to introduce a new system of payment by result. If this proved deeply unpopular with the workforce, worse was to come in the shape of short-time working and lay-offs. Genuine hardship caused inevitable unrest in an already volatile general atmosphere. Troublemakers easily exploited the situation, resulting in the commandant, like his predecessor, being hauled physically before the town's Revolutionary council. Here, he was instructed to approach the Constituent Assembly to reverse all earlier decisions made on economic grounds and to release weapons from the arsenal to arm the expanding National Guard.

The assembly did, in fact, agree to return to the previous system of payment but, in the absence of actual funds, settlement would needs be partly in the unpopular government *assignats*, already widely issued to compensate for sequestrations. This paper money carried an in-built devaluation at each exchange, and deprivation increased to the extent that the new *ordonnateur* approved the distribution of bread from the arsenal's bakery, normally dedicated to supplying the fleet. Growing hardship did not convert the arsenal's workforce overnight into rampant revolutionaries. Ordinary men, however, responsible for the welfare of their families, were becoming deeply discontented. A large workforce, vital to both the navy and the local economy, was here wide open to agitation.

Following the trend set by the assembly in Paris, provincial revolutionaries split into factions, Toulon being no exception. Thus the Jacobin Club, formed in 1790, was opposed by a new group formed in the following year. Its members were not easily labelled, but may be termed 'moderate'. Each group sought to control the municipality and, in doing so, necessarily wooed the National Guard. This factionalized the guard in turn, which climaxed its division in a public shoot-out.

The virulently left-wing, who stubbornly retained control of the authority in the town of Toulon, contrasted with the relatively moderate administration of the greater Toulon district and Var *département*. Events in the capital were causing grave misgivings in these bodies which, none the less, praised the assembly for its confirmation that a monarchy-based constitution would persist (which, of course, proved in September to be totally untrue). Despite this gesture, in May 1792 local Jacobins demanded that an armed detachment be sent to Paris in response to the appeal for forces to repel the invaders, whose advance was threatening the capital.

The bloody events in the Tuileries in Paris during the June again provoked comment from the Var departmental administration, which publicly denounced such action carried out in the name of the people. This brought about a violent response from the Toulon civic authorities, virulent protest being followed by the murder of four Var administrators by Jacobin extremists.

Early in 1792 a new commandant, the marquis de Flotte, had taken over at Toulon. He had tried to steer a middle course, avoiding outright condemnation of events in the port to date. If he thus anticipated a smooth relationship with the municipality he was disappointed, for he placed himself between two extremes. The establishment navy suspected that he harboured sympathy with the concept of authority by the people; the revolutionaries in the Hôtel de Ville objected to his continuing insistence that, as commandant, he exercised absolute authority for the maintenance of naval discipline. As with others in his situation, he found himself continually undermined by the local Jacobin-dominated administration while remaining unsupported by the increasingly ineffectual Ministry of Marine.

Worn down by the futility of his situation, Flotte requested in June to be replaced, only to be rewarded with promotion. This, and his allegation that the officials in the *intendant*'s department in the arsenal were working to frustrate his efforts, sealed his fate. In September an unidentified group of men hauled both Flotte and his chief aide from their residences, brutally hacked them to death and hung their remains in true revolutionary fashion *à la lanterne*. The *ordonnateur* himself was saved only through hasty declaration of his popular patriotic sympathies. Murdered elsewhere was the founder member of the town's moderate anti-Jacobin Club, doubly detested because he was also a post captain and, as such, seen as a representative of the deposed central authority.

Within the space of three months three *ordannateurs* had tried and failed to restore the situation at Toulon. One of them, Thiveno, wrote to the minister of marine, stating bluntly that the naval administration in the port of Toulon was in a state of paralysis and that the arsenal was now little more than a general resource for the navy, the army and neighbouring *départements*. The army, for instance, had requisitioned over 200 cannon, far more than had been the case at Brest or Rochefort.

Yet another new appointee, the minister was the celebrated mathematician Gaspard Monge. Something of a moderate, Monge knew little of the navy and its ways but is credited with being the first to fully recognize the gravity of the situation and to initiate action which, ultimately, would create the navy of the republic.

An interesting feature of Toulon's internal struggle is that, once firmly in power, the Revolutionary element dedicated itself to the task in hand. It took positive steps to assist the *ordonnateur* in maintaining calm and order in the workplace and thus to facilitate the major task of mobilizing the Toulon squadron to meet the threat of a wider external conflict.

The local army commander, Anselme, was particularly demanding, creating a major shortage in ships' supplies by requisitioning almost the entire stock of hard biscuit. He needed it to feed his army which, from September, was advancing along the coast to take Nice and beyond. He also required specialist warships for inshore support and to act as protection against privateers disrupting his supplies. For fire support, the Toulon yard readied four old frigates and, for escort duties, twenty-six *chaloupes* (fast craft with peculiarly French rigs and not equivalent to a British sloop). Their commanding officers were nominated by the local civic authorities.

By the end of 1792 the control of activities at Toulon was almost totally exercised by the '*trois Corps*': the administrators of the town, the district and the *département*. An active war was now being conducted along the coast in Piedmont, and warships were deployed by the corps – rather than the navy – on numerous 'special missions'. Commanding officers of regular warships, although appointed through the Ministry of Marine, were all placed under surveillance to establish their degree of adherence to 'patriotic' principles. Having 'Revolutionized' the dockyard workforce, the administration now virtually sidelined the commandant's organization in its identical desire to mobilize the yard's full potential in supporting the war.

The dearth of experienced officers acceptable to the Revolutionary councils was already causing difficulties in senior appointments. In August 1792, the command of the Mediterranean fleet was given to one Laurent Truguet, a local man whose lack of aristocratic background saw him promoted to post captain in January that year, and to rear admiral just seven months later. After one month's experience in this rank, he found himself commander-in-chief.

Following the debacle of the expedition to Sardinia, Truguet was replaced by the comte de Trogoff de Kerlessy. An officer of the 'old' navy, he had been purged by Jeanbon Saint-André, the influential naval representative on the all-powerful Committee of Public Safety, now effectively a ruling Cabinet. It was Jeanbon Saint-André who succeeded in re-establishing some measure of order in Brest but only at the cost of wholesale dismissal of experienced officers and their replacement by over-promoted personnel from the merchant marine and nominees ('pistols') from the local 'patriotic clubs'. Such men may have been more acceptable to rebellious lower decks but they did not make for an efficient fighting fleet at a time when it was about to be pitted against the Royal Navy, a force with a few of its own scores to settle.

Trogoff's saving grace in the eyes of Jeanbon was that he came from the ranks of what might be termed 'impoverished aristocracy'. His seniority as post captain dated from 1784 and he had seen considerable service in the 'American War'. He was probably well worth his promotion to flag rank in January 1793 but he, too, had seen only months of experience at this level when called to replace Truguet as commander-in-chief.

His situation was not enviable. Rightly concerned that his accident of birth might yet be used against him, he was still a professional officer who sought to maintain the independence of the service from the all-pervasive influence of the local Jacobin authorities. This, despite the passivity of the enfeebled Ministry of Marine in Paris and widespread disaffection from 'patriotic' i.e. highly politicized, crews on many of the ships in his command, the Toulon arsenal, upon which he depended, was all but bankrupt. It employed more people than it could possibly pay yet could not lay them off for fear of local insurrection.

The material state of the fleet had also suffered considerably. As a rule of thumb, a French ship of the line was considered to have a useful life of only ten years, a frigate fifteen. To maintain the size of the fleet as defined by Castries, it was necessary to build at least six ships of the line and four frigates per year. The term 'build' could mean either entirely new ships or the reconstruction of those veteran ships still worthy of the expense. Until 1788 this rate of build was maintained but as early as 1787 Toulon had advised the ministry of a growing backlog of ships awaiting repair due to an increasing shortage of local timber.

The Revolution also had an early effect on funding. Although the budget levels during 1789–91 appeared superficially to have increased, they had to cover the extraordinary expense of partial mobilization, primarily with the intention of assisting Spain over the 1790 Nootka Sound crisis. Only about half of the ministry's needs could be met from what was left and from the middle of 1790 Brest and Rochefort were also reporting a marked reduction in operational tempo.

Between 1789 and 1792, therefore, only eighteen rather than twenty-five rebuilt or new ships of the line entered service, although frigate numbers were on target. Not counting over-age ships, the French fleet had decreased in size and it was necessary to boost its strength by the recommissioning of old vessels that had been slated for disposal or dismantling.

Modern research, using French records, suggests that the useful strength of the French navy at this time was sixty-five ships of the line rather than the seventy-six quoted by classic analysts such as James. Although their smallest was of 74 guns, thus out-classing the numerous 64-gun British ships of the line, about 30 per cent of all French ships of the line were older than the recommended ten years of age.

From 1786, only three types of ships of the line (of 118, 80 and 74 guns) were planned to be built, all to standard design with the dimensions of the two smallest types identical. Following a competition between six of the most eminent French designers, proposals by the Brest constructor Jacques-Noël Sané were selected. The resulting ships proved to perform excellently, their size and performance greatly impressing the British.

The 118-gunners were large enough to dominate most British first rates. They were able to fight their heaviest guns in the poorest of weather and were able to throw a broadside of 619kg (1,362lb) against the 566kg (1,254lb) of their opponents.

It was Sané's 80-gun two-deckers, however, which proved his best. The British acknowledged that 'their qualities ... have rarely, if ever, been surpassed'. Not only were their sailing qualities much admired, they also carried 24-pounders on their upper deck where a British 74, which was usually pitted against them, mounted only 18-pounders.

Sané possessed a natural skill which enabled him to combine two characteristics in his ships: the ability to maintain a press of sail while giving the lower gun-deck sills sufficient freeboard simultaneously to fight the heaviest weapons. Records quote a Sané-designed 74 as having 1.68 to 1.83m (5ft 6in to 6ft) command against a British first rate's 1.37m (4ft 6in). Despite the depth of hull necessary to support such dimensions, Sané was able to incorporate more than adequate stability. In some cases, in fact, his ships were over-stiff, resulting in excessive rolling on some points of sailing, sufficient to hazard the masts. This was countered by shifting weight upwards, thus increasing roll period.

Up to 1791, when this programme began to go awry, French yards had put afloat three 118s, three 80s and thirty-seven 74s to Sané's designs. Recognizing the superiority of the 80 over the 74, Jeanbon Saint-André infuriated his fellow *représentant en mission* at Toulon, Niou, by substituting them in the arsenal's building programme.

Sané responded to lack of numbers by adopting the common British practice of cutting-down ('razing' or 'razee-ing') larger ships of obsolete design. He thus created a number of single-deckers, technically classed as frigates but carrying a previously unheard-of armament of twenty-eight 36-pounders. Even such drastic remodelling did not appear to unduly affect the sailing qualities of these old 74s: one, the *Flibustier*, was credited with once achieving a speed of 15 knots.

French frigates taken by the British were highly valued. The *Pomone*, captured in 1794 by Borlase Warren's squadron, would prove to be highly influential to British design yet, at home, she had been castigated by Jeanbon Saint-André as being a dull sailer. As with their larger colleagues, French frigates carried their batteries high, with the gunport sills up to 1.83m (6ft) above the normal waterline.

In July 1792, with war against Britain seven months distant, the commandant at Brest wrote 'with true pain' to the then minister of marine, Jean de Lacoste. Complaining, as usual, at the continuing shortage of central funding, he pointed out that dispositions were already suffering due to the increasingly inevitable neglect of the fleet. 'It is frightening', he went on, 'that the port of Brest [holds] fourteen ships of the line and nine frigates that demand either major work or scrapping.'

Mention of the *Flibustier* (above) is a reminder that, even as the fleet itself was being allowed to deteriorate at a disturbing rate, revolutionary fervour remained undiminished. Further manifestation of this lay in the wholesale renaming of warships with the intention of wiping out names connected with the old regime whilst glorifying the Revolution itself. As the policy was somewhat haphazard, doubt exists as to whether some of the allocated new names were actually used, and the following list is probably not complete. The definitive articles, always included by the French before ships' names, have been excluded.

PREVIOUS NAME	GUNS	NEW NAME
Dauphin Royale	118	*Sans-Culottes*
États de Bourgogne	118	*Montagne*
Bretagne	110	*Révolutionnaire*
Royal Louis	110	*Républicain*
Auguste	80	*Jacobin*
Couronne	80	*Ça Ira*
Duc de Bourgogne	80	*Caton*
Deux Frères	80	*Juste*
Languedoc	80	*Anti-Fédéraliste*
Saint-Esprit	80	*Scipion*
Alexandre	74	*Jemmapes*
Apollon	74	*Gasparin*
Argonaute	74	*Flibustier*
Borée	74	*Agricola*
Commerce de Bordeaux	74	*Bonnet Rouge*
Diadème	74	*Brutus*
Dictateur	74	*Liberté*
Ferme	74	*Phocion*
Jupiter	74	*Montagnard*

Lion	74	*Marat*
Lys	74	*Tricolore*
Marseillais	74	*Vengeur du Peuple*
Orion	74	*Mucius Scaevola*
Pyrrhus	74	*Mont Blanc*
Sceptre	74	*Convention*
Séduisant	74	*Pelletier*
Souverain	74	*Peuple Souverain*
Suffren	74	*Rédoubtable*
Thésée	74	*Révolution*
Réfléchi	64	*Turot*
Aglai	frigate	*Fraternité*
Capricieuse	frigate	*Charente*
Gracieuse	frigate	*Unité*
Uranie	frigate	*Tartu*
Charente-Inferieure	frigate	*Tribune*

The renamings speak volumes of the mood of the times. That the policy stems from the extreme Left is apparent, with *Sans-culottes*, Jacobin and Montagnard being represented but not, say, Plaine or Girondin. Names with obviously royal connections were changed to those strongly symbolic of the Revolution. Names connected with those regions of France that were counter-revolutionary were likewise erased. Some are particularly grim in their context, e.g. the change from *Couronne* ('crown') to *Ça Ira*, roughly translated as 'Thus will it be'. In light of what was to befall the city of Marseille, the rebaptism of the *Marseillais* as the *Vengeur du Peuple* was horribly appropriate. The *Lys*, named for the area from which stemmed the flower symbolic of royal France, became the *Tricolore*, after the nation's new symbol.

The leading Revolutionaries, many with classical education, had something of an obsession with the noble ideals of the ancient Roman republic, seeing parallels with their achievement. They did not lend their names for self-aggrandisement but saw themselves in the role of the prominent figures of that time, hence *Caton* ('Cato'), *Brutus*, *Scipion* ('Scipio') etc. Only the assassinated Marat had a ship renamed directly in his honour.

Tartu, indirectly, might also fall into this latter category. Tartu had been the commanding officer of the *Uranie* 36, losing his life in the course of the brisk duel with the British *Thames* 32 in the Bay of Biscay during October 1793. The British ship was so cut about by her heavier adversary (18-pounders versus 12s) that she was taken by other French ships later in the day. Tartu had the posthumous honour of having his ship renamed after him. As a further twist to the story, the *Tartu* was herself captured in January 1797 by the British *Polyphemus*, entering Royal Navy service as the *Urania*. The unlucky *Thames* spent three years under French colours with the name *Tamise* before being retaken by the *Santa Margarita* which, despite her unlikely name, was a British frigate that, as was the custom, had retained her name after being captured from the Spanish back in 1779. She was now captained by Thomas Byam Martin.

IN SUMMARY, the navy of the new French Republic was in no condition for a major war. Although of superior design, too many of its ships were either over-age or in need of extensive refit. Its Atlantic bases had sufficient materials to maintain their squadrons but insufficient to support full mobilization. Toulon, in contrast, had already seen its stocks badly reduced. All workforces harboured deeply felt grievances, that at Toulon particularly so. The Atlantic bases had benefited from energetic *ordonnateurs* and commandants, who had reasonably accommodated the opposing demands of civic interference and the separate existence of the navy. In Toulon, the navy was no longer under autonomous control, and could no longer look to the Ministry of Marine to reimpose discipline or direction.

Freed from the constraints of normal discipline, ships' crews had become unpredictable, difficult or impossible to control, a situation exacerbated by the necessary but large-scale over-promotion of unsuitable and inexperienced officers to replace the demolished *Grand Corps*.

Through the division of authority, the Revolution effectively destroyed the already debilitated fleet of the *ancien régime* in order to replace it with an alternative, based on acceptable Revolutionary principles. This process of renewal would, however, require time to implement and, through the Convention's ill-judged declaration of war, time is what the service did not have.

chapter three

The Naval Situation in Great Britain

DIRECTION AND ADMINISTRATION

As with any major enterprise, the Royal Navy required an agency through which it received its directives, and another that ensured that these could and would be carried out. The one was the Admiralty, the other the Navy Board.

The Board of Admiralty had the task of interfacing the purely political input of national policy requirements with the output of how to achieve those requirements in naval terms. It was, and remains therefore, a partly political and partly naval body.

Britain, being a constitutional monarchy of the style that so many French citizens still desired, had in George III a king who was entitled (and not afraid) to exercise his remaining powers to intervene in the planning and conduct of his nation's wars. Such action could, however, be taken only through the prime minister who acted, as appropriate, in the role of adviser, filter or brake. George's position was weakened increasingly by the illness which, gradually intensifying, dogged him almost throughout his long reign. Lengthening spells of mental instability on the part of the monarch obliged Pitt in 1788 to frame a bill naming the ineffectual and unpopular Prince of Wales as regent, acting as head of state during the periods when his father was incapable of functioning normally.

The prime minister was, therefore, the main arbiter of policy, directing the Admiralty through the Cabinet, but carrying the Cabinet primarily on resolutions formulated by himself and just three of its members, namely Henry Dundas, otherwise 1st Viscount Melville, the home secretary, together with William, Lord Grenville the foreign secretary, and the Earl of Chatham who, as First Lord of the Admiralty, was the navy's political head and the channel through which the Board of Admiralty received its general directives.

Chatham was a civilian but was typical of what were described as 'political admirals' or 'admiral politicians' who were, in varying proportion, one or the other. Some rarely, if ever, held major command in the service, yet served it well. Ideally, the board would be headed by a competent politician, supported by seaman-admirals with some political acumen. Needless to say, this balance was rarely achieved, not least because board members owed allegiance to opposing political parties.

To simplify decision-making, the board was rarely more than seven strong. Much routine business was decided by the First Lord alone but, in the case of important decisions, at least three members needed to sign the minutes. Available board members met most days at the Admiralty office in Whitehall, which also housed the executive staff whose task it was to initiate action on the board's decisions. At the head of this was the first secretary, whose degree of empowerment made him a considerable and often well-known figure in his own right. The Board of Admiralty's brief ranged from fleet deployment to individual promotions, via related aspects such as victualling, hydrography and naval hospitals. Its most important subsidiary was the Navy Board, directed by the comptroller.

This body was predominantly civilian in composition and had the primary responsibility of satisfying the service's material requirements. Its most significant figure was the surveyor who, together with his assistants, oversaw ship design, construction and maintenance. Having risen through the dockyard system, each was an experienced shipwright. At a time when science had yet to be wedded to ship design, such experience was crucial to the fighting efficiency of the ships specified. Through its commissioners, the Navy Board ran the dockyards, while selecting and supervising the many civilian contractors whose participation was vital in absorbing surges in activity consequent upon sudden mobilization.

About ten strong, the Navy Board was notorious for the longevity of its serving members who, enjoying a comfortable living, contrived to remain in post despite advancing years, increasing infirmity and impaired faculties. There was great scope for graft in a system that was desperately inefficient but, with the accounting methods available, it was usually impossible to establish whether a proportion of funds was being dissipated through dishonesty or simply through poor practice. What is certain is that the official manpower establishment was never achieved on the funds provided, while royal dockyards were subjected to periodic major reviews in working practices that resulted in only cosmetic improvements.

Funds were allocated by Parliament in the annual Naval Estimates. The figure depended largely upon the numbers and types of ship required by the Board of Admiralty to pursue its tasks. This, in turn, decided manpower, and it was this establishment that determined the total, the overall sum being based simply on a fixed amount per head. Allocation of money was primarily to wages, ship construction and maintenance, and ordnance.

Ordnance, of course, was the major *raison d'etre* for each of the navy's warships and it was a further peculiarity of the system that the Ordnance Board was an independent body. Because it supplied all guns and explosives to both the army and the navy, it answered directly to the Cabinet. In fairness, the system functioned well, although it was as conservative as the remainder of the service.

Where the Board of Admiralty was responsible for officer's commissions, the warrants of senior non-commissioned officers were issued by the Navy Board. These 'warrant officers' included the sailing masters, senior gunners and surgeons upon whom the efficiency of the day-to-day running of a ship greatly depended.

The Navy Board thus exercised considerable authority but, due to the diversity of its interests, was inevitably unwieldly and usually enjoyed an unsatisfactory relationship with the Board of Admiralty. Not the least problem was simply that the navy itself was expanding. New developments necessitated new administration which, instead of being allocated to existing departments, resulted in the creation of more. By 1793 there were no less than thirteen such organizations, each with its own commissioner and administrative structure and located at sites scattered across the capital and at Chatham and at Portsmouth. Several and unsuccessful were the overhauls of the Navy Board's working structure and it is perhaps not surprising that it eventually disappeared through the gradual assimilation of its functions by the Admiralty.

The general inefficiency of the Navy Board's activities had, fortunately, been largely offset in recent years by the felicitous appointment of Sir Charles

Middleton as comptroller. Although 52 years old when he assumed the post in 1778, he was still only a senior captain in rank. He had served at sea without particular distinction but now excelled as an administrator. His twelve years as comptroller saw the active and reserve fleets well provided for, his eventual departure from office leaving the service in a condition where the rapid expansion of 1793 was greatly facilitated.

Middleton was perhaps the most prominent example of the political admiral, gaining flag rank only in service ashore and never wearing his flag in command at sea. During this period, as was common, he became a Member of Parliament, only to have his outside interests curtailed when the new war saw him appointed to the Board of Admiralty. He proved equally adept at the navy's direction, eventually shouldering the heaviest responsibility as First Lord, a post that he assumed when Lord Melville resigned following impeachment. At this point he accepted a peerage, becoming Lord Barham.

Irascible, never doubting his own judgement, Barham brooked little dissent and was difficult to work with. His avowed policy, however, was to maintain a powerful primary battle fleet in the western approaches to the English Channel, both to watch activities in the French Atlantic ports and to safeguard the distant inward and outward flow of British trade. Barham would certainly have agreed with Mahan's later criticism of Howe's insistence on basing this force at Spithead rather than Torbay. Fortunately for Howe's sensitivities, Barham was not appointed to the Board of Admiralty until the year following.

HAVING RECEIVED a direct requirement from the Cabinet, the First Lord would call a meeting of the Board of Admiralty. This would assess the necessary resources, and specify to the Navy Board what to provide. On the board's behalf, the first secretary would also frame the necessary orders for the commander-in-chief (C-in-C) within whose station limits the desired action was to be taken. Routine orders to commanding officers of ships and shore stations at home and abroad were usually issued through who was at this time termed the First Professional Lord (later renamed the First Sea Lord), who was likely, but not necessarily, to be a seaman-admiral.

Depending upon the size and importance of a station, its C-in-C might be as senior as an admiral of the fleet (of which rank there was, until 1805, only one at any one time) or as junior as a commodore, who was often a senior captain promoted only for the duration of a task or appointment.

Commanders-in-chief were carefully selected for, in those days before science speeded up communication, instructions could reach them on distant stations no more quickly than a fast ship could carry them. Besides managing and, when necessary, fighting their fleets, C-in-Cs had to be very much diplomats and able to use initiative when faced with a quickly developing local situation. Unless, therefore, he was embarking upon a campaign that required specific orders, a C-in-C's instructions from the Admiralty were surprisingly lacking in detail, mainly to avoid imposing undue restriction upon his available range of options.

On an important station, the C-in-C might have several score ships under his command, organized into divisions or squadrons led by subordinate commanders. The first, and most obvious, divisions were those into which the line of battle was organized. This unwieldly formation might be several miles in length and, signalling methods being what they were, the best place for a C-in-C was in the centre of the line, approximately equispaced from either end. The Centre was thus the senior, or Red, division, all of whose ships wore red ensigns. As there was at this time only one Admiral of the Red he was literally 'Admiral of the Fleet' and would be unlikely to be holding a seagoing appointment. The Centre was preceded by the Van, or White, division and followed by the junior Rear, or Blue, division. Each of these also wore distinctively coloured ensigns.

Flagships of each division were identified by the wearing at the masthead of an ensign of the appropriate colour, plain red, plain blue or white with a red St George's cross. All ships of the line had three masts, an admiral wearing his distinguishing flag at the main, a vice admiral at the fore and a rear admiral at the mizen.

The C-in-C's ship was usually the largest, both to reflect his own status and to accommodate his considerable staff. The day-to-day running of the ship was still the responsibility of her appointed commanding officer, who carried the title of flag captain. His increased responsibilities carried no extra emolument except when his ship wore the flag of a full admiral.

Subordinate to the C-in-C and serving on his immediate staff was the captain of the fleet. Despite his title, he might also hold flag rank, his role being to act as chief of staff and adviser to the C-in-C. As such, he was privy to the C-in-C's intentions and, should the latter be incapacitated, he was empowered to act in his stead even though he might be junior in rank to the divisional commanders.

In the normal course of its activities a fleet might include inshore squadrons, flying squadrons or frigate squadrons so that, considering the force as a whole, a complex hierarchy emerged.

Due to the high incidence of disease and accident, as well as action, mortality was high by today's standards. This might involve considerable clerical work: the loss of, say, the commanding officer of a frigate could result in each of his officers being promoted by a rank with, at the bottom end, the granting of a commission to a warrant holder.

A flagship needed to be able to communicate a C-in-C's requirements to the remainder of ships in company. By day this was by means of flag hoists. Flags were far from ideal as they were difficult to read when viewed against the sun or when streamed directly toward or away from the observer. They could also be obscured by sails or, once battle was joined, by smoke. Frigates were thus commonly stationed as 'repeating ships'.

The book *Admiralty Fighting Instructions* was a standard work, revised periodically and issued to all commanding officers. Each thus knew what was expected of him but still required to be informed of exactly when. Numerous sea officers, notably Kempenfelt, who had studied French practice, had already proposed codes of signalling and, while it would be 1799 before the first official Admiralty book was distributed, the systems already in use were, despite shortcomings, quite comprehensive. During 1793 both Howe and Hood produced systems, although that of the latter was acknowledged to be mainly the work of his secretary, John MacArthur, who was an enthusiast in the field.

Flag signals had moved on from the earliest straight substitution of a flag for each number or letter. MacArthur's system, besides being able to spell out specific words, comprised mainly groups of four flags to represent numbers of up to 9,999. Each number represented a specific command or enquiry, listed in a signal book held by each ship. Many usefully posed specific questions that required a response. Others were left blank, allowing a C-in-C to allocate them for purposes appropriate to his own operations, for instance to call up individual ships.

Nothing, however, could much improve on a senior officer having a total rapport with his subordinate commanding officers, so that he knew instinctively what his admiral would require and needed no more than an executive signal. The interpretation of flag signals, their misrepresentation or their being ignored were recurrent themes at courts martial.

PERSONNEL

By modern standards, recruitment to the Royal Navy's officer class was haphazard in the extreme, yet the searching nature of an individual's experience within the service was a powerful means of filtering out the incapable. History itself bears witness to the fact that the will to win was rarely found wanting although, on occasion, aggression exceeded ability.

This was the age of the great landowner, the squire, who in the absence of the kind of centralized bureaucracy that today is taken for granted exercised virtually absolute power over all tenants within his boundaries. Magistrate or justice of the peace, he represented the law. Education, the provision (or not) of benefit and almshouses fell within his gift. Where profitable or necessary he built roads and infrastructure, and he maintained a useful two-way relationship with the church. Many great landowners were titled, others were merely 'gentry'. Some were becoming yet more wealthy as the gathering momentum of the industrial revolution increased the demand for land upon which to construct factories and the mass housing for their associated workforce.

Largely dependent upon the patronage of the landowners were the professional classes, the schoolmasters, parsons and lawyers. It was from within this now-disappeared social structure that the navy's officers were largely drawn. Connections and a good name remained important, but social status less so, as the navy expanded rapidly at the outset of such as the French Revolutionary War.

The Royal Navy of the late eighteenth century ran on the very minimum of administrative staff, and there was no regulated entry system. As the existing methods of recruitment produced suitable numbers of aspirants with the desired qualities, there was little incentive to change them. Most young men entering the service were virtually apprenticed to a specific commanding officer for the necessary three years' sea time that regulations stipulated must be served before they could be rated master's mates or midshipmen. For this period they were quaintly termed 'Captain Servants', a commanding officer being entitled to employ four such for every hundred men in his ship's complement. This strange system was one of preferment and, where a captain might take a titled lad free of charge for the social status thus derived, the majority came with a negotiated sum which greatly enhanced a commanding officer's income, for the average third rate might carry a score of 'young gentlemen' on its books.

As with most loosely regulated systems, it was open to abuse, particularly by those already well-placed within the service. Officers such as Rodney and Cochrane were, with a little exercise of a 'blind eye', able to enter infants on the books of ships in order to give them a flying start, a procedure that occasionally resulted in grotesque anomalies such as Rodney's indifferently gifted son making post captain at the age of 15.

It was evident, however, that the Admiralty was getting to grips with the necessary regulation of the system for, in 1794, the category of 'Captain's Servant' would be abolished in favour of a 'Volunteer, Class I', who had to be at least 11 years of age and who, for the first time, would be paid a stipulated wage. A commanding officer could now no longer continue with the fiction that an infant was serving aboard his ship for, as his charge would now have to appear on the ship's payroll, the risks of deception were too great.

An alternative method of entry was through the Royal Naval College in Portsmouth dockyard or through 'crammers' such as Burney's Academy in Gosport. Many such lads benefited by scholarships and studied a specified range of subjects. Although this was a logical beginning for a career, it was not popular. In addition to universal disapproval from commanding officers whose privileges were being eroded, the service itself was not in favour of what it regarded as intellectuals. It was, in any case, thought that the latest age at which a boy should go to sea was 13.

A third route for entry was via the merchant service or from the lower deck. This often produced consummate seamen (Captain James Cook was but one example) but they seldom made high rank due to their lack of social influence.

Education in the service was subordinated to practical skills. A schoolmaster might be found aboard a large ship but, to a great extent, the theoretical aspects of seagoing, particularly mathematics and navigation, were taught by the captain himself or a designated officer. There was no standard curriculum but both 'volunteers' and the midshipmen that they became were given considerable responsibility. The best were re-rated Master's Mates and understudied lieutenants at watchkeeping.

Regulations demanded that youngsters could not attend the all-important examining boards for lieutenant before they had attained the age of 20 and had served at least six years' sea time. Although each of these requirements could be 'fiddled' to a degree, the average candidate was by now a seaman of considerable experience. Practical skills and personality impressed a board more than academic attainment. In its imperfect and rather casual way the system, in general, produced very good officers.

Once passed as lieutenant, an officer joined a pool of over two thousand such. Each could be commissioned only to a ship specified by the Admiralty and, for those with few connections or little talent, the wait could be very long in times of peace. A useful middle route could be to accept a post as a sub-lieutenant (a temporary rank only) to serve as a qualified subordinate to a lieutenant-in-command who captained one of the navy's very many small ships, engaged principally against enemy privateers.

When his ship paid off, an officer's commission ended and he went ashore on half-pay, calculated at the rate that he had lately been receiving afloat. Half-pay depended upon holding himself in readiness for a further engagement, so it was difficult to accept paid employment in the meantime. Except in special cases, there were no formal provisions for a retirement pension, an officer simply going on an indefinite spell of half-pay.

Intermediate in rank between commissioned officers (or, more correctly at this time, commission officers) and petty officers were the warrant officers who were, as already noted, appointed by the Navy Board rather than by the Admiralty. Some ranks, such as those of the master and the surgeon, carried wardroom status. Others, such as the gunner, carpenter and the boatswain, remained with the ship between commissions and were termed 'standing officers'. Theirs was the key role of maintaining the overall standard of a warship while she was being refitted. The major cultural difference between warrant officers and the lower deck lay in the requirement that they be both literate and numerate. Warrant officers were rarely able to progress to commission status.

We have already noted the difficulties experienced by the yards charged with bringing forward a surge of reserve warships as war was once more declared. Even had bottlenecks not occurred, however, it would have benefited the Admiralty little, for there remained the need to recruit and train the crews to man them.

The British Parliament, effectively paymaster for the First Coalition, voted huge sums for the rapid increase in the size of the service. The number of men required was large, larger still when viewed against a British population which at this time totalled less than 9 million. In 1792 there served an official total of 15,000 seamen and marines. During the following two years, funds were approved to expand to 45,000 and 85,000 respectively. By 1797 the total had peaked at about 120,000.

By today's standard, complements were enormous. The average third rate, 74-gun ship, the backbone of the fighting fleet, had over 600 on her muster roll. A first rate 100-gun three-decker needed about 840. Due to shortages in personnel, however, most ships sailed with reduced complements.

At a time when life at sea was hard and dangerous, it was impossible to attract sufficient volunteers. The Royal Navy suffered further in this respect because hostilities immediately began to inflate the wages paid to merchant seamen. This service was also more attractive in that a crew member could sign off at the termination of a voyage to enjoy a spell ashore, a right not available to his naval counterpart.

About half the requirement was thus generated by impressment. Following the political revolutions of the previous century, the old principles governing enforced service for the British crown had received a setback in the new perceptions of personal liberty and reduced power of the state. Sheer necessity, however, had seen the rights of impressment reasserted.

There was nothing makeshift about the impress service, which was well organized. The nation was divided into thirty zones, in each of which a full captain controlled the activities of gangs, some eighty in all, whose approach to their work varied in harshness according to the degree of urgency or the manner of the lieutenant in charge. A commissioned officer, bearing an Admiralty impressment warrant, had to be present by law. His gang typically comprised two petty officers and four or five other ranks, most of whom were landsmen. Violence was commonplace, with the gang itself often having to protect itself from a mob in particularly hostile quarters.

Certain tradesmen and callings were supposedly immune from impressment, and certificates needed to be carried to this effect. Such papers were, however, commonly forged or obtained by agents for an appropriate consideration. They were, in any case, of little use during periods of the 'hot press', when national urgency was such as to render virtually anybody liable.

The merchant service suffered particularly from impressment, with inbound vessels being brought-to in the Downs and stripped of their best men, often to the extent that a master would have to hire local crews (protected for the purpose) to assist in getting his vessel to port in London. Foreigners serving aboard British-flagged ships were supposedly immune to impressment but, at this time, it was still difficult for an American to prove his citizenship. Many were thus taken, causing a growing national resentment that was to be a contributory factor to the outbreak of war less than twenty years later, at a time when the colossal struggle against France was still unresolved.

Perhaps a quarter of a ship's company were volunteers. Many of them liked the life, qualifying as 'able seamen' and, quite often, remaining with a respected commanding officer as he progressed from commission to commission. As a commanding officer was responsible for manning his ship, his reputation was very important, particularly if he was associated with prize money.

At his own expense, he would organize recruiting drives at suitable locations, usually an inn. Posters were written and produced locally appealing to patriotism, love of a fight and income. By today's standards and sensitivities they read crudely, but men of the time did not mince their words to satisfy the demands of minority pressure groups.

'Let us, who are Englishmen', one read, 'protect and defend our good King and Country against ... the Designs of our Natural Enemies, who intend ... to invade Old England, our happy country, to murder our gracious King as they have done their own ... and teach us nothing but the damn'd Art of murdering one another.' This was addressed to 'All who have good Hearts, who love their King, their Country, and Religion, who hate the French and damn the Pope'.

For obvious reasons, there was no preliminary training, so many, both volunteers and pressed men, went afloat with no previous experience. Possessing no seamanship skills, they were known as 'landmen' (or 'landsmen'). Although regarded as the lowest category, most were intelligent and quickly became useful. Many were skilled tradesmen who had been displaced by the new mechanization of the industrial revolution. Dextrous, they proved to be hard-working and reliable.

Others, charged with, or convicted for, minor misdemeanours also found their way into the service as an alternative to gaol. Neither hardened criminals nor guilty of violent crime, these were debtors, drunkards and small-time ne'er-do-wells. To these would soon be added the so-called 'Quota Men', following the government order that each county recruit a number of men proportional to its population. Most of these resulted from the offering of substantial bounties. Known as 'Billy Pitt's men', many brought disharmony and radical notions in place of useful skills and were widely blamed for the imminent rash of mutinies that would scar the navy's reputation.

A surprising number of foreign seamen served voluntarily in the Royal Navy. The main reason was that, as the war progressed, blockade and general disruption to trade caused many neutral ships to be laid up, and their seamen were content to obtain alternative steady employment in a diminishing market.

It says much for the national character that such an eclectic band of men could be forged into crews whose fighting qualities were respected the world over. Punishment and discipline were, by today's standards, brutally harsh but need to be viewed through contemporary eyes, for life ashore was itself hard. What is evident is that the will to win cannot be instilled merely through the application of an iron disciplinary regime; much must depend upon organization and example. This came through applying the age-old principle of divide and rule as, for instance, expressed by Kempenfelt to Middleton (later Lord Barham).

> … If six, seven or eight hundred men are left in a mass together … and the officers assigned no particular charge over any part of them, who only give orders from the quarterdeck or gangways – such crew must remain a disorderly mob, business will be done … without order or despatch, and the raw men put into no train of improvement … Left to themselves [they] become sottish and lazy, form cabals, and spirit each other up to insolence and mutiny.

'The only way', Kempenfelt went on,

to keep large bodies of men in order is by dividing and subdividing of them ... into as many companies as there are lieutenants ... These companies to be subdivided and put under the charge of mates or midshipmen; and besides this, every twenty-five men to have a foreman to assist in the care of the men, as a sergeant or corporal in the army. Each lieutenant's company should be formed of the men who are under his command at quarters for action. These companies should be reviewed every day ... the officers ... thus becom[ing] acquainted with the character and behaviour of each individual ... find[ing] out the turbulent and seditious, and keep[ing] a strict hand over such.

Not all beneficial activity was, in Kempenfelt's opinion, necessarily directly related to duty: '... the men should always have the full time for their meals and for repose, and certain portions of time in the week allotted for washing and mending; but at all other times they should be kept constantly employed ...' A measure of puritanism is also evident: '... idleness is the root of evil ... Motion preserves purity; everything that stagnates corrupts.'

Aggression and the will to attack at any opportunity were deeply impressed into every British naval officer: reticence was simply the shortest route to half-pay. This was not necessarily the way with the French, their rather more individual attitude arousing frustration in the renegade John Paul Jones, who wrote to the comte de Kersaint:

I have noticed ... that the underlying principle of operation and rule of action in the French Navy have always been calculated to subordinate immediate or instant opportunities to ulterior, if not distant, objects ... that it has been the policy of French admirals ... to neutralize the power of their adversaries, if possible, by grand manoeuvres rather than to destroy it by grand attacks.

Jones compared this with his own 'small scale' successes, going on to impress upon Kersaint that: 'The rules of conduct ... that serve to gain small victories may always be expanded into the winning of great ones ... and it seems to be a law inflexible and inexorable that he who will not risk cannot win.'

Certainly, the Royal Navy's record was enhanced considerably by the straits to which the French had reduced their own navy. None the less, despite the propaganda, the enemy often fought well and fought hard.

A significant incentive to the British was the prize money system, despite its being iniquitously unfair. Because a commander-in-chief on station was entitled to a one-eighth share of all monies thus awarded to ships under his command, it followed that he invariably had his most able frigate captains patrolling the most productive areas. For the Admiralty, this guaranteed that the maximum hurt was being inflicted on the enemy; for the crews, there was always the promise of a major windfall.

Should an enemy warship be captured, it was the hope of all concerned that she was of sufficient value to be purchased by the Admiralty for further service. Her value had thus to be assessed down to the very last item of equipment. From the total had to be deducted the cost of repair which, following a hard-fought action, could be substantial.

Also payable was so-called 'head and gun' money, calculated on the number of guns currently arming the prize and the number of her crew alive at the outset of the encounter. 'Head and gun' money was shared equally among the victorious crew, but prize money was divided according to a fixed scale. In 1793 this involved the sum first being divided into eighths. As already noted, it behove a C-in-C to recommend to the Admiralty that a prize was worth purchasing, a recommendation with which their lords still, of course, had to agree.

The commanding officer of the ship making the capture was entitled to two-eighths, i.e. a quarter. Should he have been operating independently of any command, no C-in-C would have been involved and he would take three-eighths. This was a major incentive for an enterprising captain and formed the basis of many a family fortune. Of the remaining five-eighths, one was shared between the ship's lieutenants, the marine captain, the master and surgeon. Another was awarded to the rest of the senior warrant officers, and one to the remaining warrant officers, their mates and the marine sergeants. This left just a quarter to be shared among the remainder of the ship's company.

A smaller frigate, with contents, might be valued at £25,000. The victorious commanding officer might thus expect between £6,000 and £10,000, then a sum greater than he would likely earn in wages over his whole career. Even the share for the lower deck would be equal to more than a year's income, although this was more an indictment of their poor wage rates than generosity on the part of the system. Where any additional 'head and gun' award was no more than pocket money to senior ranks, it might account for 15 per cent extra to a seaman's pay.

A further cause for discontent was the Admiralty's insistence on using 'prize agents' to distribute the bulk of the award. These gentlemen were masters of graft and were universally detested. Their official commission was 5 per cent of the total, to which amount they could add considerably through purchasing the share of beneficiaries who were being pressed for payment of debts. There were also various legal wrangles by which payment could be delayed, so that the agent could benefit from interest paid on the considerable sums entrusted to him.

Such delays were particularly the case when the prize had been a merchantman. She and her cargo had first to be condemned by a prize court. Then, in a mixed, or 'break-bulk', cargo it was ever difficult to distinguish between the various grades of contraband material and what was inviolable on account of being neutrally owned (although if the end-user could be shown to be the enemy, it could still be impounded).

It could thus be a considerable time before the rightful recipients saw any of their awards. In the case of Admiral Hood at Toulon, we will see that the special circumstances involved meant that over a decade would elapse before any distribution was made. Only a few fortunate commanding officers and crews ever benefited from prize money to a life-changing extent. As with a national lottery, many had small gains while most looked to the possibility of 'the big one'. Meanwhile, the hard daily routine went on.

Seamen had real grievances about their pay which, at this time, had not improved since the days of Cromwell. Not only was the private soldier, regarded as a being of lesser skills, now paid a shilling a day but the ordinary seaman's 23 shillings and sixpence (about £1.18) monthly pay was not paid until six months in arrears.

Some commanding officers cared more for running a 'taut ship' than for the welfare of their men. Particular officers could be greatly disliked for a variety of reasons. Whether the ship ran well or not, the conditions and food were very much products of their times and were very rough. Differentiation between seamen and landmen caused endless friction. Legitimate grievances could be presented by the lower deck in accordance with the Articles of War, but all too often those who presented them were dismissed without redress and, thereafter, treated as troublemakers.

Such contempt shown by officers for their men began a trend towards protest by disobedience, first by individuals, then by small groups. From 1793 the practice spread, culminating in the great mutinies of 1797–8. Throughout this period of unrest, however, the Royal Navy fought as well as ever. On the vast majority of the hundreds of British warships, men grumbled but did their duty. Concentration upon mutinous behaviour in the few has stained the reputation of the many.

THE SHIPS

For the designer, warships were, as now, an acceptable compromise between conflicting requirements. One quality could be enhanced only at the expense of another. This was the age of the broadside-armed ship, carrying guns on either side of the maximum length of one, two or three decks. Guns and their ammunition were extremely heavy and, towards the extremities of a vessel, imposed severe loading stresses. This was because the ends were finer-lined and, having smaller submerged volume than the centre sections, exerted less upthrust (or buoyancy) to support the weight. The result was that ships tended to 'hog', or sag, toward their ends.

In a wooden-built ship, hogging was destructive in opening seams and loosening joints. The one admitted water to accelerate rot and decay, the other caused a ship to 'work' in a seaway, becoming so flexible that it was not uncommon for them to be totally dismantled, either for reassembly or to incorporate their useful timbers into the structures of others.

Viewed as a uniformly loaded beam, a ship's hull could be expected to deflect in proportion to its length. The degree of deflection was, importantly, dependent upon its depth. This meant that all hulls were length-critical but that, say, a three-decker could be built rather longer than a single-decker.

Although in 1793 the great design innovations of Snodgrass and Seppings were, for the Royal Navy, still a decade away, such improvements were already being experimented with by the French and Spanish, who were much more ready to harness science to the improvement of ship design. Reports abounded of the superior sailing qualities of enemy warships. Those that were captured were often found to be flimsily built but were highly valued for their handling and extensively copied. It was not a question of speed, because the very full lines of contemporary sailing ships were inherently inefficient to the point where small differences had negligible effect. The superiority of foreign-built ships lay in their reputation for being able to lay closer to the wind and to go about without missing stays. Being totally dependent upon the wind, a sailing ship was inevitably judged by how well she could harness that element for her purpose.

As far as speed was concerned the British had, for some time, enjoyed the advantage of 'coppering'. Following experiment to nullify the effects of galvanic action between copper and a ship's iron fastenings, it became British policy from 1783 to clad the underwater sections of every warship with thin copper plate. This greatly reduced the activities of wood-boring marine worms and also the extent of fouling by weed and shellfish. Less encumbered, British ships, for a considerable period, enjoyed a definite speed advantage. This was noticeable particularly on distant, warm-water stations, where fouling was otherwise rapid and facilities for cleaning minimal.

Lord Barham, who instituted the measure, was so pleased with the results that, in his report to Melville, he was moved to a touch of rare humour: 'So much was the activity of the fleet increased that Mr. Rigby, in his witty way, observed that unless the captains were coppered also, we should have none to serve ...'

Ships, being armed principally on the broadside, were best fought in 'line of battle'. For all its faults, this formation presented an opponent with a formidable problem in that, for as long as the line remained in close order, he was faced with a continuous line of guns. To maintain station, ships required speed in hand and also the ability to manoeuvre. Dull sailers and indifferent handling were thus an immediate problem but, as an action progressed, damage to tophamper increasingly reduced a ship's ability to keep her position. If fought to a conclusion, a battle usually progressed to one of duels between individual ships.

Manoeuvrability and smart ship handling showed their true value in single ship-on-ship encounters, typically those between frigates. Jockeying for the best position from which to loose the opening broadside might well involve a close-quarter tacking duel in light weather, a situation in which, other factors being equal, the better-designed ship would have the advantage. An objective was to place one's own ship 'athwart the hawse' of an opponent, at right angles across his bows or stern. Faced only with weak end-on fire, a ship could release a broadside which would sweep the enemy's decks from one end to another, often leaving her crew in such a bloodied state of shock as to be unable to resist a rapid boarding.

Gun-decks were open from one end to the other, all partitioning being temporary and struck below before an action. This made them particularly vulnerable to end-on, or 'raking' fire. Although it might be thought that a stout transverse bulkhead at either end might defeat such tactics, the inclusion of these would have been at the cost of at least one pair of guns. It should also be remembered that actions such as these were conducted at point-blank range, where even the 18-pounder guns of a frigate could pierce a couple of feet of timber. In European waters, British success in this type of action was so marked that it bred complacency – a complacency brutally exposed when the service eventually embarked on the totally unnecessary war with the United States in 1812.

British gunnery of the time concentrated on rate of fire rather than accuracy. Although a 32-pounder was well capable of ranging a couple of miles, it was hopelessly inaccurate at such distance when fired from a heaving deck while, at the end of its flight, the ball would have lost much of its energy. Practice thus emphasized getting in so close that an opponent's hull was vulnerable. Directions speak of battle to be conducted at a half-musket, or pistol, shot, but the aggressive commander sought nothing less than to lay his ship alongside that of an enemy.

In such circumstances, the character and steadiness of gun crews were all-important. Incoming shot, particularly from the recently introduced carronade, smashed a ship's timbers into swathes of lethal fragments. Loss of life and limb was such as to make many actions unsustainable for any length of time. The noise was brain-jarring, the smoke impenetrable, the air unbreathable. Working barefoot on sanded decks, the living could barely keep upright as they slithered on the remains of the dead. Where possible, bodies and body parts were heaved overboard without ceremony while the carnage continued. Discipline, rate of fire and the ability to withstand this particular brand of hell would win the day.

Crews were large, both for the labour-intensive task of sail handling and to serve the many guns. A 32-pounder required a crew of seven, an 18-pounder six. Full crews could be provided for only one side, allowing replacement for those cut down in action. This was a potential weakness which could be exploited by an admiral content to engage only part of an enemy line, usually the rear. He would have spare ships with which he could 'double' the enemy, working around the rearguard or breaking through a developing gap. Having to defend both sides resulted in the enemy fighting with under-strength gun crews. His rate of fire, initially slower, would be slowed further with increasing damage, laying him open to boarding and being taken. This could occur before the unengaged vanguard could wear ship and beat back upwind in order to assist.

It will be appreciated that the ability to dictate the course of a battle lay very much with winning and retaining what was known as the weather gage or upwind position. It enabled an admiral to marshal his line into its correct spacing more readily and at the desired angle of convergence. It also allowed him to dictate the range although, in doing so, he sacrificed some. This was because his engaged side was that to leeward, the side towards which the ship listed under the press of wind. At the same time, his opponent was being engaged on his windward, or higher, side. Not only was he better able to open and fight his heavier guns through the lower-deck ports, but his weapons were given greater elevation and thus potential range. Many heavy-laden two- and three-deckers of the time had the sill of their lower-deck gun ports only 5 feet above the waterline when floating upright.

The very considerable gunsmoke cleared the leeward line immediately but that from the windward line drifted down towards it, probably incommoding both admirals equally. Ships of the leeward line had the undoubted advantage of being able, if badly damaged, to drop out of line, which would endeavour to close up, affording them cover in withdrawing.

As with the application of science to ship design and, to a great extent, with signalling, the French were ahead in the study and development of tactical theory. As explained earlier, they were more concerned about the successful completion of a specific mission than the seizing of a fleeting opportunity to engage an enemy squadron. Reluctance on the part of the French to get embroiled in an engagement was, inevitably, ascribed by the British to an innate sense of inferiority, which was not necessarily the case.

BRITISH SHIPS WERE classed by 'rate', of which there were six. As these were based on the number of guns officially (if not exactly) carried, their definition varied over the years. From the point of view of personnel, their ship's rate defined the number of each rank that could be entered on her books. Their officer's pay also varied according to rate.

First rates were always few in number but, being very expensive to construct, tended to be kept in good repair and were, in consequence, comparatively long-lived. They were (almost invariably) termed 'three-deckers', meaning that they carried their armament on three continuous gun-decks. To qualify as a first rate, a ship had 100 or more guns; by 1793, this commonly meant 110. This was in keeping with the general tendency of all classes to increase in size slowly to the very limits imposed by then-current shipbuilding techniques.

Stability limitations obliged armaments to be of mixed calibre, with the heaviest weapons naturally on the lowest deck. Some first rates were still carrying 42-pounders on the lower gun-deck but, in practice, both gun and ball were too heavy to maintain a satisfactory rate of fire, and they were being phased out in favour of the very effective 32-pounder.

Ships of the time featured a marked 'tumblehome', their beam being at its maximum near the waterline but decreasing with height. As a feature it reduced topweight and the length of the many transverse deck beams. It was also thought that, if the higher guns were located farther inboard, it would improve a ship's stability, a quality recognized as desirable but imperfectly understood.

On the middle deck were to be found 24-pounders and, on the upper, 18- or 12-pounders. On firing, the guns ran back inboard until restrained by their tackles. This required space, but the progressively narrower beam of the higher decks was compensated by the smaller weapons mounted on them.

Not counted in the official establishment of guns (and this was true of all six rates) were those mounted topside on the forecastle or quarterdeck. These might include a brace of long-barrelled chase guns and a number of carronades. These weapons had been in use with the navy since 1779 and represented a major shift in a science that had long remained almost static. Standard cannon were massively constructed, particularly at the chamber end, to allow for the enormous stresses induced by the almost instantaneous combustion of the powder charge on firing. Improved methods of corning powder had seen the process change from a virtual explosion to something like a controlled burn. The difference was measured in microseconds but reduced the stress sufficiently for a gun to be made lighter.

Long barrels improved accuracy and, particularly with slower-burning charges, increased muzzle velocity and range by allowing the ball to be accelerated along the bore for the full period of the burn. As the British preferred close-range engagements, however, such refinements were something of a luxury. At short range, a high-velocity ball would pass straight through an enemy vessel and, in carrying further, would waste much of its energy.

The carronade took all these factors into account, firing a heavy ball with a relatively small charge. The projectile was brought to a halt by the target's hull, expending all its energy in a single, timber-shattering impact. Because the charge was smaller, the gun sections could be made much thinner and, as accuracy at close quarters was not a problem, the barrel could be much shorter. The resulting gun was so much lighter that it could be carried high in the ship and mounted on a new-style carriage. This usually dispensed with wheels (or 'trucks'), absorbing recoil forces with a slide arrangement. The barrel was elevated by a stout screw and the whole could be traversed on a pivot. Being so compact and requiring less manhandling, carronades could be served by crews as small as two.

Such guns required precision in manufacture, possible only through the advances made in the industrial revolution. Metals were now of more consistent quality, casting techniques had improved and final machining carried out to greater dimensional accuracy. These benefits were fully exploited by the Carron company, which gave its name to the weapon.

Used as a short-range component of a more standard armament, the carronade (some of which fired 68-pound balls) was very effective. Inevitably, however, the commanders of some smaller warships became over-enthusiastic about its qualities, substituting it for the majority of their long guns. Several were thus badly worsted in duels with opponents armed with standard weapons, who simply lay beyond carronade range to pound the unwise into submission.

The French navy had adopted the carronade in both ships of the line and in frigates but to a smaller degree than the British. A contemporary French record mentions a total of 210 such pieces in service, forty-six of them aboard ships of the Toulon squadron. Carronades were carried in smaller numbers in French frigates than in British, but contemporary

French analysis of actions concludes that the difference was not decisive.

Where the British carronade fired solid shot the French equivalent, the *obusier de vaisseau* introduced in 1787, used 36-pound explosive shells. These, like the 'bombs' long thrown from the mortars of 'bomb ketches', were hollow roundshot (literally, a 'shell') filled with powder and fitted with a rudimentary fuse. Both the British and the French had experimented with shells during the earlier American War of Independence, with the former reaching the conclusion that, at the current level of technology, the weapons were more danger to the user than to the target. The French, less conservative, persevered, their ships carrying a proportion of explosive shot, which were believed to have been the cause of accidents.

Second rates were classed in 1793 as three-deckers bearing between ninety and ninety-eight guns. In length, they were often no more than 10 feet shorter than first rates, but they were considerably cheaper to operate as flagships on account of their lighter armament. In place of 42-pounders on the lower tier a second rate invariably carried 32-pounders. On the middle deck she had 18-pounders rather than 24s and on the upper deck either similar 12-pounders or lighter 9-pounders. This resulted in 100 less crew members and a less cramped ship, while the increased rate of fire of the lighter armament went some way towards compensating for a lesser broadside weight.

Third rates were officially the smallest ships powerful enough to serve in a line of battle during a major action. Classed as carrying between sixty and eighty guns, they comprised the largest category in the navy. Until the middle of the eighteenth century, 80s had been constructed as three-deckers but by 1793 these had virtually disappeared in favour of the two-decked version. Remaining 60-gun two-deckers, together with their 64-gun derivatives were, by now, also thought to be too small to be considered ships of the line, their largest guns being 24-pounders. None had been built in the preceding decade.

The dominant third rate was the 74-gun two-decker, which represented a good balance of size and armament and could fairly be termed the workhorse of the fleet. Generally with good sailing qualities, 74s were not over-armed for their size carrying, as a rule, twenty-eight 32-pounders on the gun-deck and twenty-eight 18-pounders on the upper deck. Twelve or fourteen 9-pounders were sited on the quarterdeck, with a further four on the forecastle. By now, some of the 9-pounders would have been landed in favour of 32-pounder carronades.

Designers continued to push lengths to the practical limit, adding small proportional increases in beam. The usual objective was to provide further space and displacement for another pair of great guns or to substitute 24-pounders for the upper deck 18-pounders. Such experiment was rarely worth the effort, resulting in crank ships that were sluggish sailers or leaving the sills of the lower-deck gun ports too close to the waterline to be opened in boisterous conditions.

A 74 was a popular command, being too small to be blessed with the chore of flagship (except in minor circumstances) yet large enough to be of considerable consequence. As a rough yardstick, first, second and third rates were spoken of as 'battle ships', and lesser vessels as 'cruising ships' or, more simply, as 'cruisers'.

With the virtual disappearance of the 60-gun ship, fourth rates were almost invariably 50-gun two-deckers. Too small to be included in a line of battle (although the *Leander* served at the Nile) a 50 was able to undertake aggressive patrolling or to act as leader, perhaps wearing a commodore's broad pendant, to a group of frigates. In this role, she might act as a minor flagship.

The hull of a 50 was deep in comparison with its length, conferring strength but usually at the expense of sailing qualities. Her armament was suitably scaled, comprising 24-pounders on the gun-deck and 12-pounders on the upper. Topside, there was a mix of 6-pounders and carronades.

Until the 1780s the navy built two-decker 44s, carrying both 18- and 12-pounders. Classed as fifth rates they were, like the smallest three-deckers, over-ambitious and unlikely to be able to operate their lower gun tier in a blow. The design pre-dated that of the true frigate which, by 1793, formed by far the largest component of the fleet's fifth rates. They were the smallest ships to be commanded by post captains.

British frigate design was heavily based on the French concept of a two-decker carrying no armament below the level of the upper deck. The lower deck (which, otherwise, would have been termed the gun-deck) could thus be located close to the waterline, allowing the upper deck, which supported the main battery, to be set about 8 feet above the standard waterline. For the size of ship, this was a good compromise between locating the gun ports high enough to be opened in heavy weather yet not so high as to cause stability problems.

With their dashing popular image, frigates were popular commands, particularly with the strong likelihood of independent operation. The latter was an important consideration as such duties promised not only the chance of prize money but also, in the event of a smartly fought action, the opportunity of attracting the attention of promotion review boards.

Based loosely on the design of the captured French *Renommée*, British frigate construction may be said to have begun in 1756 with the *Southampton* and *Richmond* classes. They were comparatively small, 32-gun vessels, their armament comprising twenty-six 12-pounders on the upper deck, with four 6-pounders on the quarterdeck and a further pair on the forecastle.

Heavier, 18-pounder batteries were, for some time, limited to the two-decker 44s but the shortcomings of these ships, together with reports of French interest in up-gunning their own ships, led to British interest. Rumours regarding the armament of vessels completing for the American Continental Navy, as it came to be known, probably decided the British to start building classes of 38- and 36-gun, 18-pounder frigates in 1778, actually pre-empting the French by about three years.

By 1793 the 12-pounder frigate had all but been abandoned. The capture of the French *Pomone* in the following year would provide the British with an exemplar, the reproduction of whose stable form would allow a further increase to include 24-pounders. Carrying a total of forty or more heavy cannon and carronades, these ships would be classed fourth rates.

Mainly under the impetus of foreign competition, frigate size increased at a rapid rate. Many of the larger examples on the British list were of French origin, but an alternative means of producing large and strong hulls fairly quickly was to cut down, or raze, two-deckers. Known as 'razees', most had been 64s of middling usefulness. Some were successful but most were judged to have their single remaining gun-deck too close to the waterline.

The smallest rated ships were sixth rates, under the captaincy of commanders. The difference between these and the numerous unrated ship-sloops was mainly one of scale, the sixth rate carrying between twenty-two and twenty-eight 9-pounders, typically augmented by eight 24-pounder carronades, while the sloops had up to eighteen 6-pounders, backed by 12-pounder carronades.

Although posts aboard sixth rates were eagerly sought by newly promoted commanders, the ships were not built in large numbers, not least because their usual duties would make them easy prey for enemy frigates. Commerce protection and patrol were their usual lot and, for these, sloops could usually perform equally well while having the advantage of being built more cheaply and in greater numbers.

The term sloop was imprecise, embracing brig- and ship-rigged categories with two and three masts respectively, some with quarterdecks and/or forecastles, some without. For lieutenants-in-command they provided valuable experience in that the enemy employed large numbers of speedy corsair-style craft, commonly termed *chasses-marée*, to prey on commercial shipping. Often privately owned, they were strongly manned with large, highly motivated crews. Resulting duels, to prevent the taking of merchantmen, could be as bloody as anything between larger vessels.

BRITISH SHIPBUILDERS preferred to build predominantly in British oak which, in conjunction with good design and adequate maintenance, was extremely durable. The wood's qualities depended greatly, however, upon its slow rate of growth. Over the years, profligate use of oak had been matched by a lack of any national policy regarding the replenishment of plundered woods and hedgerows. This naturally resulted in shortages and a significant rise in price, for the transport of large timbers overland was prohibitively expensive. To be viable, timber needed to be sourced close to the water over which it could be transported. Indeed, shipyards still tended to be clustered close to extensive woodland, yet not too far from a major dockyard, whose resources were often required to complete the hulls produced by comparatively unsophisticated small yards.

Shortages were felt most keenly in particular components which had to be cut from grown timber, notably knees (the brackets that supported transverse deck beams) and futtocks (sections which, scarfed end to end and doubled, formed a ship's main frames). To alleviate the problem there was a large-scale shift to German oak, but this timber's tendency to rot became apparent only after several ships had been built from it. Several classes of frigate were built of softwood while, at the opposite end of the scale of alternatives, some were built of teak in Bombay. The lifespan of 'fir-built' frigates was, typically, only ten to fifteen years, but teak construction was no guarantee of longevity, the Bombay-built *Andromeda*, for instance, being hulked after only twelve years' service. It will be appreciated that not the least reason for the importance of the Baltic trade to Britain was that it was the source of many indispensable shipbuilding materials, the supply of which had to be maintained at all costs, even to the extent of hostilities.

Chronic shortages of specific components persisted, however, leading directly to the general introduction of iron components, which had been used in minor applications by the British and other nationalities for at least seventy years already.

PART TWO *Hostilities*

chapter four

The Process of War,
January–August 1793

INTOXICATED BY REVOLUTION, France at the beginning of 1793 none the less faced a daunting combination of threats. Engaged in a process that could no longer be checked, she was creating internal stresses that would soon erupt into civil war, that most savage of conflicts. Simultaneously, she was beset by enemies on whom, with a casual lack of diplomacy, she had declared war. Arrayed against her were Austria and Prussia, Spain and Portugal, the kingdom of the Two Sicilies, the United Provinces and Great Britain.

Britain lacked full commitment in that her prime minister, Pitt, believed that the nation's interests were primarily extra-European. Growing concern that rabid Revolutionary ideas might successfully take root in Britain had led to a train of flawed logic. This postulated that insurrection thrived on general dissatisfaction. Dissatisfaction could be allayed by spending public money on socially popular schemes. Extra taxation to raise this money would only increase dissatisfaction and funds, therefore, had to be diverted from an existing vote. As happens all too often, this proved to be the defence budget. The inevitable outcome was a considerable cut in the strength of the army.

Perhaps fortunately, therefore, the military was in no state to be squandered in ambitious expeditions to Europe when France declared war. Defensively, its role would be to protect the home islands and foreign possessions against any enemy attempts at invasion. Offensively, it would be employed in raids and incursions against enemy shores, transported and supported by the Royal Navy.

From the outset, the coalition exhibited its weakness in its inability to agree common war aims. Austria, in particular, sought to conquer such territory as would command maximum bartering power at the eventual peace. Several of the allied states were short of war funds and Britain found herself subsidising most of them. In return, she was able to extract an agreement that the restoration of the French monarchy was not to be a primary war objective. To have adopted it would have been to accept that France would have to be beaten into unconditional surrender, altogether too ambitious an outcome. A common aim, however, was to remain beyond the reach of what was described as the 'general convulsion which appeared to threaten the total subversion of every social principle and every wise reputation of what is called government'.

A first requirement for the British was manpower to boost the strength of the fighting services. The small standing army was speedily augmented by the usual course of hiring German mercenaries, initially 8,000 Hessians. Because most of the available regular troops were on standby for service abroad, militias were mobilized for home defence. As conscription was not yet a politically acceptable option, landed gentry were officially encouraged to raise companies of fencibles. These, by definition, were limited to home service but the system none the less proved to be the foundation of many a fine regular regiment.

The navy, of course, had its own methods of recruitment, although rapid expansion soon brought problems. In time of war, for instance, rates paid to merchant seamen, particularly to those engaged in risky trades, soon increased to levels that made the pay of the regular navy look grossly unattractive. To offset both this and some of the general perceptions of life in the service, the official bounty offered to volunteers was supplemented by many municipalities from public funds. Where this reflected a degree of patriotism, it had also the practical purpose of simplifying the meeting of manpower quotas, soon to be set by government.

With so many officers languishing on half-pay there was, at the outset, no difficulty in mustering the required numbers. Despite this, inducements generally favoured officers over ratings.

For the actual conduct of hostilities, there existed no real War Cabinet. In practice, the prime minister, together with the home and foreign secretaries, with irregular contributions from the king, comprised an *ad hoc* committee which drove the remainder of the Cabinet on policy matters. Not for a year was the post of secretary of state for war created, and even then it was considered so minor a task that the home secretary, Viscount Melville, assumed it as an addition to his other duties. These included serving as treasurer of the navy under the First Lord of the Admiralty, the Earl of Chatham. During the period covered by this narrative, therefore, the British contribution to the coalition had a distinctly amateurish air, with a tendency to dissipate available resources.

The Royal Navy's tasks were little different from those of earlier conflicts. As the French traditionally practised war on commerce, or *guerre de course*, the defence of trade loomed large, as did the capture of the overseas bases upon which enemy privateers depended. The West Indies were much prized as a market and source of wealth by both the British and the French and, again, it could be expected that the ownership of key islands would be hotly contested. Reinforcement of the West Indies stations was, therefore, an imperative.

The disposition of the bulk of the Royal Navy was much influenced by that of the French, based in four major locations. The strength and disposition of the latter at this time are neatly summarized by William James, the first edition of whose *Naval History* was published some thirty years later. His assessment was as follows:

LOCATION	SHIPS OF THE LINE				FRIGATES					CORVETTES
Guns	120	110	80	74	64	40	38	36	32	26 or fewer
Brest	1	5	7	26	-	10	-	24	-	23
Lorient	-	-	-	10	-	1	-	5	-	-
Rochefort	-	-	-	12	1	2	-	14	-	11
Toulon	2	-	3	19	-	5	2	13	2	13
Totals	3		5 10	67	1	18	2	56	2	47

Of these, at the start of hostilities, forty-six ships of the line, forty-six frigates and twenty-five corvettes were still 'in ordinary', i.e. laid up, or under repair and maintenance. Ten ships of the line and eight frigates were under construction.

By some margin, the most powerful French squadron was that based on Brest. From this very secure location at the western tip of Brittany, it was nicely poised to operate in either the English Channel or the open Atlantic, for which forays it could conveniently be augmented by contingents from Lorient or Rochefort.

Toulon, base to the Mediterranean squadron was, like Brest, protected by its geography against direct attack from the open sea. With Italy yet to be unified, and still comprising several states, only the navy of Spain could seriously challenge that of France in this theatre.

At any particular time, the nature and extent of British naval activity in the Mediterranean fluctuated largely according to the state of relations with France and/or Spain and the threat that they posed to national interests or alliances. Gibraltar had already been developed as a fleet base, though while it was conveniently located for watching the Spanish fleet in its southern bases of Cadiz and Cartagena, it was a long distance from Toulon.

The common procedure of 'close' blockade meant maintaining a battle squadron off an enemy's base, thereby severely limiting his options. Imposing considerably less strain on either ships or men was the 'distant' blockade. This involved stationing only a frigate squadron in the enemy's offing, supported by the odd 74. Their task was to summon the main strength of the battle fleet at the first hint of the enemy breaking out. Either option required the availability of basing, repair and maintenance facilities within practical sailing distance. At this time, therefore, the island of Minorca was strategically important to the British, its deep-water base of Port Mahon being only 250 miles from Toulon.

Not surprisingly, Minorca had already seen two considerable periods of British occupation but, just ten years earlier, by the terms of the Peace of Versailles which had officially ended the American War of Independence, the island (together with Florida) had again been ceded to Spain. The presence of Spain in the First Coalition was thus essential to the Royal Navy's ability to invest Toulon if the effort of again capturing the island was to be avoided.

William James' voluminous statistics allow us also to arrive at a brief summary of the strength of the Royal Navy in 1793. The table below permits a rough comparison with that for the French fleet.

Rate	FIRST	SECOND	THIRD	FOURTH	FIFTH	SIXTH
Guns	100–120	90–98	64–80	50–60	32–44	20–28
Number	5	16	92	12	79	35

At the beginning of the year, only one first rate was fully commissioned, the remainder being under repair or in ordinary. Of second rates, the corresponding figure was 4 out of 16; for third rates, 21 out of 92; for fourth rates, 7 out of 12; for fifth rates, 35 out of 79; for sixth rates, 15 out of 35.

It will be noted that while the French had readily available over half their strength in the three major categories, the British had to hand less than a quarter, and under one half in lesser classes. It was fortunate that it was impracticable for the French to concentrate their strength.

During 1793, therefore, as British yards strove to bring ships forward from reserve and recruiting services scoured the land for the crews to man them, the Royal Navy was numerically inferior and found itself severely stretched. It appears to indicate that it was not expected that the French would declare war. Indeed, just a year earlier the prime minister, noted for having less acumen for war than his father, had declared: 'Unquestionably, there has never been a time in the history of this country when, from the situation in Europe, we might more reasonably expect fifteen years of peace than at the present moment.'

It was in Britain's favour that partial mobilizations against Spain in 1790 and against Russia in 1791 had been valuable exercises in proving the thoroughness of Lord Barham's *matériel* preparations.

In time of war, overseas possessions are both blessing and liability. Garrisons needed to be rapidly strengthened, causing a further drain on the already inadequate strength of the British army while requiring the services of warships to transport them. While some larger islands assisted through the raising of forces of local levies, the alliance of the Spanish was welcome, not least for removing a further threat.

On paper, the Spanish fleet was a formidable force, the design and construction of its ships highly regarded. As with the French, however, its infrastructure had been badly run down, with dockyards under-resourced and ship maintenance skimped. As allies, the Spanish were regarded by the British as unreliable, while the Royal Navy held the fighting qualities of their fleet with scant respect. In the words of Nelson himself (then newly appointed to command the *Agamemnon* 64, having spent five years on half-pay): 'I never saw finer men-of-war ... very fine ships, but shockingly manned.'

Spain at this time supported a fleet of over 200 ships, seventy-six of them ships of the line. Of these, fifty-six were in commission. Indeed, of the whole, about 80 per cent were ready for sea, an extraordinarily high proportion. In 1795 Spain would make her own peace with France but, for the period of this narrative, remained an ally of Britain.

A further short-lived ally would be the Netherlands, fated to be quickly overrun by French forces. Their fleet, too, was of considerable size, being reckoned at 119 ships, forty-nine ships of the line. Where the British acknowledged the excellence of Dutch seamen, their ships were not rated so highly. Not only had their general condition been allowed to deteriorate but their design was found wanting. Due to the uniquely constricting feature of the shallowness of home waters, Dutch ships needed to be of limited draught. In order to displace a given amount, their designers inevitably produced beamy ships with little depth to their hulls. The first factor made them poor performers to windward while the latter meant that hulls lacked the longitudinal stiffness required to tolerate heavy armament, particularly near the extremities. It was thus no accident that the largest Dutch ships were their ten 74s. Their frigates were well constructed but, again due to weight restriction, they carried few guns above 12-pounders at a time when their foreign equivalents shipped an 18-pounder main battery.

Of the minor allies in the Mediterranean region, Portugal possessed ten ships of the line, equivalent to third rates of between sixty and eighty guns. It also had fourteen frigates. Less than half of the total strength could be mustered at any one time.

Often referred to simply as 'Naples', the Kingdom of the Two Sicilies supported only a small fleet, but the king placed a valuable division of four good 74s and a brigade of troops at the disposal of the British commander-in-chief, Mediterranean fleet.

Despite its name, the kingdom comprised the island of Sicily and the southern half of the Italian peninsula. It was thus of considerable strategic value to the British, although its main base at Naples was a considerable distance from Toulon and its workforce was badly affected by French-inspired republicanism.

Although the Royal Navy's Channel and Mediterranean fleets would bear the brunt of containing the French, their strength could not be boosted at the expense of other commands. Since the loss of the American colonies, the North American station had diminished in significance, but that of the Caribbean was as important, and as demanding, as ever. British interests stretched from Jamaica in the west to Trinidad (then Spanish), hard by the South American coast, a chain of islands some 1,500 miles in length and mostly in British or French possession.

The constant wind pattern and the considerable sailing involved in adequately covering the theatre required the maintenance of two separate forces, one based on Jamaica, the other in the Leeward Islands. Owing to the presence of French bases and the wealth of British commercial traffic around the islands, the opportunities for the enemy to disrupt trade were considerable. British fleet dispositions reflected this, having their strength in frigates and minor warships, backed by a number of line ships that was steadily reduced as the actual threat from the enemy became more accurately gauged.

Beyond protection of trade, the navy was endlessly involved in combined operations, moving troops from one garrison to another or against enemy-held islands. Such captures denied them bases for privateering while providing useful bargaining chips at the eventual peace talks. A separate problem lay in the islands' workforce, mainly imported West African slaves. Understandably, these embraced French Revolutionary ideals wholeheartedly, and trouble, however sporadic, was easily fomented and widespread.

Reports quickly reached Britain that francophone Haiti was of royalist sympathies, leading the poorly advised Pitt to initiate action from Jamaica. With an eye also to the acquisition of the rich adjoining territory of Santo Domingo, a campaign was launched that was to drag on fruitlessly for five years. Following a fearful toll in lives and expenditure, the whole enterprise ended in failure.

Smaller but equally vital, the East Indies station covered the Indian Ocean from the Cape to the Indies, including the waters around the subcontinent, on which France still maintained commercial enclaves. To the east of the great island of Madagascar lay the two French possessions of Ile de France and Ile de Bourbon (now Mauritius and Réunion respectively) which were capable of supporting a French frigate squadron.

For the moment, Britain's Dutch coalition partners were facing the immediate threat of a rampant, militaristic France. As Mahan so shrewdly pointed out, however, the greater long-term cause for concern was from Britain herself, ever hungry to extend her empire. The United Provinces had colonies at the Cape and in the valuable islands of Java and Ceylon. They also possessed minor islands in the West Indies and considerable tracts of land in South America. When, shortly afterward, France overran the United Provinces, restyling them as the puppet Batavian Republic, Dutch territories abroad became fair game, with Britain taking most of them and retaining them at the peace.

Ironically, it had been Britain's firm stand over the Netherlands that had been a major cause of the French declaring war. With the French occupying the Austrian Netherlands and threatening the United Provinces, there had been every prospect of the whole nation, its fleet and its foreign possessions passing into French hands. British war strategy was thus to intervene in the Netherlands while seizing French overseas territories, in the process inflicting the greatest possible damage to the enemy's fleet. Without the support of the Spanish fleet as ally, the French would then be vulnerable to incursions against their own coasts. Such were the ambitions of Melville, but they proved to be beyond the nation's ability to realize with the forces available.

Although British military activities in the Caribbean and the Indian Ocean are beyond the scope of this narrative, they continuously absorbed resources that could have been employed to critical effect closer to home.

THREE WEEKS BEFORE the execution of Louis XVI and a month before the official declaration of war, there occurred an incident which, although minor in itself, included the first hostile shots of a naval war that, with little interlude, would continue for a further twenty-two years.

On 2 January 1793 the British 16-gun brig *Childers* (perhaps more correctly a 'brig sloop', to differentiate this twin-masted type from the three-masted 'ship-sloop') entered the Goulet, the approach to the French base at Brest. From here the port may be observed clearly, but it is not certain whether the *Childers'* commanding officer, Robert Barlow, was acting under orders or on his own initiative. Either way, his was a highly provocative act in the prevailing state of international relations.

Bordered by high ground, the waters of the Goulet were commanded by fortifications. Only when one of them put a warning shot over his mastheads did Barlow break out his national ensign. This served only to enrage the French gunners, who opened fire from either shore. With the flood tide under her, with little wind and unable to elevate her guns sufficiently to respond, the situation of the *Childers* appeared unhealthy. With the aid of sweeps, however, Barlow's men brought her head around and, playing a fitful breeze, her master clawed her, painfully slowly, to the safety of open water.

Unpractised, the French artillerymen hit their target only once, a massive 48-pounder ball smashing one of the brig's toy 4-pounders into three pieces. The shot itself was brought home as a trophy.

THE FRENCH MINISTER of foreign affairs, Charles-François Dumouriez, was a career army officer of experience and political acumen. He had so far survived having been a favourite of the king, mainly by virtue of his belief that the 'enemy' Austria could be seriously undermined by striking at the Austrian Netherlands. His great opportunity was created through the Prussian invasion, when he was instrumental in inspiring the mobilization of the French citizen-army that barred the route to the capital.

It was Dumouriez who directed Kellermann's movements before and after his success at Valmy. French forces followed up the ensuing Prussian withdrawal, that under the minister heading for Belgium. Hopes that the population would rise spontaneously against its Austrian rulers were not realized but success at Jemappes saw Dumouriez in Brussels by 15 November 1792.

The policy makers of the Convention, notably Danton, envisioned a Revolution-based 'Greater France' whose eastern boundary would follow the Rhine north to the sea. Dumouriez's success in Belgium thus met with considerable approbation but, typical of the paranoid atmosphere within the Convention, also caused suspicions to be voiced that the minister was engaged in creating something of a personal fiefdom. Such suspicions were fuelled by Dumouriez's calculated strategy of encouraging an 'independent' Belgium that would deny the southern Netherlands to the Austrians without provoking the yet-neutral British into declaring war. To pursue this policy, he had to get the Belgian clergy on his side, which meant greatly playing down the Revolutionary drive to radicalize the profession. Having given them the necessary undertakings, Dumouriez went on to request funding from them for a national army. This was one step too far for the Convention, which ordered that all decrees so far made should apply also to Belgium.

As already noted, it was the reopening of the Scheldt to free navigation in November 1792 that moved the British government towards declaring war. Pitt's first response was to mobilize the militia, both to act as a counterweight to an obvious increase in revolutionary enthusiasm within the kingdom and to permit an intervention by regular forces in the Netherlands should it prove advantageous. The pro-British order, re-established by Prussian military intervention five years earlier, was looking decidedly shaky. Should the 'patriots', many of whom had sought refuge in France, again take advantage of the situation to create a state of near civil war, the British could see the French taking immediate advantage. As the former were bound by treaty to support the House of Orange, hostilities thus looked likely even without the execution of Louis.

Dumouriez did indeed have plans to extend his sphere of interest beyond the Scheldt and commanded sufficient respect to enter negotiations by proxy with the British at the highest level during the horror-struck days following the French king's death. As Britain hovered on a war that would upset the French minister's intentions, he sought to play down the Convention's expressed policy of exporting revolution and to justify the Scheldt navigation problem as being no more than the rectification of an anomaly. However, even as the British pondered, unconvinced, the die was cast by the Convention itself declaring war on both the British and the Dutch on 1 February 1793.

The great rivers traversing the southern Netherlands form a natural and formidable impediment, easily defended at the 'barrier towns' where lay the essential bridges. Even before any declaration of war, the French posed a threat sufficient for the Stadholders to request British military assistance. The British were slow to respond and now, as Dumouriez advanced, hastily cobbled together a small expeditionary force.

The French leader was taking a considerable risk for as he marched north toward the rivers his supply lines became ever more extended and vulnerable. They required protection at a time when he was losing personnel, for his citizen soldiery, their first wave of patriotic fervour diminishing in the bitter cold of a soggy Flemish winter, melted away to return to their farms. His strength was further diminished by the need to invest those defended towns that he had not the resources nor the time to capture. With the knowledge that a coalition army was moving westward to place itself across his line of retreat, Dumouriez took Breda on 26 February. He was now just 10 miles short of the Maas River that would bar further advance. Fifteen miles to the north-west, therefore, his leading elements laid siege to the small fortified town of Willemstad, prior to attempting a crossing of the Hollandsch Diep.

On 1 March, before the French made their move, 2,000 British troops under the Duke of York were landed downstream, at Hellevoetsluis on the opposite bank. This deep arm of the North Sea was well suited to naval support and the frigate *Syren* provided guns and crews to man several shallow-draught Dutch craft, able to work close inshore to enfilade French positions. The enemy's siege batteries were taken and Willemstad relieved in what was the first British military success of the war.

As Dumouriez continued to conciliate with the Belgians, his army was badly defeated by the Austrians near Maastricht, then at Neerwinden. His situation now unsustainable, the French general was obliged to seek terms. On the understanding that he was now disillusioned with the Convention, and was prepared to work against it, he was allowed to march his army out of Belgium without any further action being taken against it. By the end of March, it was gone.

Having tried, unsuccessfully, to turn the loyalties of his men, Dumouriez was visited by his minister of war, who sought some explanation for his bizarre conduct. Dumouriez's response was to detain the minister and his party, then to turn them over to the Austrians. Shortly afterward, they were joined by the general and his senior officers. For the moment, the Netherlands were secure, but the reprieve was only temporary.

It has already been noted that the British Admiralty placed the highest priority on reinforcing the West Indies stations, where the standing forces were indeed weak. Based on Jamaica was a 50-gun flagship, three frigates and six smaller vessels, while the Leewards were usually covered by a pair of 50s, two frigates and four smaller vessels. As the French normally maintained three or four ships of the line in the area, usually based on Martinique in the east, they could, had they concentrated and moved smartly, have inflicted considerable woe on the inferior British force. An important point to bear in mind is that the north-east trade winds blow steadily over the greater part of the year, so that any enterprise launched in the days of sail from the eastern end of this great island chain would be likely to have had the initiative.

Although the French declaration of war had been a surprise, the existing inadequate active strength of the Royal Navy could be increased rapidly. This was thanks to Charles Middleton (Lord Barham) who, having recently departed the Navy Board, had left the system in excellent order. All ships 'in ordinary' had been grouped into divisions, each of which had been allocated a superintending master. Assisted by the simplified logistics of large classes of ship built to a near-standard design, equipment and stores for each division were housed in lay-apart storehouses adjacent to fitting-out berths. Sequential routine docking meant that a good proportion of reserve ships had clean hulls, enabling them to be brought forward quickly. On his departure, Middleton could inform Melville that 'upwards of ninety sail of the line' were in good condition and provided for.

Urgency was added by the knowledge that Rear Admiral Pierre Sercey had sailed from Brest for the West Indies at the end of February with three 74s and supporting ships. It was not known that his task was to escort home a convoy, vital to France in a period of poor harvests. At the same time, it was noticed that a new squadron, drawn from the French Atlantic bases, had begun to be assembled in the anchorage to the lee of the Quiberon peninsula, its purpose unknown.

In the West Indies, Vice Admiral Sir John Laforey had moved his Leeward Islands squadron immediately against the French-held island of Tobago which capitulated with little opposition. It was thus in hopes that most local French garrisons would hold royalist sympathies that Rear Admiral Alan Gardner sailed on 24 March 1793 with a pair of 98s, five 74s, two frigates and a tender. In his first flag command, Gardner's intent was to take Martinique from the enemy, using nearby Barbados as his base. It would, however, require a further year and a larger enterprise to achieve this objective.

THE NAVY'S MOST EXPERIENCED sea officer was Lord Howe, who commanded the Channel (or Western) squadron. At 67 years old, he was elderly for the task but had accepted it in 1790 at the personal request of the king. It was his second spell in the command and he had previously served as First Lord, this at a time when senior service personnel were commonly involved in high politics (and were frequently blighted by them).

Howe's area of responsibility ranged from a point to the east of Portsmouth south to Gibraltar. It thus included all French bases except those in the Mediterranean. At a time when practically all British naval assets in home waters were to be found on the south coast, scattered from the Nore in the east to Cork in the west, the Channel squadron could be restyled the Atlantic fleet for operations in the deep ocean.

Howe maintained a close interest in the French fleet gathering inside Quiberon. Its purpose remained unknown but, as the opportunity had not been taken to sail quickly to, say, the West Indies, to strike while British strength was still weak, it was assumed that it had a major task in view. This might have been the escort of a considerable convoy or even an expedition to Ireland but, while the Admiralty made its dispositions and brought forward reserve ships with all despatch, Howe's course was to remain vigilant, informed and ready to counter any move on the part of the enemy until such time as he had the means to initiate decisive offensive action.

The admiral was strongly against close blockade, considering it not worth the wear and tear on ships and personnel. His policy was to maintain the bulk of his strength on the English south coast (whence he exercised it constantly) while employing a fast frigate squadron to watch the enemy closely and give warning of any movement. The accepted procedure was to use the anchorage at Torbay, the closest that offered the best combination of space, holding ground and protection from the south and west. Howe, none the less, preferred Spithead, with the nearby facilities of Portsmouth dockyard. The fleshpots of Southsea, in addition, offered far more than the under-developed wastes of the West Country. In this, Howe drew a strong later censure from Mahan, who declared it too distant. Which, indeed, it was.

All, in fact, was not well with the French fleet. In command was the Flag Officer, Brest, although ships from Lorient and Rochefort were attached. Vice Admiral Morard de Galles was a career officer whose competence had been proven in the Indian Ocean squadron where, during the Seven Years' War, he had served under Suffren. Then, it had been a matter of resourcefulness, of making-do in the face of official neglect. Now, with his own flag, he was responsible for a fleet crewed by men who knew their rights but who neglected their responsibilities. In the new state that France had become, the fleet went to sea virtually with the consent of its citizen complements and Morard was aware that the enforcement of the customary standard of service discipline could generate a backlash that could see him 'investigated', relieved of his duties, imprisoned or executed. Several of his commanding officers had been promoted for their Revolutionary spirit rather than their ability. Elevated beyond their capabilities, they ran poor ships. Exercises conducted between Quiberon and Belle Ile saw watches failing to muster in the strength necessary to carry out major fleet movements such as wearing ship. Accidents were frequent. Morard de Galles had problems enough without challenging Howe.

Keeping the fleet offshore had at least the advantage of placing crews beyond the influences of the ports where, particularly at Brest, outright mutiny was always likely. Increasingly, however, a further reason became apparent. Immediately to the south was the region of the Vendée, one of several which had retained a majority of royalist supporters and which now were breaking into open revolt. This counter-revolution had to be crushed by military means; it was the task of the fleet to prevent the British from aiding the insurgents by an assault from the sea.

SINCE OPENING THE WAR with Britain and Spain, those directing French affairs had been active. Undaunted by the array of enemies that they had created, they focused the fierce energies released by the Revolution into gearing up the spirit and resources of the nation to overcome any force that opposed it.

In truth, the coalition faced by the French was a force far less than the sum of its parts. Both Austria and Prussia had been recent allies of France and tended more toward hostilities with each other, each vying for control of what, eventually, would emerge as a united Germany. It was in the gift of Spain, another late ally, to threaten the French with her not inconsiderable fleet and army which, acting in concert, could have campaigned along both the Biscay and Mediterranean shores. That they did not was due to lam-entable standards of government and military direction and, free of any real threat from this quarter, the discordant mass of the French armies could be concentrated in the east.

With Italy yet a collection of smaller states, Spain was free to establish naval command of the western Mediterranean, but both the material state of her fleet and the quality of its direction had deteriorated. Until the British could assemble a Mediterranean fleet worthy of the name, using the greatest asset of their allies – their geography – the French, prevented only by their own deep divisions, could act with any squadron they cared to deploy.

The lack of cohesion between the coalition states allowed the French armies, as alarming in their fervour as any fielded by the Mahdi, to succeed in detail. In Belgium, in the Italian border country, in the high Savoy and deep into Germany, the Revolutionary cohorts drove back their disunited opponents, responding to Danton's call to answer their challenge by 'hurling at their feet the French king's head'.

Wars, however, are expensive and the French economy, already fragile, was under severe pressure. One major cause of the original revolt, the price of bread, was now controlled by law, pleasing the populace but hardly suiting the producers, many of whom moved out of cereal production. Wholesale confiscation of property had seen the issue of government interest-bearing bonds (*assignats*) by way of compensation. Being transferable, these soon went into general circulation but, poorly underpinned by genuine resources, their value fell rapidly, creating a fresh cause for discontent.

As the price of 'secondary essentials' rose, interested factions within the Convention, as usual, made political capital. Representatives of the radical *Sans-culottes sections* (termed the *Enragés*), notably the fiery left-wing *abbé*, Jacques Roux, fanned the unrest to push the Convention toward ever more extreme agendas. Such activities were sufficiently alarming to bring about a temporary, and unlikely, meeting of minds between the Montagnards and the more moderate Girondins. Interfactional squabbling, yet more rancorous as military success stagnated, then reversed as Dumouriez first retreated, then defected.

Greater threat generated greater response. Encouraged by divisions among the Revolutionaries and thoroughly upset by ever harsher decrees, ordinary people began to rebel *en masse*, particularly in highly religious or royalist-sympathetic areas such as the Vendée. The assembly required an army to repel Coalitition forces advancing from the east. This was created by a national levy, of which the initial demand for 300,000 proved to be an unpopular measure with the population at large. For a while, the despatch of regular troops contained the problem but it was now a case of Frenchman fighting Frenchman.

A more conciliatory attitude on the part of the Convention would have helped defuse the situation, but it reacted as it had done to Dumouriez's earlier proposals in Belgium. Armed 'rebels' and returning *émigrés* would now be summarily executed. Priests, denounced by six or more parishioners, would be deported.

This new culture of curtain twitching and denunciation gained further impetus through the formation of Surveillance Committees. Originally charged with monitoring the movements of foreign nationals, their activities were quickly extended to their fellow citizens, whose very hope of employment soon depended upon a committee's approval.

This culture, nurtured by the *Enragés*, quickly developed to the point where it caused embarrassment to the Convention. Apparently at last aware of the bad name that was being acquired by France through the arbitrary punishments being meted out by almost any group or organization with an axe to grind, as long as it was in the name of the Revolution, Danton at last sought to concentrate such power back where it belonged: with the state. He proposed the formation of a Revolutionary Tribunal, in the hands of which would reside the power of life or death. To exercise such authority in a manner acceptable to the mob, much of which now had a taste for violence, the tribunal would need to be severe. 'Let us be terrible,' said Danton, 'so that the people need not be.'

This recentralization of authority took a major step forward when, on 6 April 1793, the Convention appointed a nine-man Committee of Public Safety to supervise executive decisions. This cabal rapidly assumed the status of a government cabinet and was to gain for itself an unholy reputation.

Within the Convention, the truce between the Montagnards and the Girondins collapsed, mainly through the latter's close association with the disgraced Dumouriez. Matters degenerated to the extent that a concerned Danton attempted to mediate, only to be rebuffed by the Girondins, who retaliated by demanding the arraignment of the influential Marat before the tribunal. This over-confidence was their undoing, for their case was totally inadequate to substantiate a major charge and, in overriding the immunity of a deputy, they laid themselves open to similar treatment. True to form, the *Enragés* and *Sans-culottes* demanded and received Jacobin support in a *putsch* aimed at demolishing the whole Girondin group. The Insurrection Committee demanded nothing less than the arrest of all leaders of the faction but the Convention, fearing its own disintegration, referred it to the Committee of Public Safety for a decision.

On 2 June the Left organized a large-scale march on the Convention to reinforce its demands. Rowdy behaviour within the chamber resulted in a mass exodus of deputies who, once outside, found themselves beset by an excited crowd, estimated at 8,000 and barely controlled by an angry National Guard. To an accompaniment of jeering, members had to return to the chamber and their deliberations. Twenty-two prominent Girondins were duly expelled and placed under house arrest.

The proscription of their leaders triggered a resolute Girondin response. Having signed a mass protest against the Jacobin coup, they returned to their constituencies where, for the most part, they organized opposition to the extremists running the capital. Many in the provinces were fearful and sickened by the course of events so far, detesting the militants who were increasingly gaining power in local politics. Power in the large provincial cities traditionally rested with the large employers. Their concern was for the effects of the Revolution on their markets; their employees feared in turn for their jobs. In the great commercial cities, such as Marseille, Lyon and Bordeaux, the powerful merchant class rebelled against dictatorial rule from Paris, carrying with them the professional class – lawyers, academics and clergy – who were already suffering from central diktats. They also carried along many of the skilled working class, artisans who felt less liberated by events than threatened by them.

Regionally, there occurred 'peasant revolts', usually isolated and which quickly ran their course. That in the Vendée was something different. Deeply religious, its inhabitants were largely impoverished and uneducated, employed at mere subsistence levels. Towns were viewed sceptically by the peasantry as centres for control and taxation. For leadership, a Vendéen turned naturally to his priest who, as well as giving spiritual guidance, was the usual source of education, nursing and help for the destitute. Not surprisingly, therefore, the new constitutional clergy imposed by Paris caused immense dissatisfaction. This was made the worse by disillusionment for, just three years earlier, the king had invited all to submit their grievances in the national collection of the *cahiers de doléances*. These, it was understood, would be the basis of a fairer society, one which addressed their legitimate complaints. Instead, the government had murdered their king, imposed endless decrees, demanded a contingent for a conscripted army and had persecuted their priests. The Vendée peasantry detested the new order as much as the new order loathed the 'enemies of the nation'. Their eventual response was equally savage.

The trigger for a general uprising in the region was the decree of 6 March 1793, ordering the closure of all churches served by a refractory priest who had refused to take the new oath. Within days, crowds began to attack the homes and business premises of officials administering the new order. There were clashes with detachments of the National Guard, following which matters erupted in the small town of Machecoul, scene of a prolonged and pitiless massacre in which 500 are held to have died.

Within a fortnight, Paris had moved in 50,000 troops. Although this number sounds formidable, over 90 per cent were newly mobilized raw recruits. Spread over a large area, they were nowhere in strength sufficient either to awe or to subjugate the furious peasanty. Control exerted even by regular army units ran no further than the towns that they garrisoned. The countryside, a wilderness of *marais* drained by a complex web of ditches, belonged to the people. One by one, they reclaimed their towns and, by May 1793, the Vendée had become what has been termed 'a state within a state'. At its head stood a Grand Council whose religious head, the Abbé Bernier, addressed republicans at large to explain their aims and in justification of their action: 'To recover and preserve for ever our ... Roman Catholic religion', continuing:

> you ... subverting all the principles of religious and political order, were the first to proclaim that insurrection is the most sacred of duties. You have introduced atheism in place of religion, anarchy in place of law, men who are tyrants in place of the king who was our father ... you, whose pretensions to liberty have led to the most extreme penalties ...

As an indictment of the new regime, the statement could hardly have been bettered and it caused fury in the Convention, at which it had been aimed. For the while, circumstances dictated that the Vendée situation be accepted, but its time would come. Meanwhile, mindful of the fact that the French themselves had on more than one occasion sought to cause mischief by exploiting Irish dissatisfaction, the Committee of Public Safety was concerned that the British would take advantage and land a force to aid the Vendéens. For this reason Vice Admiral Morard de Galles was obliged to keep his mutinous fleet anchored uncomfortably under the lee of the Quiberon peninsula.

Pitt's priority, however, did not lay in the re-establishment of the French monarchy. Neither did he, with his slender military resources, wish to become embroiled in further Continental adventures. A landing was still well in the future and, when it eventually came, it was of French royalist sympathisers.

DELAYED BY MANPOWER shortages and other priorities, the Admiralty could only slowly build up the strength of Lord Howe's Channel fleet. As spring passed into summer, however, the French fleet remained largely inactive. It slowly grew to three three-deckers, three 80s and no less than fifteen 74s, accompanied by a frigate squadron.

The latter force was occasionally detached on independent missions, which enabled the watching British to get a rare chance of action. On 27 May the *Sémillante* 32 was intercepted by the British frigate *Venus* of approximately equal weight. Following two hours of close-quarter gunfire the Frenchman's defence faltered but, even as the British closed to board her, reinforcement appeared in the shape of the French *Cléopatre* 36. Damage to the combatants reflected the different modes of engagement. The British always aimed to hull their opponents and the *Sémillante* was visibly settling from damage received. The *Venus* was much cut about aloft as the French aimed to reduce their opponent's ability to sail and manoeuvre. Chivalrously, the *Cléopatre* was more concerned for the survival of her colleague than carrying the fight to the *Venus,* which was fortunate to escape.

The *Sémillante* survived this drubbing, which occurred north-west of Cape Finisterre, but her saviour was not so fortunate. Just three weeks later, in the western English Channel, the *Cléopatre* fell in with the British 36-gun frigate *Nymphe*. Action was sought by both commanding officers, but fifty-five bloody minutes later the Frenchman, having had her mizen mast and wheel shot away, lost manoeuvrability and was unable to prevent the British taking her by boarding.

Frigate commands were a fine training ground for the navy's rising stars. Their operations permitted periods of independence and they saw more action than ships of the line. In this case, the *Cléopatre* became the first such prize of the war and, being a fine vessel, was purchased by the Admiralty for further service. The *Nymphe's* commanding officer, Edward Pellew, thus made his name and the fortune of his family, not least because he secured with the prize the French signal codes, for which the Admiralty Board expressed its pleasure.

Pellew went on to become famous in the later hounding to destruction of the French 74 *Droits de l'Homme*. Rising rapidly in the service he finished the Napoleonic Wars as Admiral Sir Edward Pellew, Lord Exmouth. In this era of apparently unremitting savagery, it is pleasant to record that Pellew was so impressed by the fighting qualities of the *Cléopatre's* dead captain that he sent his widow financial assistance. The gallant captain, identified simply as 'Citoyen Mullon', was interred at Portsmouth.

It was already apparent that while ship-for-ship the British were getting the better of these minor encounters, their opponents in no way shirked action and fought hard. Removed from the Revolutionary hothouse of the main body of the fleet, crews of smaller vessels appeared to observe correct standards of discipline.

Lord Howe finally sailed with the Channel fleet, then fifteen ships of the line, on 14 July 1793, over five months after the commencement of hostilities. Standards of ship handling appeared deficient and, following a damaging collision, the fleet returned, anchoring in Torbay. On the 25th Howe learned that an American master had reported seventeen French ships of the line 30 miles west of Belle Ile. It was now known that Sercey's squadron was expected back, escorting a convoy from the West Indies, so Howe sailed again. Baulked by a persistent westerly, he remained in the area, gaining two more ships of the line as he waited. Finally getting away as the wind veered to the north, Howe's fleet comprised four three-deckers, nine 74s and four 64s, supported by nine frigates and five smaller craft. The force arrived off Belle Ile on the 31st, almost immediately sighting Morard de Galles who, cruising off and on, was indeed awaiting Sercey's arrival.

For about thirty-six hours Howe tried to bring the enemy to action but the latter, holding the weather gage in fickle winds, was able to decline. Battle would probably have been beneficial to the French, who now returned to their usual anchorage and state of rebellious and corrosive inactivity.

Not the least problem faced by the French fighting services was the imposition by the Committee of Public Safety of the so-called *Députés en mission*. These appointees accompanied, and often overrode the decisions of, commanders in the field. Their virtually unlimited powers were often matched by a general lack of knowledge of military matters. They could invoke the threat of any punishment in order to drive men to greater effort. If things went badly, senior officers could face demotion or death. Conversely, almost by whim, quite junior officers could find themselves elevated to high rank, as in the case of Villaret-Joyeuse.

The *député* responsible for the navy was Jeanbon Saint-André, prominent Montagnard and president of the Convention. With limited background in naval affairs, he ascribed the run-down state of the fleet to the deliberate policy of the king. This was a total misrepresentation against one who had always taken great interest in the service. Jeanbon Saint-André eschewed manoeuvre and evolutions, instead exhorting commanding officers in Nelsonian phraseology to lay their ships alongside those of the enemy. Larger crews, imbued with Revolutionary spirit, would then carry the day by boarding. Unfortunately the French seamen, although unquestionably brave, generally had not sufficient sea time to hone the necessary skills, so that boarding was usually on British terms.

The commissioner's greatest folly was to disband the corps of gunners on the grounds that it comprised army personnel trained exclusively to fight at sea. This made them 'elitist', as the new creed of total equality meant that any soldier could demand equal and similar duty. The fact that serving and aiming great guns on the heaving deck of a warship bore no resemblance to fighting on land was a fact so obvious that it could have been hostage only to pure dogma.

THE FRENCH MEDITERRANEAN squadron, although junior to that based on Brest, was an important instrument of national policy. Deployed from Toulon, it operated in the western basin of the Mediterranean as counterbalance to the fleets of Spain and the Italian states. War with Britain, however, usually demanded a reinforcement of the Brest squadron in order to be able to create local and temporary naval superiority for any major operation in the Western Approaches. It thus became standard British policy to prevent any such reinforcement. It will be apparent that this was best exercised through containing the Toulon squadron in the Mediterranean rather than by hunting it down in the Atlantic. Gibraltar, and the advanced base at Minorca, thus became of critical importance for the maintenance of a large British presence.

British diplomatic relations with coalition partners, with the possible exception of some Italian states, were not particularly cordial. As Minorca could be used only at the behest of the Spanish, a reliable base in northern Italy was an attractive proposition. Those at Spezia, Leghorn (Livorno) and Genoa were, however, in the states of Tuscany and Genoa, those most immediately threatened by the French, who had already seized Savoy and Nice from the neighbouring state of Piedmont. An important factor at this time was that the merchants of Leghorn and Genoa were making huge profits by exporting grain in coastal convoys to the French, who were suffering repeated poor harvests.

Interest for the British thus centred on the more distant Naples and Sardinia, both of which sought naval protection. To these states Britain guaranteed to establish and maintain naval supremacy as required, to safeguard commerce and to provide transport by sea. In return, Naples pledged 6,000 troops (to whose maintenance Britain would contribute), four ships of the line and four smaller vessels. The smaller kingdom of Sardinia promised a very respectable army of 50,000, again subject to British subsidy.

Anticipating imminent British naval activity in the south, the French Convention reversed usual procedure. With the vigour so typical of its activities, it reinforced the Toulon squadron by five ships of the line transferred from Brest, and three more from Rochefort. Commercial traffic on the south coast suffered as its seamen were impressed by the state to bring the warship crews to full strength.

Until Britain clearly formulated her policies for war in the Mediterranean her would-be allies did not commit themselves too completely. A second tranche of 20,000 men and marines had been approved by the British Parliament in February 1793, but time was required to recruit and to train them, at the same time as dockyards laboured to bring ships forward from reserve.

Like the French fleet, that of the Spanish was divided: on the one hand there was the disease-stricken Mediterranean contingent at Cartagena; on the other, the Atlantic squadrons based on Vigo and Ferrol, where nineteen ships were being readied.

A degree of diplomatic wrangling preceded the despatch of the British fleet, as the Admiralty had requested of the Spanish that their ships should be placed under the command of the British C-in-C. The request was refused.

WITH THE OUTBREAK of hostilities, the Admiralty entrusted the Mediterranean command to Vice Admiral Samuel, Lord Hood. Like Nelson, he was son of a country parson but had a brother, Alexander, two years his junior, who had made a similarly successful career in the Royal Navy. In 1793 both were rated Vice Admirals of the Red, Alexander becoming Lord Bridport in the following year, having served with distinction under Howe at the action known as the 'Glorious First of June'. (Confusingly, two other brothers Hood, also Samuel and Alexander, were serving at this time as post captains. Although first cousins of the above, they were over thirty years younger.)

Lacking family connections, the elder brothers did not immediately enjoy the patronage that, at that time, was so important a part of the successful officer's career start. Samuel, like Alexander, began as a captain's servant, a somewhat hand-to-mouth existence. Only through the captain that had 'taken them on' did they become acquainted with influential people, who included Pitt and Grenville, the foreign secretary.

Samuel Hood was posted at the unremarkable age of 32 but, given command of the *Vestal* 32, proved his personal qualities by taking the similarly sized French *Bellone*, having fought her to a standstill. He was also fortunate in the Admiralty's deciding to purchase his prize, a fine frigate which, taken into the navy, gave sixteen further years of service as the *Repulse*.

Already 56 years of age when he received his flag in 1780, Samuel Hood then survived two contentious episodes which appear to indicate that the Admiralty, in essentially unforgiving times, could take a very fair view when errors were either unavoidable or made for good reason.

The first occasion was the repeat encounter with de Grasse's French squadron in the Chesapeake in September 1781. Rear Admiral (of the Red) Thomas Graves was senior officer and commanded the British line, as was customary, from the centre. Rear Admiral (of the Blue and, therefore, junior) Samuel Hood commanded the rear division from the *Barfleur* 98, captained by the younger Alexander. Due to a poor approach, the British line engaged the enemy at an angle, rather than parallel as tactics prescribed. Only the van division under Rear Admiral (of the Blue) Francis Drake ever became fully engaged, the remainder being beyond gun range.

Superficially for the British, it was no more than a tactical reverse (although one 74 had to be scuttled on account of damage received) but for de Grasse it was a significant success. Graves had been prevented from assisting the army of Cornwallis, besieged in nearby Yorktown, and the latter's resulting surrender had dire consequences for the British cause in North America.

Following the action, Hood was highly critical of his C-in-C, disputing that signals had been displayed. In truth, it was yet another example of how rigid adherence to the line-of-battle resulted in inconclusive actions. Graves escaped censure, going on to gain distinction (and a peerage) for his handling of Howe's van division at the 'Glorious First of June'. Hood's criticism of his superior was also overlooked, probably because it indicted the system, which stifled initiative, rather than the man. Shortly afterward, indeed, Hood was temporarily advanced to Rear Admiral of the Red.

In January 1782, just four months after the debacle off Cape Henry, Hood found himself relieving Kempenfelt in the West Indies. Now with Francis Drake as his second-in-command Hood proved his worth by brilliantly outmanoeuvring de Grasse at the minor encounter off St Kitts.

During the following month, command of the station had been assumed by the very senior figure of Admiral (of the White) Sir George Rodney, who was returning from sick leave. Hood reverted to the Blue as Rodney's second-in-command. His flag was still worn in the *Barfleur* second rate, although his cousin now had a different command. Rear Admiral Francis Drake remained as junior flag officer.

On 12 April 1782 Rodney sailed with a powerful fleet of thirty-seven ships of the line and nineteen smaller. Again, the quarry was de Grasse, who was moving a large collection of transports prior to a planned French assault on Jamaica.

Contact was made near the Saintes, a clutch of small islands south of Guadeloupe. The battle was interesting in that Rodney broke the enemy's line by taking the British centre division through it. Astern of him, Hood followed his admiral's action in taking the rear division through. The end result was to break the enemy into three groups, none of which was in coherent fighting order.

Hood's personal triumph was to have the enemy flagship, the great 110-gun *Ville de Paris*, strike her colours to his *Barfleur*, de Grasse becoming his prisoner. Four other French ships were taken, but it was now sunset. Inexplicably, Rodney ordered his fleet to lie-to for the night, allowing his defeated enemy to withdraw.

Hood, fully expecting a signal for 'general chase', was furious at being kept leashed. Although later allowed to lead a flying squadron, with which he apprehended two more of the enemy, Hood did not shrink from criticism of Rodney. The latter's extravagant praise of his subordinate contrasts ill with Hood's stinging rejoinders regarding the squandering of the chance of virtually annihilating the fleeing French. Even Rodney's initiative in breaking the enemy line was ascribed to advice received from his flag captain.

Hood again escaped censure for his intemperate criticism ('No more fit for his station than he himself was to be Archbishop of Canterbury') because the Admiralty Board knew that he was correct. Although he then further tempted fate by his poor assessment of Rodney's relief, Admiral (of the Blue) Hugh Pigot ('Very unequal [to his] very important duty [as he had] scarce seen salt water since the year '63'), Hood was created an Irish baron by the king for his 'great and eminent services'. As his abilities and aggression were never in doubt, the Admiralty Board was unable to convey any displeasure and thus, effectively, to disagree with the sovereign's assessment.

The decade of peace that followed in 1783 with the Peace of Versailles slowed Hood's advancement, but he made Vice Admiral of the Blue in 1787 and of the Red in 1793. At this point, and with the opportunities offered by a new war, he was appointed commander-in-chief, Mediterranean.

Although the preceding years of peace had seen Samuel Hood pass his peak, he was thought by Nelson to have the spirit and energy 'of a man of forty'. Generally well-liked in the service, he possessed qualities that were well suited to pursuing a task through to its conclusion. His sharp criticisms, although they never showed himself in poor light, was invariably directed at those who warranted it, often superiors. Advancing years had also somewhat tempered an earlier impulsiveness.

BRITISH NAVAL PRESENCE in the Mediterranean in February 1793 was minimal. The station ship, the 50-gun *Romney*, wore the flag of Rear Admiral Samuel Goodall. There were also a frigate and four smaller vessels whose only serious duty had been the protection of trade against opportunist pirates, active off what was still called the Barbary Coast.

The French at Toulon had at the outbreak of hostilities seventeen ships of the line ready for sea and a further fourteen refitting, under repair or still in build. Given time, they could thus muster a force comprising potentially two 120s, four 80s and twenty-five 74s, supported by twenty-seven frigates and corvettes.

Fortunately for the allies, the spirit of the Revolution had greatly reduced both the efficiency of the dockyard and the effectiveness of the fleet. By dint of receiving reinforcement from Brest, sufficient ships had been assembled to make an attempt at invading Sardinia but, as we have seen, the results were disastrous. The British Admiralty knew well, however, that it could not depend upon this comedy of errors continuing for any length of time and sought to put together a credible Mediterranean fleet with which to oppose it. Its assembly, however, depended upon greater priorities elsewhere, available manpower and the capacity of home dockyards to deal with the sudden surge of work involved in bringing forward other ships from reserve.

Although Barham had done much to improve the efficiency of the yards, the level of payment for their civilian workers remained considerably less than that for those in commercial yards. This resulted in flagrant misappropriation of stores as 'perks', despite every effort to contain the practice. Punishments included fines of up to £200, public whipping or transportation for up to fourteen years. The tariff was savage but the dockyards were an integral part of the lives of the townsfolk and a strong vein of sympathy was apparent in the local magistracy. Those punished could often find themselves local heroes.

There was also the question of unrest, both spontaneous and organized, in the workforce. This was forty years before the action of the Tolpuddle

Martyrs, but skilled men who knew their value in a war emergency were prepared to use group pressure to improve their lot. 'Artificers', it was noted, 'manifested ... dispositions to take advantages of the times ... to combine together for the purpose of extorting ... an increase in wages or ... of opposing some order or regulation.'

It became law that those who exhorted the workforce to successful strike action would be guilty of treason. Those 'affording them support by voluntary contributions' would face charges of sedition. These were the reactions of government facing the threat not only of armies but of Revolutionary ideas. On the whole, however, the grievances of the dockyard workers were, like those on the lower decks of the navy itself, reasonable. It is interesting to note, none the less, that when mutinies began shortly afterward trouble centred on the service rather than in the yards that supported it, although there would be a level of unrest officially described as 'riots' at both Plymouth and Sheerness.

Despite problems, ships were commissioned steadily from reserve and, with an eye to the increasing urgency attending developments in the Mediterranean, Hood, the commander-in-chief designate, was instructed by the Admiralty to send out his growing fleet to reinforce Goodall in several batches. Each would be headed by one of his divisional commanders, the final group by Hood himself who, upon his arrival, would formally assume overall command.

Hood received his first Admiralty letter on 24 March 1793, directing him to order Rear Admiral (of the Blue) John Gell to proceed into the Atlantic, covering a convoy of East Indiamen, thence to cruise off the Azores in the general protection of trade until 25 April when, in his flagship, the *St George* 98, he would arrive at Gibraltar with one 74 and two frigates to complete with water and provisions, then to await Hood's or Goodall's instructions.

If little sense of urgency is apparent in these orders, neither is there in the next, dated 5 April. By these, Vice Admiral (of the Blue) Phillips Cosby would sail on the 10th with his flag in the *Windsor Castle* 98, in company with the *Princess Royal* 98 (which would become Goodall's flagship upon her arrival) and three 74s. They were to proceed southward, covering any commercial shipping in that sector, and to cruise from there in the general support of trade until arriving at Gibraltar on 15 May.

Here, Cosby would take Goodall and Gell temporarily under his command.

Also to come under Cosby's jurisdiction at Gibraltar were four smaller vessels engaged in convoy escort. Even with these attached, the concentration would still not have grown sufficiently to counter the French Toulon squadron, which probably explains the apparent lack of urgency.

A third squadron was ordered away on 8 May under Vice Admiral (of the White) William Hotham. His flag was in the first rate *Britannia*, and she was accompanied by three 74s, one 64 (Captain Nelson in the *Agamemnon*) and a brace of frigates. Hotham's first duty was to meet an inbound convoy to the west of Ushant and then, having shepherded it into the Channel, to await Hood's instructions.

An interesting detail is Hood's very slight seniority to Hotham. At the beginning of that year, 1793, both were Vice Admirals of the Blue, the junior division. In this rank, Hood enjoyed three years' seniority. In the February, both were promoted, Hood directly to the Red, the senior flag, but Hotham to the intermediate White. (In February 1799 with both in their mid seventies, Hotham would finally catch up when both were made Admirals of the White.)

Hood himself was ordered to Portsmouth on 4 May to break his flag in the *Victory* 100. Here, shortly after Hotham's departure, he received his orders. He was to sail at 'the first opportunity of wind and weather' with such store ships and trade that required protection, to link with Hotham in the chops of the Channel and proceed to Gibraltar. There, he was to take the combined groups under his command, obtain the latest intelligence and, unequivocally, to 'use [his] best endeavours to seek the French Fleet and to bring it to action'. Should the latter, as expected, remain in Toulon it was to be watched, particularly with an eye to the protection of trade, not only British but also that of the coalition partners.

The admiral was advised that ambassadors and representatives of each of the allies were in negotiation to decide the most effective means of acting against the common enemy, and that it was incumbent upon him 'in pursuance of His Majesty's said pleasure' to cooperate fully with the commanders of the partners' fleets and armies. In the event that he was still in any doubt, the letter repeated that 'the leading object of your Instructions is to give Battle to the Fleet of France and to secure … free and uninterrupted navigation of the Mediterranean'.

Two days later, on 20 May, Hood was ordered to get under weigh as soon as he could muster seven ships of the line that were ready in all respects. In accordance with instructions, the *Victory* sailed from Spithead on the 23rd in company with five 74s, two 64s, two frigates and three smaller. One hospital ship, a store ship, two fireships and a clutch of East Indiamen completed the assembly which, two days later, met up with Hotham.

Aboard the *St George*, Gell's flagship laying in Gibraltar, the log for 20 June recorded laconically: 'At 10 arrived V. Adm. Hood in the *Victory* and V. Adm. Hotham in the *Britannia* and part of their fleet'. A near month had elapsed, accounted for by the necessity of Hood's meeting and escort of a valuable 76-ship Mediterranean convoy. This had been badly delayed and Hood notes it having been met on 7 June.

In all, Hood now had assembled at Gibraltar two first rates of 100 guns, three second rates of 98, twelve 74s and two 64s. There were seventeen frigates and smaller. These numbers varied continually, however, as ships joined or sailed or were despatched on convoy duty.

An urgent requirement for Lord Hood was to establish a diplomatic rapport with his allies and, through this, to formulate an appropriate plan of action. There existed British diplomatic representation in Turin (Piedmont), Florence (Tuscany) and Genoa (Genoese Republic). Despatches from Turin were increasingly critical of British delay as French forces tightened their grip on those parts of the state that they had seized, establishing themselves so that eventual recovery would be the more difficult. Those from Genoa continually emphasized the assistance being rendered to the French through an unbroken flow of supplies. Pressures on the new C-in-C had begun to accumulate but, in truth, the Admiralty could not move any more rapidly than diplomacy, and the treaties made by the British foreign secretary, Lord Grenville, were still being formalized – that with Sardinia on 25 April; with Spain on 25 May; with Naples on 12 July; with Prussia on 14 July; and, finally, with Austria on 30 August.

Problems in relations with the Spanish were already becoming evident. Just days after the conclusion of the alliance Lord St Helens, the British ambassador in Madrid, was complaining that 'they are infinitely more untractable [sic] and difficult to deal with as friends than as enemies'. He mentioned the hostility of the Spanish minister of marine, only one of many who were convinced that British policy would be to ensure that the Spanish and French fleets would be pitted against each other, weakening both so as to allow the Royal Navy to emerge with uncontested superiority. As the minister had the ear of his chief minister, St Helens counselled extreme caution on the part of British officers in their dealings with their Spanish counterparts.

Hood, in any case, was not one to value Spanish support particularly highly and his blunt response led St Helens to advise Grenville in London that the admiral was of the opinion that the two fleets should not work 'in absolute conjunction'. In any joint enterprise it was proposed that one squadron should undertake the active role, while the other should contain the remaining enemy force.

As instructed, Hood completed rapidly with water and victuals at Gibraltar and sailed again on 28 June, escorting a Mediterranean convoy eastward until it could be safely detached under the escort of a pair of frigates. Progress was frustratingly slow and the fleet was still short of the Balearics when, on 8 July, it fell in with the Spanish Cartagena squadron, which reported itself stricken with pestilence and returning to port. Its otherwise available strength, however, was given as twenty-six ships of the line and ten frigates.

For their current state of health the Spanish gave as their reason the fact that they had been sixty days at sea. Nelson in the *Agamemnon* noted: 'From the circumstances of having been longer than that time at sea do we attribute our getting healthy … Long may they remain in their present state.' Later, he wrote: 'All we get here is honour and salt beef. My poor fellows have not had a morsel of fresh meat or vegetables for near nineteen weeks.'

On 16 July, following a 'most tedious' passage, the *Victory* and her squadron raised Cape Sicié, south-west of Toulon. Behind the scenes, diplomatic work had already begun inasmuch as Hood had sent ahead Captain John Inglefield in the fast-sailing *Aigle* frigate to the port of Genoa with a letter for John Trevor, the British envoy in Turin.

Trevor had an important role in events, expecting to receive the Earl of Mulgrave, colonel of the 31st Regiment but acting as representative of Henry Dundas, Viscount Melville. While not yet officially filling the new post of secretary of state for war, Melville was very much the articulator of policy. His instructions to Mulgrave were that, having arrived at Turin, he was to persuade the Austrians to increase their military contribution from the current 8,000 men to, if possible, 20,000 in order to recover the Piedmontese territories of Savoy and Nice, currently occupied by French Revolutionary armies.

Diplomatic efforts (ultimately unsuccessful) were in train to attract Switzerland into the coalition, her troops being highly valued. From this source, and from Germany, it was hoped to raise a further 15,000 or more. Mulgrave's task was to coordinate these efforts with those of the British representatives in Italy and with Hood.

Should this accumulation in strength be realized, Melville's objective was 'to capture Marseilles, Toulon and Corsica', with later designs on Brest. This vague plan appeared to depend upon first defeating French military forces in the north, thus enforcing a partial withdrawal from the south. As the small British army was already fully committed in Flanders, in the West Indies and in the anti-insurrection role at home, Melville's grand design would depend upon close and successful coordination between the coalition partners. Judged against developments, it would appear that the secretary of state's aspirations were based on good intelligence and were not unattainable.

Melville's interest in Corsica was based on its boasting good anchorages within 150 miles of Toulon, ideal bases for coalition operations against the south coast of France. Formerly Genoese territory, Corsica had been ceded to France as recently as 1769. Its very independently minded people had little affinity with the French but were well disposed toward the British. The aged and unofficial Corsican leader, General Paoli, once exiled in Britain, had been judiciously reinstated by the French Convention but, sickened by events on the mainland, he had distanced the island from them. Corsica was another pocket of royalist sympathies, hardened by the unacceptable behaviour of commissioners sent there by the Convention.

In April 1793 the Toulon republicans demanded that Paoli came to the mainland to explain his attitude. Wisely, he declined to comply, instead summoning leading figures from all the island's communities. They gave him full backing and Corsica effectively revolted against French rule, confining its representatives to the towns. It was readily apparent to the British that, if the Royal Navy could prevent any French intervention, Corsica would come over to the coalition by dint of its own effort.

From Turin, John Trevor had reported back to Hood in gloomy terms. During the month's delay in the anticipated arrival of the British fleet, the French had established up to 18,000 troops in Nice and had dug well in. At the moment, the coalition could oppose them with some 20,000 Piedmontese and 7,000 Austrians. Because further Italian reinforcement was being withheld due to petty internal jealousies, additional Austrian assistance had been sought.

Trevor reported further that one Captain Masseria, personal representative of General Paoli (and paid a retainer by the British) had arrived at Leghorn to confer but had been sent packing by the Tuscan government, itself both nervous of the French and anxious to maintain the highly profitable grain trade.

Trevor also had useful intelligence on French fleet dispositions. With Hood delayed, the Toulon squadron had been urged to strike quickly against the Spanish fleet and to destroy it in detail. This fleeting opportunity had, however, passed unexploited owing to the poor material condition of some French vessels, together with the general state of indiscipline and indifferent leadership. Three frigates, none the less, were at Leghorn and two more at Genoa, all designated escorts for grain convoys. A Levant squadron comprised five frigates, backed by four more at Smyrna and one detached at Salonika. More immediately relevant to Hood were two unspecified French warships off Corsica while, at Tunis, the Bey of which the French were cultivating, lay a 74, four frigates and three smaller ships.

The first hostile brush with the French occurred when Captain Inglefield, having received his despatch, began to warp the *Aigle* from the mole at Genoa where she had been moored stern-on, 'Mediterranean fashion'. The port was, of course, neutral territory and, laying close aboard the British vessel were the French frigate *Modeste* and the corvette *Badine*. As the *Aigle* got under weigh, so both the French ships did likewise, obstructing her. It was deliberate provocation, probably spurred by the knowledge that the *Aigle* had been captured from the French a decade earlier. A strong diplomatic representation followed Hood's expressed displeasure at the incident. It was met with an anodyne response from the Genoese authorities; but the *Modeste* would discover, just three months later, that the Royal Navy had its own way of responding to calculated insult.

PROBABLY NOT UNCONNECTED with the fact that his father was comptroller of the navy, Thomas Byam Martin, on being promoted to the rank of commander, was given his choice of ship in the *Tisiphone*. Built as a fireship, she had been converted to a 20-gun ship-sloop and was reputed to be a fast sailer.

Having received Trevor's despatch from Turin, Hood, while still at Gibraltar, had placed Martin under the orders of Captain George Lumsdaine for a special mission. The latter, in the *Mermaid* frigate, was to accompany the *Isis* 32, laden with gifts for the Bey of Tripoli. He also carried important despatches for the British consul at Tunis. These were to be passed to Martin, when near that port, for personal delivery.

Duly entering the Bay of Tunis in a gale of wind, Martin was confronted by the sight of the French *Duquesne* 74 and a frigate squadron at anchor. He saw his primary duty as reporting the enemy presence to his superior officer. Duly overhauled and brought back, Lumsdaine assessed the situation and sent away the *Mermaid* to report directly to Hood while he joined Martin in the *Tisiphone* to accompany the *Isis* to Tripoli as ordered.

Having thus discharged their duties, as they had thought, Lumsdaine and Martin were more than surprised on their return to discover that their admiral had 'expressed his dissatisfaction with much warmth' and, upon being summoned aboard the flagship, were informed of Hood's intention of court-martialling both for disobeying orders.

Hood, of course, had been playing something of a wily game. Apprised of the French squadron at Tunis he had sent the *Tisiphone* there in the hope that the senior French officer would 'in the rashness of [his] republican feelings' take the ship. Such an action would give Hood the necessary pretext for sweeping the enemy out of every neutral port. Lumsdaine was duly tried but was exonerated, the majority of the board feeling that he had used reasonable discretion. Because he was obeying the orders of his senior officer, Martin never faced a court.

The affair did neither officer much harm in that Byam Martin died an admiral of the fleet and Lumsdaine a vice admiral. It did, however, say much for the character of Hood and illustrates the touch of ruthlessness necessary in an effective commander-in-chief in time of war.

Perhaps, also, the admiral felt a little guilty at his readiness to put the *Tisiphone* and her crew in such danger. In the following October, the enemy frigate *Modeste*, which had caused such offence at Genoa, was cut out there, taken and commissioned into Hood's fleet. Martin was promoted post captain to take her command.

WITH THE CIVIL WAR intensifying, and major cities and regions openly hostile to the legislature in Paris, a coordinated effort on the part of the coalition might well have reversed the course of the Revolution. But its forces were divided, by both geography and inclination. The Spaniards, entering France by the Pyrenees, were far distant from the Sardinians attacking across the Alps in Savoy. These failed to assist the royalist strong-hold of Lyon, besieged by the troops of the Convention from mid July. During that month Austrian, British and Dutch forces advanced into French territory, capturing the fortress of Valenciennes. Simultaneously, the Prussians probed into the Vosges. What had begun promisingly, however, collapsed when the British and Austrians decided to operate separately, followed by a similar split between the Austrians and the Prussians.

French military forces, which should have been greatly divided and everywhere under pressure, were thus able to contain the threats from both within and without. Internal dissent was now countered increasingly through the policy of terror, as decreed by the now smaller Committee of Public Safety. Although courts were never quite as indiscriminately ruthless as often portrayed, often discharging as many as they condemned, this was offset by the sheer number sent for trial.

Terror was now the means by which those put in a position of respon-sibility discharged that responsibility. The threat of summary punishment permeated from the War Cabinet to the humblest of levies. Terror became the cement that maintained the fabric of the Revolution at the time when it looked most vulnerable. It is generally held to be the means by which the Revolution survived.

Acting with fierce energy, the committee organized the famous *levée en masse*. All France was to be mobilized. Unmarried men would fight, with improvised weapons if necessary. Married men would manufacture weapons and generally support those who fought by manning the rear echelons. Women would tend the injured and sew uniforms and tents, assisted by their children. This was total mobilization, war across national boundaries even as forecast by the comte de Guibert.

In areas where the spirit of Revolution commanded only borderline support, the posting of conscription notices fomented more seats of mass opposition. None, however, prospered, snuffed out by the universal threat of summary punishment (even battalion-sized units were issued with mobile guillotines). In return for this enforced absence from its farms, the peasantry was promised that the last seigneurial rights would be abolished.

Military units were all accompanied by *représentants en mission*, the dreaded commissars who would have officers shot in front of their men for incompetence or non-enforcement of discipline. In extreme cases they insisted that, in the name of equality, the duties of commander be rotated in turn throughout the unit.

Although life afloat to an extent insulated ship's crews from the immediate effects of these draconian decrees, the steady drip of half-baked fraternalistic dogma eroded their will and weakened the sense of total unity that defines efficient companies. The response of authority was not to inspire the lower deck with that trust in direction that saw gun crews fight to the last round but to threaten the officers with death should they fail to do so. The same fate awaited the commander of any ship of the line that was surrendered, unless that ship was sinking under him. Any that allowed a line of battle to be broken would suffer likewise. No smaller ship could be surrendered to an enemy of less than twice its strength while, in combat, no quarter was to be given.

AS HE QUIETLY FULMINATED at the easterlies that slowed his passage from Gibraltar, Hood could have had little inkling of what lay ahead. His Admiralty orders promised a standard routine of blockade, patrol and convoy. The major task of bringing the enemy to action depended very much on whether that enemy was minded to leave the security of his well-defended Toulon base. Information was scanty for, as late as 1 August, the First Lord, Chatham, mentioned in a letter to Hood: ' I am very anxious to hear what the real situation is of the French force at Toulon, of which we have very little and very imperfect intelligence.'

Although the admiral was almost certainly aware of the extent of the civil war wracking France, and that much of the Midi embraced policies more moderate than those being imposed upon it by a far-off Paris, he took the robust view that he was at war with France and that all French were to be assumed hostile. His first imperative was to foster the required easy working relationships with Britain's coalition partners, whatever his private opinions of their fighting qualities.

Events ashore had, in fact, progressed somewhat. Wisely, the Convention had extended feelers to investigate the possibility of a negotiated settlement with the intractable south. If a little magnanimity could defuse the situation, suitable retribution could wait awhile.

Both the far south and the Rhône valley, however, remained implacably opposed to the new order and were capable of committing like excesses to demonstrate the fact. On 27 July, therefore, as Hood offshore reassembled his fleet, scattered and damaged by a fierce three-day gale, the Revolutionary General Jean-François Carteaux occupied Avignon, which effectively put a wedge between the federalist hotspots of Lyon and Marseilles/Toulon.

Carteaux's army had, in fact, been drawn from the so-called Army of the Alps, whose coalition opponents remained more interested in mutual disagreement than in pushing westward to exploit the opportunity of aiding the Girondist moderates while they were still a force. For Lyon, therefore, once it had been invested, it was only a matter of time. Its capture, some ten weeks later, was accompanied by savagery designed deliberately to cow remaining opposition elsewhere. The termination of the siege also freed republican military strength, which was immediately directed at the dissidents in the south.

The British appreciated that too little grain could be grown in the dry south to support its population. As communications with the north were still comparatively primitive, the region depended upon its imports from Italy and North Africa, and these were now effectively cut off by blockade.

As in Corsica, the region had been greatly antagonized by the activities of the two *représentants en mission* sent by Paris, but remained more committed to a France of moderate change than it was to defection. ('Although the Convention has denounced them as traitors,' Nelson wrote, 'yet even these people will not declare for anything but Liberty and Equality.')

The moderate civic leaders of Toulon, incensed by the proscription of the Girondists in Paris and at the unjustified execution of the faction's leading members, expelled the Jacobin *représentants* on 13 July. As it was all too plain, however, that the Convention retained its grip on the better part of the nation, there could be no thought of recant: the Revolutionaries showed no mercy. The Toulonnais prepared to defend themselves.

A majority of the town's citizens had appeared, understandably, not to favour armed opposition, but had been galvanized by the activities of Carteaux's army nearby and by the knowledge that a second column was advancing along the coast from the area around the Italian border. Fearful of retribution, they fell in behind their leaders, who declared loyalty to the now-imprisoned dauphin, the young Louis XVII. Then, almost certainly with grave misgivings, they decided to seek assistance from the enemy coalition, whose presence was very apparent in the offing.

In the naval base, personnel were polarized between the Revolutionary cant of the crew from the recently arrived Atlantic fleet ships and the natural moderation of those aboard the existing Mediterranean squadron. Their senior officer was Contre Amiral (Rear Admiral) Comte Trogoff de Kerlessy, who was anxious to play down his aristocratic background. For obvious reasons he thus avoided risk of confrontation and, consequently, exerted little authority. His second-in-command, Contre Admiral Saint-Julien, was of Revolutionary sympathies, as were the crew of his flagship. As already noted, however, such crews were more concerned with rights than with obligations. For the moment, there was no chance that Hood would be able to realize the key requirement in his Admiralty orders, that of bringing the enemy fleet to action.

PART THREE *Toulon*

chapter five

Occupation and Expectation, to September 1793

EVENTS IN TOULON had been stimulated by Jacobin excess. Popular clubs had sprung up throughout the *département* but, where they were ostensibly to assist in the organization of the region's defence against any incursions from the east, they had, in reality, been more concerned with assuming power by a coordinated effort. To this end, representatives were in close touch, meeting almost daily in defiance of opposition from more moderate elements who, a silent majority, appeared powerless in the face of the vigour and determination of the left-wing activists.

Prominent opponents of the movement began to experience unpleasant deaths, succumbing in ones and twos at the hands of orchestrated mobs or of groups of men who had the entrée even to the city gaol. The latter persons were never apprehended, but their identities were known and remembered. Aimed mainly at members of the middle class, their activities pre-dated the September massacres in Paris. This was deliberate policy, for it had been declared that, while the aristocracy of the nobles and the clergy had been overthrown by the Revolution, the *bourgeoisie* ('the strongest aristocracy of all') still flourished.

The autumn of 1792 was Toulon's nadir, the time of the thug. Moderates were cowed into deserting the committees and institutions through which the town functioned. All authority was now through, or controlled by, the Jacobins. Maintenance of law was precarious and partisan. Employment depended in large measure on accepting the situation with as much grace as possible, although it had to be borne in mind that, to a large section of the town's poorer community, and to those eager to take advantage, the new order was to be embraced wholeheartedly, for they believed themselves to be on the threshold of great things. It would be a difficult birth and pain had to be accepted.

Even the architects of events in Toulon began to feel that things might have gone too far, however, and they took the precaution of sending representatives to Paris to present their case and to pre-empt awkward questions. They need not have worried, for the emissaries discovered a capital in bloody turmoil, with a National Assembly little interested in the problems of a distant, provincial city.

To the east of Toulon, General Anselme's campaign into Italy was going well, reducing the state of hyper-excitement and permitting the Var departmental elections to be held in September 1792 in something like normality. Turnout was low, however, and the Jacobin candidates had little difficulty in gaining power.

By October the Revolutionary army had taken Villefranche and Toulon was busy with the preparations for Truguet's abortive expedition to Sardinia. It was the patriotic duty of radicals to cooperate fully in such an enterprise and, once again, there was a sense of purpose as means were found to keep the arsenal busy. Further elections, for district and urban representation, were thus conducted toward the end of the year in a calmer atmosphere, which tended to obscure the fact that, again with low turnouts, the popular representatives had firmly grasped power, and by a fully democratic process.

Toulon's town council now largely comprised men of no previous experience and of no great education. It firmly approved the news, early in 1793, that the king had been executed and set about restoring a sense of order and a return to the rule of law. Paint was applied over the cracks of Jacobin excess by renaming the club the Republican Society and its resolve was underlined with the imposition of the first death penalties on those who continued to act with violence. 'Without the exercise of virtue', it was stated, 'your revolution will be in vain.' This was a new departure for the more extreme fringe elements, which thrived in the general state of unrest and which had no reason to welcome normality.

With the general return of order, the populace was relieved of much of the threat of lawlessness, the primary concern of every household. In the absence of this major preoccupation, however, townsfolk naturally concentrated upon the next most pressing issues: employment, the cost of a loaf and the falling value of money. Popular opprobrium had been directed at the old order, blamed for responsibility through mismanagement, graft or unspecified counter-revolutionary activities. Now that the Jacobins were firmly and obviously in power, and being equally powerless to effect instant improvement, they began to be blamed instead.

The coming of war transformed matters inasmuch as considerable numbers of workers, both skilled and unskilled, were drafted into the arsenal. As many had been recruited from around the country they were unaffected by problems peculiar to Toulon and acted as a counter to radicalism. Also resident in the arsenal were two *représentants en mission*, sent by the National Convention to enforce efficient working practices. These enjoyed every cooperation from the Jacobin administration, which began to dismiss recalcitrant employees, a previously unthinkable measure. Dockyard workers and naval personnel were also obliged to leave the militia in order to prevent the resulting continual absenteeism. Thus, the National Guard, previously an instrument of Jacobin policy, saw its party ties weakened and uncertainty grow in its ranks as to the direction in which affairs were heading.

Even as it had underlain the widespread grievances that had launched the Revolution four years before, the price of bread remained a major issue. At a local level this was due in part to naval blockade interrupting grain supplies from Ligurian ports. General unrest also stemmed from the unpopularity of the *assignats* which, imposed upon workers as a portion of their wages, were steadily depreciating in value. Traders were increasingly reluctant to accept them as payment, many charging a premium to do so and thus adding a further twist to the spiral of hardship.

General disaffection was staved off during the first half of 1793 by the local authorities, supported by the *représentants*, approving pay increases of the order of 150 per cent, with the further concession of issues of bread. Concessions were, however, of limited use for, sensing their growing bargaining power with the extra demands of war, workers' committees demanded an end to the issue of paper money and a freeze on the price of staples. Powerless to refuse them, the authorities acceded to their demands, but the lot of the average worker remained measurably worse than it had been under the monarchy and, for this, he blamed the controlling Jacobins.

The currency of the local administration was considerably undermined by a succession of events which began in March 1793 with the hang-dog return of the miserably unsuccessful expedition against Sardinia. A month later, the authority of the replacement commander-in-chief, Trogoff, was challenged when the crews of two recently returned frigates refused to put to sea again. Their failed demand for shore leave, as a right, hardened into a total lack of cooperation with their officers.

Now, by their own actions, inextricably bound into the workings of the navy, the civil authorities took both crews ashore for interrogation. What emerged was a story centred upon the senior captain, François-Gabriel de Basterot of the *Melpomène*, who at only 30 had been fast-tracked for promotion due to the general shortage of officers. On the recent voyage his behaviour had, indeed, been somewhat unusual but was less that of someone conspiring against the new republic than of one suffering from nervous exhaustion. None the less, he was charged with involvement with *émigré* counter-revolutionaries and, as scapegoat, faced with court martial. Despite every evidence that the crews had been exercising their new democratic right to question and debate every order given to them, making Basterot's authority unenforceable, the hapless captain was declared guilty as charged and summarily guillotined before the assembled fleet.

The incident was significant in that the Revolutionary authorities, having gained power, were faced with the consequences of the mutinous behaviour that their new order encouraged. It also demonstrated that officers were still likely to be blamed for the indiscriminate actions of their crews, a situation here exacerbated by Basterot's minor aristocratic background and his having joined the service under the old regime.

There existed also the paradox of mutinous crew members addressing the local Republican Society, where they were enthusiastically received, although this same club represented the forces that were striving to get the fleet on to a war footing despite the depredations of its own policies.

Commanding officers, for their own good as much as for the benefit of the service, had to accept the realities of the situation but, having done so, were entitled to expect to be able to maintain discipline in the name of a central authority. As this authority was now the republic rather than the crown, it was to the republic that they looked for support, only to discover that they, as a corps, were still generally regarded by those in power as potential enemies of the people. They also found that local committees exercised greater authority than did the Convention in Paris.

It was events in Paris, however, that were to shape those in Toulon, fatally damaging the Jacobins' credibility. Late in the May the Girondins were expelled from the Convention, their leaders confined under house arrest. Delegates thus proscribed returned to their provincial constituencies, burning with desire to prevent a single group perverting a popular revolution to its own ends. The result in several major cities was the so-called 'federalist' backlash. Minor employees and merchants, the middle-class *bourgeoisie* hated by the activists of the Left, greatly concerned at the course of events, felt sufficiently emboldened to unite and to challenge the Left's authority. Perhaps to their surprise, they discovered that they were supported by many of their employees, the humbler working folk that the militants assumed were the mainspring of their cause. Brave parades by a few thousand such as in Lyon or Marseille did not, however, yet constitute a major threat to those in control in the capital. Further, had the federalists enjoyed more eventual success, complications would have emerged through their being polarized between royalist and non-royalist sympathies.

Matters came to a head on 13 July when Jean-Paul Marat, who typified the clique that espoused bloody death as reward for the slightest suspicion of anti-revolutionary foot-dragging, was himself assassinated. Interestingly, his killer, the young Charlotte Corday, had been motivated not by the death of the king but by the conviction that Marat was a leading cause of the intensifying civil war that was plunging France into outright anarchy.

Marat lay virtually in state, to be viewed for days by much of the populace as preparations were advanced for an elaborate martyr's funeral. This led to a series of events, climaxed on 10 August by an ambitious travelling spectacle which enacted, in allegorical form, the progress of the Revolution to date. This, the so-called Fête de l'Unité et L'Indivisibilité, celebrated the first anniversary of the overthrow of the monarchy, and was designed as a consecration of the new constitution. Such cavorting may well have cheered Parisians, reinforcing their belief in themselves as the dynamo of the Revolution, but they could not disguise the fact that all was not well elsewhere.

Although, at the end of July, General Carteaux's republican army had taken the city of Avignon, driving a wedge between dissidents on the Mediterranean coast and those in the area of Lyon, foreign armies were advancing across France's borders while, in the Vendée and the Midi, opposition thrived. It was, however, never likely that the federalist forces in Lyon, Marseille and Toulon would unite in a common front, while Carteaux's active presence was a potent reminder that, once demolished in detail, those forces would face the worst of state retribution.

In the Convention, the considerable figure of Georges Danton strove to promote the policy of appeasement, to meet with the forces of counter-revolution in order to agree a mutually acceptable compromise. He failed in the white heat of extremist anger that followed the death of Marat, and was dropped from the Committee of Public Safety. In place of pragmatism there thus emerged the policy of organized terror.

Accused of allowing the price of bread to exceed by far that obtaining during the monarchy, the Convention responded by denouncing hoarding. All those holding stocks of a wide range of essentials were ordered, on pain of death, to declare them. All had to be available on the open market. Regulating officials would be appointed in every region to oversee harvests and to ensure that no wily peasant withheld any part of his crop. *Représentants en mission* would everywhere ensure that the republic imposed its will, if not by edict then by force and, if necessary, terror.

Facing threats to the Revolution, both within their borders and without, the authorities initiated an attempted total mobilization, a *levée en masse* for the creation of a huge conscript army. In the south, however, events had moved ahead of the Convention's ability to control them.

In both Marseille and Toulon the Jacobins were on the defensive, their clubs in close touch in an attempt to keep the situation under control. To the general population, however, had come the realization that it was being cowed by a comparatively small number of resolute extremists who were imposing the policies of a far-off Convention whose actions transcended the mores of decent folk.

As the silent majority began, haltingly but with increasing confidence, to find its voice, the oppressed from the whole region began to migrate to the coast. They were not necessarily pro-royalist nor anti-revolutionary so much as merely fearful for themselves and their dependants and bewildered by events and contemptuous of pip-squeak representatives of a new order who strutted among them exercising extreme and terrible authority. The local *sections,* the committees of citizens' representatives, had been proscribed by the new authorities, who determined that any discussion would be tightly controlled. Now, however, some nine months later, there came strengthening calls for the committees' reinstatement.

Deciding on a show of strength, the Jacobins staged a procession through Toulon's narrow streets. But the armed mob, with its bellowed, orchestrated demands of death for all who supported reversion to the old system, had lost much of its power to shock and to intimidate. Onlookers were now repelled by the spectacle.

Previously a feared instrument of Jacobin authority, the National Guard was now a force of very uncertain individuals. The power that had spawned them appeared to be on the wane and there was a fair chance that they would be called to account for past actions carried out in its name. In a somewhat craven *volte face* they backed a new and strongly worded demand that the eight *section* assemblies be permitted to reconvene and that the process of government of citizens' affairs return to something like the earlier normality that now appeared so desirable.

With a surprising docility, the Jacobins stepped down, transferring power back to the district assemblies, which quickly moved to appoint an overall General Committee. This comprised thirty-two members, drawn from every *section*. They came from the *bourgeois* aristocracy, so detested by the Convention and who, mostly, had earlier experience, together with arsenal and military representatives, artisans and clergy. In Marseille the handover process was rather more difficult, but ended similarly.

In a symbolic move to extirpate Jacobin philosophies, that club's meeting place was destroyed although, in the spirit of reconciliation, some of its members were invited to participate in the new neighbourhood assemblies. Probably because of the lack of any practicable alternative, some officials were left in post. These included magistrates, some committee leaders and National Guard commanders.

By coincidence, power in Toulon reverted on 14 July 1793, the fourth anniversary of the storming of the Bastille. Measures were put in hand to appoint new district and departmental assemblies but, due to the course of events, the process was never satisfactorily completed.

An inevitable and unpleasant result of the changeover was the establishment of a Popular Tribunal to try those accused of excesses committed under the Jacobin regime. So many were taken into custody that most had to be imprisoned afloat. The vessel so employed was the *Thémistocle*, a new, Lorient-crewed 74 that was awaiting repair following an on-board fire and explosion caused by explosive shells during the abortive Sardinian expedition.

It is a sad indictment of the new and 'moderate' administration that its courts handed down far more sentences of capital punishment than had those of the 'extremist' Jacobins. Of the four local *représentants en mission*, two managed to escape but both their colleagues died as a direct result of their incarceration. All had been die-hard Montagnards and, as it was this faction that was held primarily responsible for the creation of a state of civil war, the local population was absolved from being bound by any of the Convention's decrees.

Sectional representatives of Toulon and Marseille declared a unity of purpose with pledges of mutual support. The effectiveness of this was soon confirmed when the Toulon authorities refused a demand from the Ministry of Marine in Paris to initiate a naval blockade of Marseille as a prelude to operations aimed at rectifying the situation there. Mutinous behaviour on the part of the crews might, in any case, have made compliance with the order impossible. Two French frigates, obliged to shelter in Marseille from superior Spanish forces, were detained there when their crews refused to sail again.

It is essential to understand that the new regime in both cities was not totally anti-revolutionary, representing as it did the views of ordinary folk exasperated with extremism and insecurity. Decrees passed by the Convention prior to the purge of June 1793 were still observed. A joint open statement from the Toulon *sections* made it quite clear that they adhered to the principles of the republican constitution on condition that it promoted respect for the individual, his property and law and order. It deplored the unpredictability and violence inseparable from Jacobin control, and the fact that the Convention, the national government, was riven with factional anarchy.

For Rear Admiral Trogoff and other senior naval staff the situation was delicate. Having adapted their outlook and procedures to accommodate the dangerous eccentricities of the new Revolutionary order, exerted primarily at a local level, they were now obliged to work with a municipal structure that had reverted to something like orthodoxy. At the same time, however, they were acutely aware that the situation was precarious, amounting as yet to no more than a successful local revolt. Authority, on paper, had been recentralized to its proper location, the Ministry of Marine, yet the functions of this organization remained hobbled by the Convention and it existed, as matters stood, in an enemy camp.

Trogoff had already been experiencing trouble with central government. In June a Spanish squadron had appeared off the Ligurian coast. The implications for the vital coastal trade were obvious and its presence served as a reminder that it was only a matter of time until a British force came to join it. From both regional and local level, Trogoff was urged to give battle to the Spanish before the British reinforced them. However, despite a haranguing from the *représentants* about their duties to the state, his seamen showed little enthusiasm and the admiral was convinced that any sortie was doomed to failure. He contacted the minister of marine, requesting that he order the Toulon squadron to remain in port. He also emphasized that he was only acting C-in-C Toulon in Truguet's absence and that, as he had not been otherwise advised, he expected Truguet to return to his command after he had explained to the minister his reasons for failure in Sardinia.

Although the naval officer corps had played no obvious part in the overthrow of local Jacobin authority, its broad approval was evidenced by the fact that several senior ranks and an *ordonnateur* served from the outset on the new sectional assemblies. This left Trogoff in an impossible situation, complaining to Paris that, despite his continuing loyalty to the state, he received no support or direction in return, still being expected to supply two Revolutionary armies in addition to his own squadron.

Wisely, Trogoff distanced himself somewhat from the new sectional authorities. All too aware of Carteaux's army near Avignon and the advance of a large detachment from the Army of Italy, marching westward toward Toulon, he feared for the future of this modest counter-revolution and, reasonably, for himself. He resisted a demand from the new authorities to immobilize part of his squadron, maintaining that as the fleet was an instrument of the state, only the state, through the minister of marine, could so instruct him. The reason for this strange requirement had been the intention to use the crews to contribute to a military force to counter the expected reaction from central government, whose record to date suggested that conciliation was unlikely.

Trogoff's every action suggests that he was endeavouring to remain true to his profession and to retain independent authority for his fleet. Effectively a hostage to events at Toulon, however, he could now anticipate only a vengeful hostility from a state administration which he still firmly supported and to which he looked for direction and sustenance.

The revolt in the Midi, which had broken out in evident anticipation of the collapse of extreme Montagnard dominance of the Convention, soon began to look isolated in the face of energetic reaction from Paris. Cold realization set in following the defeat near Aix-en-Provence of an ad hoc military force raised jointly by Toulon and Marseille. This had set out with the quixotic intention of linking with other federal forces around Lyon before marching on Paris itself. More volunteer band than army, its resolve disintegrated before General Carteaux's battle-hardened veterans.

As already related, Admiral Lord Hood made his landfall near Toulon on 16 July 1793, just two days after the moderates had regained control of the city's administration. Official British knowledge of the state of affairs in the region was, as yet, rather sketchy and the admiral had a comparatively open brief. As instructed, he detached a frigate to Genoa with despatches for the British envoy in Turin. The general attitude of the Genoese Republic appearing to place the continuing lucrative grain trade with the south of France above its loyalties as a coalition ally, Hood also deployed several minor warships, both to interdict the trade and to watch the port of Genoa. The former duty was excellent training for junior commanders as the trade was conducted for the greater part in fast-sailing local craft known as *tartanes*, which were single-masted and lateen-rigged.

The home secretary, Henry Dundas, 1st Viscount Melville, was a more powerful influence on affairs than was the foreign minister, Lord Grenville. It appeared to be his policies that lay behind the efforts of the still-forming coalition to assemble a multi-national army with the specific primary objective of recovering Nice and Savoy, that had been seized by the French Revolutionary Army of Italy. Somewhat enigmatically, Dundas charged Hood, should circumstances permit, with the capture of Toulon, Marseille and Corsica. Even to contemplate the seizure and retention of major cities in metropolitan France suggests that Dundas had excellent local sources of information.

With a blockade declared, British ships exercised their right to stop, search and, when appropriate, to seize every ship or cargo destined for the two French ports. This factor forced up the price of bread yet further. The hard-pressed general public were now fearful at the almost unique situation where, on the one hand, their vengeful countrymen were gathering their strength to obliterate what they interpreted, incorrectly, as a regional anti-revolutionary movement while, on the other, the nation's traditional enemy was, with allies, assembling a considerable naval force, capable of putting ashore a military expeditionary force of significant size.

The young Captain Horatio Nelson, commanding the *Agamemnon*, expressed the hope that an efficient blockade would force the French Toulon squadron to emerge to seek battle in order to relieve the stranglehold. He could not have begun to perceive the true situation ashore. Prospects for action, however, initially appeared to be good. Even as Hood arrived, two French frigates ran foul of the *Illustrious* 74 in darkness. The British ship, commanded by Thomas Lenox Frederick, was not a lucky vessel, and, indeed, would be lost by grounding soon afterward. Her crew still relatively inexperienced, she failed to apprehend the enemy. The French 18-gun ship-sloop *Éclair* was not so fortunate when, cut off, she was brought to action and taken by the frigate *Leda*. Promptly put 'under new management' the Frenchman was commissioned into Hood's fleet, beginning thirteen years of useful employment with the Royal Navy.

Sensing an opportunity to gain intelligence on the enemy's strength and disposition, the wily Hood decided to offer the French an exchange of prisoners, the *Éclair*'s crew against similar number of British. He selected Lieutenant Edward Cooke of his own flagship to act as representative. The choice was excellent, for Cooke proved to be resourceful. Hood instructed him to elicit any information that would assist him in deciding his plan of campaign.

In what was described simply as 'a French prize', Cooke entered the outer roads of Toulon under a conspicuous white flag of parley. This proved to be an unfortunate introduction, as the plain white *pavillon* was also the banner of the deposed Bourbons and, whatever the allegiances of the French at Toulon, most embraced some form of republicanism.

The British were curtly instructed to hoist the new French ensign (a white field, defaced in the upper hoist by the new tricolour). This, of course, was not immediately practicable, but then neither were British prisoners immediately available. Admiral Hood must have found it intriguing that, instead of informing the British to make themselves scarce on pain of being fired upon, the French agreed to a second meeting three days later. Cooke was able to return with a few ex-captives but, more importantly, with information that sixteen French ships of the line were ready for sea, with five more undergoing repair. From a neutral skipper he was also able to learn of the generally anxious state of the populace, a significant number of which had been arrested for voicing the need of some sort of contact with the British.

Admiral Hood awaited developments patiently for, in blockade, patience was a prerequisite, and the Toulon squadron was, at the moment, his main concern. These were the days when command of the sea permitted a blockading squadron to approach to a point just beyond the enemy's cannon shot, enabling an admiral to see at first hand a port's geography.

The Admiralty, as opposed to Dundas, had included nothing in its instructions about occupying either Marseille or Toulon and Hood, therefore, was not allocated the means, although a substantial number of regular army units were being carried in lieu of marines. Respecting the home secretary's comments, however, Hood must have looked thoroughly at the enemy's coast, comparing the chart with what lay before him.

From seaward, even close in, the town and arsenal would, at this stage of their development, have been hardly visible. They lay in the eastern arm of a small bay known as the Petite Rade. This lay secure in the embrace of two fortified promontories, whose batteries easily covered the narrow navigable fairway. Wrapped around this already difficult entrance was, however, the peninsula of Saint-Mandrier, the bulk of which was of formidable aspect. Steep and rocky, rising to over 400 feet, it supported heavy batteries that commanded the outer bay, the Grande Rade. These fortified headlands made any plan for direct assault from seaward suicidal.

The spacious outer bay is sheltered from the south and south-west, becoming unsafe only during the easterly *levanters*. Its defensive advantages were first utilized by Henri IV in the sixteenth century. Under 100 miles from the Italian border, it was also necessary that it be defensible from the landward direction and, for this purpose, the major feature was the arc of mountains at its back. At their highest no more than 2,000 feet, they are none the less, rugged and often precipitous. The continuity of the ridge is broken by gorges and passes of varying degrees of defensibility. The town and dockyard were thus backed by a mass of rock that presented a physical barrier between the port and its hinterland.

Both town and arsenal were enclosed by a defensible city wall, lapped by a moat which was partially tidal. The port comprised two basins, the Old and New Harbours. Adjacent to the former, the *Darse vieille*, was the maze of narrow streets that comprised the seven *sections* of the old town, stronghold of the *ouvriers* who laboured in the dockyard, together with many seamen and their families. At the eastern end of the harbour wall was the *quartier* of Saint-Jean, bastion of the Jacobin Club. At the other was Saint-Pierre, the power base of the opposing moderates. Appropriately halfway between them was the town hall, for the control of which the two factions had conducted a bitter power struggle. Adjacent to the New Harbour, now the *Darse Vauban*, was the more recent and spacious suburb of Saint-Roch, popular with the town's notables and senior officials of both the service and the arsenal.

An early reminder of the hazards of blockade hit the British in the shape of an unseasonal *mistral*. Roaring out of the Rhône valley on 17 July, and under a clear blue sky, the northerly quickly rose to gale force, raising the dangerous sea familiar to all who navigate the Golfe du Lion. Close inshore, where the effects are pronounced, Hood's ships fought and failed to hold their position.

Several ships suffered damage, the most serious being that by the *Robust* 74. This ship, in service for years, sprang and seriously weakened her mainmast. The injury must have been particularly galling to her commanding officer, the Hon. George Keith Elphinstone. Already a post captain for nearly twenty years, Elphinstone saw in this new war a last chance to further his flagging career. In this he would succeed brilliantly, but the beginning was hardly auspicious.

In addition, the *Berwick* 74, already considered a dull sailer, suffered sundry damage to her spars, including a broken bowsprit. She was obliged to proceed to Gibraltar for repair but three others with broken topmasts were able to extemporize and to keep going. One frigate, the *Meleager* 32, was also damaged sufficiently to make her run for Mahon in Minorca.

From Hood's point of view, the most serious result of the blow had been that his fleet was now widely scattered. Should the French squadron be looking to break out from its base, now was its opportunity. Rear Admiral Trogoff, however, had other problems on hand.

While the British offshore reconcentrated and repaired their various damages, the situation in Toulon became more complex. As the days following the Jacobin overthrow became weeks and July became August, little appeared to be happening beyond the circulation of wild rumours regarding the remorseless approach of the republican armies. Radical elements in the town once again began to find their voice. Intense anxiety for the future, matched with food shortages due to the biting of the blockade, rendered townsfolk and dockyard workers vulnerable to street-corner rhetoric.

Within the sectional committees, left-wingers again asserted themselves with confidence while, within the arsenal, the still extant Central Workers' Committee began to foment unrest. Having let matters drift too far, the authorities pulled them up with a round turn, arresting two of the ring-leaders and summarily condemning them to death. Their imprisonment, pending execution, sparked disturbances that even included a rescue attempt.

Suitably alarmed, the moderates adopted a firmer stance, dissolving all workers' committees in favour of a small security committee which was empowered to act quickly on its own authority. The causes of the growing counter-rebellion had not, however, been removed and pressure on the new authorities began to build ominously. Growing numbers of refugees fuelled the problem, each a mouth to feed and each adding to the tales of atrocities committed by the Revolutionaries, depressing even further the morale of the citizenry of Toulon

Powerful divisions also existed in the French Toulon squadron. Admiral Trogoff had become too closely associated with the new municipal regime, with the result that the crews of those ships that had recently arrived from Atlantic ports as reinforcement had largely ceased to recognize his authority. In contrast to the comparatively non-aligned attitude of locally raised crews, those from Brest and Rochefort were still powerfully motivated with Revolutionary ideals and looked to Trogoff's second-in-command, Saint-Julien, for leadership.

Rather oddly, from the point of view of command structure, Saint-Julien de Chambon (described by Hood as being 'of a turbulent mind') was also ranked rear admiral and enjoyed identical seniority. He remained true, however, to central Revolutionary principles and, when the disillusioned Trogoff took to spending long periods ashore, he became firstly the adopted leader of the Atlantic crews, then the *de facto* commander-in-chief.

THE FIRST MOVE in what became known as *la grande trahison* occurred on 23 August 1793. Two days earlier, General Carteaux's forces had taken Aix-en-Provence, and the *sections* of Marseille, having already seen their armed delegation routed at Avignon, realized that their city was virtually defenceless. The hoped-for collapse of central Montagnard authority had not come about and their only fate was now likely to be a highly unpleasant one at the hands of Carteaux's men who, in victory, had already shown a penchant for undisciplined and unrestrained savagery.

On 17 August Marseille had sent representatives to Toulon in order to discuss what joint action the two cities could take in their own defence. For the moment, however, Toulon shrank from the unthinkable as Marseille proposed contacting the British fleet, ostensibly to sanction humanitarian cargoes of grain for populations already showing signs of deprivation.

This proposal was, in itself, an indictment of the French fleet's inability even to contemplate fighting a convoy through the blockade. If, ran the reasoning, the state was unable to fend for its citizens, then those citizens were entitled to fend for themselves by any means to hand. Desperation is a powerful impetus for action.

Urgent deliberations on 22 August involved representatives from regional and departmental level, and it was decided that a delegation, speaking for the Bouches du Rhône *département* as a whole, would approach Admiral Hood. They would be granted plenipotentiary powers to negotiate not just guaranteed grain shipments but also, and unbelievably, the British protection of the city of Marseille from a French army.

The *Victory*'s log for 23 August records simply 'French Carteel [sic] from Marseilles joined fleet'. At that time, Hood's main strength was laying inside the Iles d'Hyères, in the secure anchorage under the lee of the Giens peninsula, while his light forces watched a seemingly quiet Toulon, 20 miles to the west.

The admiral appeared not to have been unduly surprised at the French overture, the ports and fleet apparently having become his focus of interest. On 10 August he had adopted the official line in a letter to the British representative at Genoa. 'There is nothing ... I have more at heart than to render substantial service to the King of Sardinia', he wrote. But he then went on to underline the importance of keeping his fleet concentrated rather than dispersed on operations where individual vessels would be exposed to damage: 'You must be aware ... that every place where a ship can put her Head has guns mounted, and a few accidental shot may ... make her totally unserviceable.' He looked forward to the fleets of Spain, Naples and England each having its own 'distinct line of acting', suggesting that he still did not anticipate close cooperation or joint action.

The Earl of Mulgrave also reported his arrival on 10 August. He had been sent on ahead to Turin to act as negotiator and now, reiterating his intention to follow his instructions to assess for Hood the situation with respect to Sardinian forces, made also the point that 'Toulon, Marseilles and Corsica are the main objects pointed at in my instructions'. From the outset, Dundas's primary objective had been the reduction of the French navy's ability to operate freely and thus to dictate the course of events in the Mediterranean.

Boarding the *Victory*, the Marseille commissioners were accorded all usual courtesies but were surprised at the absence of their colleagues from Toulon. This, however, had been due to Saint-Julien who, emboldened by the support of so many of his crews, had fired on the craft, preventing its departure.

The French delegation explained that Marseille had openly declared for the monarchist cause, owing allegiance to Louis XVII, the infant dauphin and imprisoned son of the executed Louis XVI. At a meeting aboard the French frigate *Nemesis* on 22 August the city's administration and *sections* had set up a General Security Committee, whose chosen representative was Jean-Abeille, now leading the delegation.

At this point it becomes apparent that Hood's duties, as defined by the Admiralty, differed from those intended by Dundas, who appeared to be acting on privy information. Whatever his personal desires, Admiral Hood could do little for Marseille: it was very large and he had not the means. He had, on the day previously, been obliged to despatch an urgent note to the Spanish admiral, Langara, requesting him to be ready to relieve the Royal Navy off Toulon as a shortage of water would necessitate its withdrawal within the week. Langara responded unhelpfully that he could not leave his current location, for he was operating in support of a Spanish army which had crossed the border into the French province of Roussillon.

Again Hood appealed for at least a squadron and as many troops as possible. He also approached the courts of Naples and Piedmont for the urgent despatch of five or six thousand troops. An unexpectedly favourable situation had arisen, he stated and he had not the means of taking advantage of it.

Slow communication proved to be the downfall of Marseille. Langara did not respond until the 26th, confirming that he was acting now with the greatest urgency to withdraw two or three thousand of the best troops (they were later to be castigated by the British as 'dregs') to be embarked in four of his vessels. By this time, unfortunately, a column of Carteaux's army had already broken Marseille's inadequate defences and, on 25 August, the city had surrendered to its awful subsequent fate.

It is difficult to believe anything other than that Admiral Hood saw in Toulon a more valuable and more easily defensible objective, which lent itself to a fulfilment of the Admiralty's instructions as well as being more within his limited capacity. The great prize, the French Mediterranean fleet, was obviously vulnerable to destruction by diehards once any agreement became known, and so it was essential to move quickly. There was considerable risk for, from the west, Carteaux was still advancing. From the east, in addition to forces already detached, the Army of Italy was also falling back in the direction of Toulon, a result of resolute action by the Piedmontese, anxious to reclaim Nice.

Hood's first necessary action was to draft a proclamation to the Toulonnais, based on the proposals made by the Marseille commissioners on the 23 August. 'His Britannic Majesty's Fleet ... having no other view than that of restoring Peace to a great Nation upon just, liberal and honourable terms' would guarantee protection to the city on various conditions which included, *inter alia*, the hoisting of the old national flag (the 'Standard of Royalty') over public buildings as a firm indication of an intention to return to a monarchical rule, the disarming of the warships and the handing-over of fortifications to British or allied garrisons. All were to be held in trust by the British so that, upon the eventual peace, 'the Port, with all its ships in the Harbour and Forts of Toulon shall be returned to France with the stores of every kind'.

The wording of the proclamation was to prove unfortunate in several respects. In effectively stipulating a return to the monarchy it clearly went against the wishes of the majority who, while terrified of the route that the Revolution was following, still supported the replacement of the *ancien régime*.

Hood had also caught the mood of the commissioners who, although they could offer little material support, clearly saw themselves as partners, even allies, in an adventure founded upon desperation. Their conditions accounted for Hood's insistence that all was held in trust. By definition, nothing had been surrendered and nothing was, therefore, disposable according to the wishes of a victor.

As a matter of urgency, Hood again called upon Lieutenant Cooke, this time to enter Toulon, seek out the missing commissioners and to present the British terms. In view of the fact that he, of necessity, would be the sole British authority present, he was given some powers of negotiation. His resulting experiences were worthy of a Patrick O'Brian novel.

Leaving the *Victory* at Hyères in a captured local craft at about 2 p.m. on the 24th, he delayed his final approach to Toulon until after dusk. It was overcast and windy and, on his previous trip, Cooke had noted that the French guard was slack after nightfall. Sailing in unobtrusively against the backdrop of a high shore, Cooke anchored and, together with a midshipman, transferred to an open boat which they boldly rowed through the ranks of enemy ships. Making to enter the inner camber they were, however, obstructed by the barrier of a taut chain and, while attempting to negotiate this, they were challenged by a patrol boat. By sheer good fortune, its commander was known to Cooke from his earlier visit. Without demur, he facilitated their passage.

A representative of the town's General Committee was also summoned through his good offices. There was, however, no welcome and, having delivered the despatch, Cooke and his colleague were not permitted to land, settling down uncomfortably in their small craft to await a response.

With day breaking, the pair were allowed finally to come ashore in the quarantine area. Hours passed before, during the afternoon, there arrived a message which decided Cooke to send the boat back and to wait on alone. As another dusk came down, a horse and guide at last arrived and, following a two-hour trek over devious paths, he reached the location where the committee awaited him.

Having argued long and hard, the committee's members were still in a state of some emotion but let it be known that they agreed that the British would take over the town and installations, and that all officers, both civil and military, would cooperate fully with the commander-in-chief's requirements. Significantly, the committee insisted that the conditions of the new National Constitution of 1791 be observed. The fleet would be brought into the inner harbour. British commitments in return would include 'doing their utmost' to protect Toulon, to supply such grain as would be required and to make payments in coin (i.e. rather than partly in the detested *assignats*).

Soon after midnight the meeting broke up and Cooke left with two committee members as guides. They reached a pre-selected point on the coast at daybreak but, in boarding a local craft, they attracted a crowd which, suspecting something, was not well disposed toward them. Cooke himself managed to convey the importance of the mission and they were allowed to proceed, eventually arriving back safely at Hyères.

Cooke's accompanying midshipman, meanwhile, had himself been apprehended. He was taken before Saint-Julien, who studied his papers and questioned him closely. Although the admiral threatened to hang Cooke should he be captured, the young officer was allowed to go.

Admiral Hood's preliminary business with the French was, however, not yet finished and, once again, Cooke's services were called upon. He embarked in the little 9-pounder frigate *Tartar*, whose commanding officer, Thomas Fremantle, sent him ashore in a pulling boat at an agreed point near Cap Brun, to the east of the town. By ill luck a French frigate had elected to anchor nearby. She sent away a longboat in pursuit of Cooke's craft and this, armed with a swivel gun, gave the British a hot time until they were able to scramble ashore.

The coast here was rocky, backed by a low but precipitous cliff. Having slipped, the enemy frigate had got into extreme range and, presenting her broadside, loosed it at the British party, still scrambling up the cliff. Bothered 'very much' by the dirt and rock fragments raised by the hostile barrage, Cooke safely made the top and gratefully gained the cover of a patch of woodland. Here he was able to gain his breath as the enemy shot created a 'confounded noise' as it tore through the foliage above and around.

Having walked to Toulon, a good 6 miles distant, Cooke was greeted warmly but was told that Saint-Julien had detained some of the town's deputies and had declared his intention of returning the place to the republican cause. With the strength at his disposal, this was no light threat and Cooke knew that he needed to communicate the fact to Hood with some urgency.

In company with a senior officer of royalist sympathy, Captain le Baron d'Imbert of the French 74-gun *Apollon*, Cooke made a further circuitous trip to the coast, where they took passage in a Genoese fishing boat. Hood held an immediate council, deciding to put a force ashore without further ado. Cooke was directed to go ashore with the preliminary party of sailors on the following morning. At his signal, the remainder of the force would join him and they would first occupy the key strongpoint of Fort la Malgue.*

The Toulon in which the British were about to land was still dangerously factionalized. As Cooke shivered in his open boat during the night of 24/25 August, the General Committee had argued with heat and some bitterness over the wording of Hood's intended proclamation.

As could be expected, the committee embraced all shades of opinion, from outright monarchist support to vehement objection to any involvement with the British. It is unlikely that any decision would have been reached except for the knowledge that, in revolutionary eyes, Toulon was already tainted and all would certainly be punished by the state's advancing forces.

Opposition in the town centred upon left-wing activists in the arsenal, whose enthusiasm was buttressed by expressions of support from the crews of Saint-Julien's Atlantic ships. Most local crews remained of moderate opinion. For the greater part, their homes and families were in the immediate area and there were real fears for their future.

Baron d'Imbert, the delegate who was to accompany Cooke on his return, was the most vocal of the pro-royalists. A minor aristocrat who had

* In justice to the resourceful Edward Cooke, it is appropriate to record that he would go on to render distinguished service in the months of ground fighting that lay ahead. He was rewarded suitably in the following year by promotion to post captain, being given command of the big 40-gun ex-French frigate *Sibylle*, in which he accompanied the *Victory* on her return to England. Still in her command, Cooke encountered the French frigate *Forte* in the Bay of Bengal in February 1799. Fought to a standstill, the enemy was taken and purchased into British service as a 44. Cooke, however, did not live to enjoy the rewards of his endeavours, dying some three months after the action from wounds received. Edward Cooke's personal courage would have been exceptional had not such conduct been commonplace in the Royal Navy of that era.

survived the purge of the officer corps, he had been appointed temporary commanding officer of the *Apollon* when her previous captain, Prévost-Lacroix, had been executed with Captain Basterot for 'counter-revolutionary activities'. The evidence is that d'Imbert was something of an opportunist, greatly overstating the level of royalist sympathy in locally crewed ships. Although he enjoyed no great degree of trust, he was at that time the best channel available to the committee, which used him to help draft an address for delivery to the ships' crews.

This was an urgent consideration for, once the committee had determined that the best course was to seek British assistance, the hostility of Saint-Julien was a potential major obstacle. Should he carry the fleet with him and have it oppose Hood's entry, disaster threatened, for the British would simply haul off, resume their blockade and allow events ashore to take their course.*

D'Imbert's address implied (falsely) that the nation in general had abandoned the Convention in Paris and had declared for King Louis XVII. The British were there to assist in a smooth return to some sort of constitutional monarchy and the French fleet would need to be temporarily immobilized to encourage the process to run with no hitch.

In those days, when news travelled slowly and was complicated by rumour and counter-rumour, an official address such as this, read by a senior officer, carried the weight of authenticity. On this occasion it was delivered simultaneously to each crew, being met with varying degrees of incredulity but, for the moment, acceptance.

The proposal to disarm the ships immediately, however, aroused vocal resentment on some. Heated debate followed, with officers realizing that the whole premise was unsubstantiated and, therefore, not as yet to be trusted. This conclusion fuelled outright anger, the officers leading their men in open defiance, voicing accusations of betrayal and treason.

Those representatives of the *sections* that had come to assist in delivering the address had, in some cases, to be hurried ashore for their own safety. In no time, the bulk of the fleet was in open revolt at the proposal and

---

* It might be mentioned with advantage that 'blockade' did not mean the bottling-up of the enemy fleet in his port, for the intention was that he be given every encouragement to come out and fight. As Nelson was to write, at a later date, to the Admiralty: 'I beg to inform your Lordships that the port of Toulon has never been blockaded by me; quite the reverse. Every opportunity has been offered the enemy to put to sea, for it is here that we hope to realise the … expectations of our country.'

Saint-Julien was popularly acclaimed commander-in-chief in place of the rarely seen Trogoff. Saint-Julien immediately set about organizing the fleet for resistance. In securing the inner harbour he narrowly missed capturing Lieutenant Cooke who, as already related, had to make good his escape overland. All ships were put on an action alert and boat patrols were mounted to intercept any more attempted contact by the British.

Following a 'tumultuous' (but, to one account, 'indecisive') council of all commanding officers aboard his flagship, Saint-Julien ordered the navy to assume control of the fortifications commanding the harbour entrance. These were currently garrisoned by a jittery National Guard which knew not where its loyalties lay. Without resistance, naval detachments thus took over the batteries in the forts of L'Aiguillette and Balaguier on the western promontory and, beyond, those on the Saint-Mandrier peninsula. Although the western side of the harbour approaches were now under Saint-Julien's control, the eastern side, including the major strongpoint of La Malgue, remained occupied by forces loyal to the town's *sections*.

Then, when no attack immediately materialized, indecisiveness reasserted itself. The local crews found that their concern for families and homes out-weighed other considerations and they accepted an argument that the town was behaving treasonably not against France but against a tyrannical republic. Following debate, the fierceness of which is well recorded, a compromise was reached whereby Toulon's proposed cooperation with the British would go ahead, while all naval personnel who remained loyal to the Revolution would be 'repatriated' to home ports on the Atlantic coast. One French account mentions that Hood had authorized Cooke to offer that these crews be paid, in coin, all their considerable arrears of pay, which amounted to a substantial inducement to 'go quietly'.

All evidence points to days of French agonizing, with either side alter-nately threatening and cajoling. Where, however, the arguments of the 'hard Left' in the fleet and the *sections* were largely idealistic, those of the moderates were driven by the dreadful fear of the Revolutionary armies, a fear all too graphically expressed by the many refugees arriving from Marseille. Logically, the British had more to gain by cooperation and under-standing, the Revolutionaries only by indiscriminate barbarism. Grand treason, for all its grave implications, was thus the more attractive choice for the people of Toulon.

Left: Henry Phipps, 1st Earl of Mulgrave (1755–1831)

Above: Vice Admiral the 1st Viscount Hood (1724–1816)

Above: Henry Dundas, 1st Viscount Melville (1742–1811)

Right: Captain the Hon. G. K. Elphinstone, 1st Viscount Keith (1746–1823)

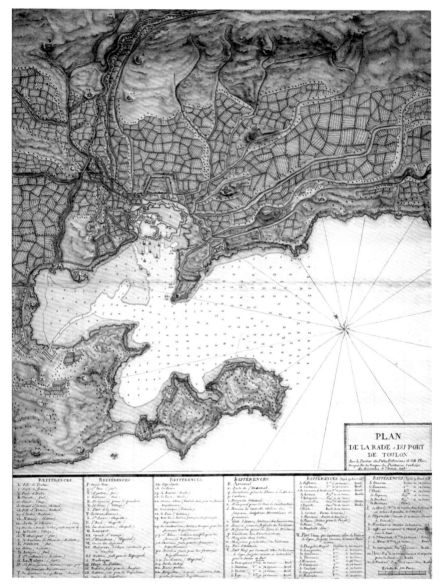

Contemporary French map showing the Coalition's
positions about Toulon. Note the dominating location
of the western promontory and the shallow nature of
the western end of the Petite Rade.

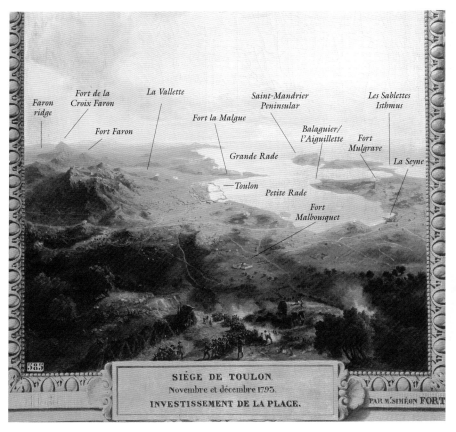

Faron ridge
Fort de la Croix Faron
La Vallette
Saint-Mandrier Peninsular
Les Sablettes Isthmus
Fort Faron
Fort la Malgue
Balaguier/ l'Aiguillette
Fort Mulgrave
La Seyne
Grande Rade
—Toulon
Petite Rade
Fort Malbousquet

585

SIÉGE DE TOULON.
Novembre et décembre 1793.
INVESTISSEMENT DE LA PLACE.

PAR M. SIMÉON FORT

Of almost photographic accuracy, this French impression may be compared directly with the map opposite. Salient points are keyed.

LE PORT VIEUX
Vu de l'atelier

Réduit de la Collection des Ports de
Par le S.ʳ Ozanne Ingénieur de la

DE TOULON
de Peinture

France dessinés pour le Roi en 1776
Marine pensionnaire de Sa Majesté.

A Paris chés le Gouaz Graveur rue S.ᵗ Hyacinte la première porte cochere à gauche par la Place S.ᵗ Michel.

Above: Toulon. Old Basin. Note, left to right, a local craft setting up a lateen rig, a single-decker approaching launch (bows first), a frigate careened and being burned off, ships 'in ordinary' and a masting hulk.

Below: British ships anchored off the Gros Tour. The Inner Road, or Petite Rade, is to the right, the Outer Road, or Grande Rade, to the left. Clearly shown are the fots of Balaguier and l'Aiguillette. Although they dominate the anchorage they, themselves, are dominated by the heights beyond.

LE PORT NEUF
Vu de dessus

DE TOULON
le vieux Môle

Réduit de la Collection des Ports de
Par le S.ᵗ Ozanne Ingénieur de la

France dessinés pour le Roi en 1776.
Marine pensionnaire de Sa Majesté.

À Paris chez le Gouaz Graveur rue S.ᵗ Hyacinte la première porte cochère à gauche par la Place S.ᵗ Michel.

Above: Toulon. New Basin. Somewhat removed from the Arsenal proper, the New Basin lacks the bustle of its neighbour. The pure white ensigns of the frigates date the picture to before the Revolution.

Below: A view of the eastern promontory showing the Gros Tour and, in the distance, the Cap Brun battery, capable of denying a large area of the Grande Rade. Many of the ships must be either Spanish or mercantile.

Above: Nicholas Pocock's 1807 painting of Nelson's five flagships. The Victory, which wore Hood's flag at Toulon, is depicted in the right foreground. From the left, the others are the Agamemnon 64 (Nelson's command at Toulon), Captain 74, Vanguard 74 and Elephant 74.

Below: Built in 1788, the *Commerce de Marseille* 118 was the largest prize to be taken by the British from Toulon. Although Sané-designed, she proved to be weakly built and was hulked after three years' further service.

Left: The young Napoleon at the siege of Toulon. This impression by Louis-Charles Bombled has the smack of authenticity although, compared with on-the-spot sketches by Granet, the battery works look very permanent.

Below: Final evacuation of the Coalition's military forces from Toulon. Relays of ships' boats are transporting troops to Allied warships anchored offshore. The fortification is probably that of Fort Saint Louis.

Above: Published four months after the evacuation from an on-the-spot original by Archibald Robertson, this aquatint depicts the blowing-up of a magazine ship. Visible in the distance is the blazing Arsenal and Sir Sidney Smith's *Swallow Tender*.

Below: The night of 18/19 December 1793. An anonymous pen-and-ink sketch. The annotations read: 1) Windsor Castle barge, 2) Victory's boat, 3) Spanish barge, 4) Swallow armed tender, 5) Hero [sic] 74, 6) Themistocle, 7) Powder frigate, 8) Frigate that had been exchang'd by the Sardinians for the Alceste, 9) Old Corvette, 10) Arsenal with 8 sail of the line etc on fire afloat as well as several parts on shore, 11) Old Arsenal, 12) Town of Toulon, 13) Part of the Heights of Pharon [sic], 14) Malbosquet [sic] throwing shells, 15) Grand Tour abandoned, 16) Fort Balaguier firing, 17) Fort Equilette [sic] firing, 18) Neapolitan fortified hill, 19) Spanish fortified hill, 20) Fort Mulgrave on les Hauteur des Grasses.

Faced with *force majeure*, his ships threatened with bombardment by the federalist forts should they show signs of resistance, Saint-Julien's new-found sense of resolute leadership deserted him. He also could not fail to be influenced by Hood's squadron, now at full strength, being reinforced by the arrival on 27 August of the Spanish fleet under Admiral Langara.

A final plea by Saint-Julien on the 27th was met with a powerful rebuff from the now grimly determined General Committee. This was about to signal to Hood to enter the Grande Rade, the outer roads, and ordered Saint-Julien to obey the British instruction to bring all warships into the inner harbour. Failure to do so would result in bombardment by red-hot shot. For a growing number of sailors this was the last straw. Fighting the British was one thing but being fired on by one's townsfolk was a very different matter. The dribble of men going ashore quickly became a flood. With admirable courage, but little conviction, Saint-Julien ordered his depleted force to stand-to for immediate action.

Then came a perfectly timed intervention from the put-upon and long underrated Admiral Trogoff. In a dramatic reappearance, he broke his flag at the masthead of the frigate aboard which he had been awaiting the moment. Finally convinced of his abandonment by the minister of marine, filled with a loathing for Jacobin extremists, he committed himself to ordering his fleet to comply. Those ships that were still sufficiently crewed got under weigh, some more reluctantly than others. Others, short-handed, remained at anchor.

Saint-Julien, in a last flourish, led his Revolutionary minded crews ashore, encouraging them to march westward to join up with the army of General Carteaux. The admiral himself did nothing of the sort. Once ashore in now hostile Toulon, he feared for his life and went to ground in a safe house, not to be seen again until he emerged to surrender to coalition forces.

AT 47 YEARS OF AGE, Captain the Hon. George Keith Elphinstone was no longer a young man. He had come to the attention of his superiors back in the American War of Independence when, in 1780, he had shown considerable aptitude for combined operations. In command of a force of troops, he had played a decisive role in the American defeat at Charleston, the colonists' greatest reverse of the war.

Now, in Toulon, having patched his storm-damaged *Robust* into something of an operational condition, he was selected by Admiral Hood for further work ashore. This was an age when it was common for a commanding officer to lead his men into combat ashore and on 28 August Elphinstone received the following order:

> As I am about to take possession of the town and forts of Toulon and mean to appoint you Governor of it [sic], I do hereby authorise you to accompany the troops into the Great Fort and to take upon you the charge and command of it, as well as of the town, and all Officers both Civil and Military are to obey you as Governor. [Signed] Hood.

All British troops, only 12,000 all told, were transferred to a selected group of ships, the *Robust*, *Egmont*, *Colossus* and *Courageux* (all 74s), the *Meleager* 32 and *Tartar* 28. At 7.30 on the morning of 28 August, the squadron stood in towards the coast near Fort Sainte-Marguerite, some 2 miles east of the 'Great Fort', i.e. Fort la Malgue (now spelled 'Lamalgue'). This, the first objective, had, as required, raised a blue flag.

The troops, under Elphinstone, would be followed by about fifteen hundred seamen. These, commanded by the ubiquitous Lieutenant Cooke, would have the main responsibility of taking over and manning the shore batteries. Cooke was ordered to assume the style of 'Lieutenant Governor'.

Most ships had to contribute to the force, their contingent being noted in their logs. The *Britannia*, for instance, recorded first transferring two companies of the 69th Regiment to the *Courageux* to be landed then, later, putting ashore a force of one lieutenant, two midshipmen and fifty seamen via the *Meleager* frigate. Forty-five men, with a similar command structure, were detached from the *Princess Royal*, and so on.

Elphinstone's own account of proceedings can hardly be bettered:

> It was near 9 before all the troops were on shore ... I began the march keeping the high ground towards Fort la Malgue and from the heights I first discovered the Spanish fleet at a great distance. About midday the British troops got into Fort la Malgue and so soon as the necessary guards were taken by them to render the place secure, the troops were assembled on the parade, and I had the honour to proclaim Louis XVII King of France in French and English to the apparent joy of all present. Soon after this a deputation came and said there were many displeased I had not proclaimed the Law and Nation, to which I replied that to whatever the Commander-

in-Chief had agreed I would bring myself to fulfil but I apprehended *that could go no further than the Constitution the late King had himself accepted of* [author's italics]. With this the late French governor of the Fort made the French acquainted and by their applause they seemed perfectly satisfied. I then proceeded to read my authority to govern and had the keys delivered to me. Soon after, deputations came from different orders of Toulon to pay their compliments, and to request that I would send troops to the City as they apprehended tumult on the part of the factions and by the seamen from St. Julien's Fleet who were landing in crowds. I ordered the 69th Regiment into Toulon and pointed all the cannon of the different Forts towards the Fleet. Four ships slipped their cables and came into the inner harbour and about 3 o'clock I received information that St. Julien had fled and that all ships had submitted.

During the evening of that first day Hood sent Elphinstone his congratulations, giving him a free hand with respect to troop dispositions with the proviso that, of the forts, 'Lamarge' was to take precedence. He added that he was sending a general proclamation which would be published by the town's *sections*. He added that General Casteaux was known to be on the march from Marseille. His force was estimated at about ten thousand and any attack by him was likely to be supplemented by another from the east, whence two separate groups from the Army of Italy were advancing under Generals la Barre and Lapoype.

The critical opening phase appeared to have been negotiated without any major hitch, and Cooke was able to note that by the following morning, there were about five thousand men ashore, the British having been joined by about fourteen hundred Spanish troops, 'including 200 Bombardiers'. The force was in the process of being distributed around the defences and Cooke judged that the number was sufficient to defend the town 'tolerably well'. Alas, the very ease with which the allies assumed power underlines the old dictum that wars are much more simple to get into than to get out of.

The following day, the 29th, was one of furious activity and consolidation. For Elphinstone, civic duties intruded heavily upon his military responsibilities. As he related:

I repaired to the City of Toulon and was there, upon reading my authority in the presence of the Committee General of War and Safety, presented with the keys. Those of the Gates and Arsenal I delivered to the Fort Major, such as related to the Civil Government I returned after the ceremony that had taken place at la Malgue. I secured the Town Gates and with the chief of each department concerted proper measures for the general defence of the place, and fixed on the requisite number of troops for all the out-garrisons. In the evening ... Spanish Marine troops landed at Fort la Malgue and were ordered into town.

The mood in the town was sullen, with little evidence of rejoicing. Those opposed to the occupation kept their counsel and their voices low in the presence of military patrols that were themselves nervous and well prepared to employ force to maintain order. For the ordinary citizen, the immediate and predominant concerns of insufficient food and general law-lessness had been allayed, revealing the deeper worry regarding the con-sequences of the grand treason of which unavoidably he was now a part.

For the moment, Toulon was not directly threatened and, as his patrols slowly and deliberately extended themselves beyond the outskirts and into the hamlets dominated by the brooding heights beyond, Hood's natural optimism asserted itself. In writing to Sir Philip Stephens, Secretary to the Admiralty, he expressed it as his opinion that the largely irregular revolu-tionary armies, then advancing on Toulon, would make little impression on the place.

In truth, the allied landing had not been a moment too soon for, even on the day of the landing, Elphinstone had reported that 'the army of la Barre from Nice arrived at le [sic] Vallette only two miles hence. On hearing that I was in la Malgue he retreated to Brignole without halting'. That the enemy had penetrated as far as la Vallette should have been a matter of some concern, for the village was situated at the southern end of the deep valley separating the dominating high ground of the Mont Faron Ridge from the height of Le Coudon to the east. With the allies yet to occupy positions commanding these approaches, la Barre had missed an opportunity.

Early on 30 August advanced elements of Carteaux's army were reported at the village of Ollioules, 4 miles north-west of Toulon. This was an advance guard commanded by Colonel Mouret and, to reach Ollioules, also located on the Toulon side of the high ground of the hinterland, it had advanced through a deep gorge that would have been virtually impassable had it already been garrisoned.

Carteaux's brutal reputation had preceded him and, with the allied outposts clearly not yet effective the town's General Committee became understandably agitated that a sudden attack might develop. At its behest, therefore, Captain Elphinstone sent out a patrol in the direction of Ollioules. As back-up, he ordered to arms 300 British troops of the 11th and 25th Regiments, together with a similar number of Spanish. The French were also given a first test of cooperation by being required to contribute 300 National Guardsmen, six pieces of artillery and wagon transport.

The preliminary patrol returned at mid afternoon with a group of peasants, reportedly wounded by enemy dragoons, and the news that the enemy were, indeed, in Ollioules and nearby Sanary. In and around the former location were an estimated 600 enemy troops, with ten cannon and a cavalry detachment. Captain Elphinstone set off immediately with his infantry, leaving the still unready French contingent to follow. More local inhabitants were encountered, hurrying from their villages and advising that they were held very strongly.

A half-mile short of Ollioules, a party was detached under Captains Wemyss and Haddon to displace a group of the enemy which was establishing itself on a low eminence to the right. As a further precaution, Elphinstone also sent Lieutenant Knight with a squad to secure an as yet unoccupied rise to the left. Both tasks were reported as 'admirably executed'.

Elphinstone and his ADC, Ensign Forster of the 30th Regiment, then reconnoitred the village in person. The position was, as reported, a strong one, the stone houses being located on the side of a hill and fronted by a ravine. This was spanned by a stone bridge that was covered by two cannon. All visible windows were 'filled with musketry'. Just above the village was a ruined castle in which were located two more cannon. Flanking the village were vineyards, partially concealing the remainder of the enemy infantry.

The day was well advanced. It was 6.30 p.m. and the light was already diminishing, but the French from Toulon had not yet shown. Elphinstone had either to attack or retire and, in the Royal Navy, retreat was never considered an option.

He sent messages to the established flanking parties to occupy the enemy covering the bridge with continuous, steady fire while the main force used the shelter of a low stone wall to advance to within 200 yards. On the order, Captain Douglas of the 11th rushed the bridge at the head of his men. A hail of musketry tore up the dusty, summer surface over which they ran, encumbered by kit. Douglas fell, mortally hit. Others beside him were cut down; others injured. The momentum of the charge was maintained, however, and the bridge crossed.

On reaching the comparative shelter of the houses beyond, the troops fanned out to complete the job with their bayonets. Superior training proved triumphant over raw valour. The republicans broke, retreating up the hill under a sporadic, valedictory fire. In the gathering dusk, they were allowed to retire without pursuit. In fact, new to determined action, they fell back 20 miles, to rejoin their main force at the village of Le Beausset, to the north.

According to Lieutenant Cooke, who was following, at Elphinstone's order, with a further force from the garrison of Fort la Malgue to act as a rearguard in case of an allied defeat, the action lasted just fourteen minutes. Allied losses comprised eight British and three Spanish dead, with six and two respectively wounded. Interestingly, no mention was made of republican casualties but French sources speak of only one dead and three injured. Fatefully, one of the latter was Carteaux's artillery commander, Major Dommartin. His loss and eventual replacement would prove to be critical to the whole campaign.

Short of ammunition and unsure of enemy strength in the vicinity, Elphinstone was pleased enough to leave the scene and return in some triumph to Toulon with thirty prisoners and horses, two standards (one of which he presented to Admiral Hood) and drums and three cannon. The last were described by Cooke as 'two sixes and a three pounder, brass, the most beautiful guns ever beheld'.

To hearten the populace, the trophies were put in display in the open space of the town's Champ de Bataille. Also, 'for the amusement and information of the public', a captured letter was reproduced and distributed. Addressed to Mouret, this expressed Carteaux's view that he would have '*le plaisir sous deux ou trois jours au plus tard, de corriger la ville de Toulon comme celle de Lyon, et de battre à plate couture les coquins d'Anglais et d'Espagnols*' ('the pleasure in no more than two or three days of correcting [i.e. punishing] the town of Toulon like that of Lyon and of thrashing the English and Spanish devils'). Rhetoric maybe, but many who read it, with the examples of other towns before them, must have experienced a whiff of apprehension.

Although the republicans had numbered nowhere near the 700 to 800 in strength claimed by the British reports, the skirmish at Ollioules put heart into the defenders. That the allied infantry met up with the National Guard during their return march to Toulon was played down in the general jubilation. Elphinstone praised Moncrieff as heading the column 'with a degree of intrepidity worthy of imitation', while the senior Spanish officer, Don Montero, was credited 'with equal valour'.

Captain Elphinstone's presentation of an enemy standard to his admiral was acknowledged by Hood as 'a flattering testimony of your attention to me'. His letter, dated 4 September, was addressed to 'His Excellency Governor Elphinstone'. There exists, however, some confusion at this time with regard to dates and individual status. Elphinstone quickly found the dual role of governor and military leader to be over-demanding, writing 'On the 30th [August], after great fatigue of business until 3 o'clock in the afternoon, I found myself obliged to go out with the troops to Ollioules', which implied some reluctance. He went on:

> Next morning, the 31st [I] represented to your Lordship by Sir Hyde Parker [i.e. Rear Admiral Sir Hyde Parker, serving as Hood's First Captain aboard the *Victory* and who, eight years later, would be Nelson's senior officer at the battle of Copenhagen] that I found myself inadequate to deal with the complicated Government of Toulon and to manage the very important Military Government of la Malgue and its dependencies at the same time I was to lead the troops in the field and to request more assistance or some other arrangement. On the afternoon of this day I was informed on board the *Victory* of the intention to send Admiral Goodall [i.e. Rear Admiral Goodall of the *Princess Royal*] to be Governor of Toulon and Don Frederick de Gravina to command the Spanish troops.
>
> On the 1st September I had the honour to attend your Lordship to the Government House at Toulon and by your order addressed the [General] Committee, assuring them of your intention to fulfil the agreement made and protect them, but the mode of governing must remain with your Lordship. I then presented Admiral Goodall, their new Governor ...

On 29 August, however, i.e. before the Ollioules affair, Hood had already redefined Elphinstone's status in a letter of authority dictated aboard the *Victory*. This stated unequivocally:

> Whereas I have taken possession of the great Fort of Malgue [sic], and all others dependent upon it, and it being absolutely necessary they should be in the Charge of an Officer of proved zeal and ability ... I do hereby constitute and appoint you Governor of them, strictly charging and commanding all Officers Civil and Military and others to obey you as Governor.

Following their reverse at Ollioules on 30 August, Carteaux's forces were quiet for a week. With their colleagues in the east not yet evident in force, Elphinstone was able to investigate the fortifications which formed a protective line on that side of the city. These comprised La Malgue and the nearby positions of Saint-Louis and the Grosse Tour (sited on the eastern promontory enclosing the Petite Rade); Sainte-Catherine (immediately to the east of the city walls, set in a hollow and covering the road to Italy); L'Artigues (on the first high ground to the north-east of the city, now termed the Corniche du Faron); and Fort Faron itself (in a dominating position on the first spot height but, itself, commanded from the higher main ridge beyond). On 3 September he was able to report that he was 'under no apprehension for their [the forts] safety at present, nor do I think that the enemy have either sufficient force or enterprise to attempt of them without a much greater accumulation of strength'.

Although for the moment this was a reasonable assessment, it carried a hint of contempt. This was not prudent for, whatever its disciplinary failings, a French Revolutionary army was highly motivated and, fired-up for battle, capable of desperate courage. Nor did it want for strength, for a considerable proportion of the Army of Italy was now withdrawing westward in the direction of Toulon. It had suffered a reverse in Nice, but the main impetus was the National Convention's realization that the Midi insurrection was the greater danger, being a direct challenge to its authority.

Estimates varied that there were between 5,000 and 12,000 French troops arriving from this quarter alone, led, as Cooke commented disparagingly, by one who was 'a dancing master at Toulon, since converted into a General'. Pickets posted on the main ridge of Mont Faron watched the activities of large bodies of men in the extensive woodland of the deep east–west valley that separate Faron from the wild high ground farther to the north. Cooke's optimistic assessment continued, being that Carteaux, with an estimated 7,000 men, lay to the west, awaiting the arrival of the full strength of la Barre and Lapoype in the east. Time, he considered, was on the side of the allies as 'the rains are coming on fast, which will distress the enemy very much, as they laid their account to wintering in Toulon'.

The proximity of the enemy is evident in that Elphinstone recruited agents, principally poachers, to enter the enemy's camps and there barter their wares while garnering useful information. 'If these men bring good and real intelligence I shall reward them well but', he cannily added in his report to Hood, 'not so as to lavish public money.' A certain naivety is evident here for, as nobody could be certain where individual French sympathies lay, there had to be doubt regarding who was spying on whom.

Amid a welter of other concerns, Admiral Hood had still not quite been able to define the limits of the boundaries of responsibility between Goodall and Elphinstone. One senses the exasperation of the latter in a submission to Hood:

> I beg leave to observe to your Lordship that the only authority under which I now act is your Lordship's original appointment as Governor of the Forts of la Malgue, etc., and the town of Toulon, which latter is superseded by the appointment of Rear Admiral Goodall. It therefore becomes necessary to make a distinction and complete separation of that that is to fall under his charge and that which is to remain with me ...

While Elphinstone pronounced himself satisfied with the ability of the eastern chain of fortifications to resist la Barre and Lapoype, he could entertain no such confidence regarding the approaches from the west. General Carteaux had quickly identified Toulon's major weaknesses. The first was that a major fleet required both the Grande and Petite Rades to be secure anchorages. This meant that the perimeter to be defended was very much longer than that required for protecting the city alone. Allied military resources would, therefore, be spread that much more thinly, exposing weaknesses. His second observation was that the anchorages would be untenable if his forces could occupy the western of the two promontories that embraced much of the Petite Rade, upon which Toulon and its arsenal fronted and in which the Anglo-Spanish fleet would need shelter from the sometimes powerful easterly *levanter*, which could be expected until the end of October. If he could also take the Saint-Mandrier peninsula, then communication by sea, upon which allied strategy depended, would be all but impossible.

Carteaux's thrust through Ollioules, deflected by Elphinstone's force on 30 August, had been in response to reports (probably from Saint-Julien's seamen) that the allies yet held the western approaches to the city in no great strength. Unopposed, Colonel Mouret's force would have progressed to secure the village of La Seyne, on the western shore of the Petite Rade, as well as the powder magazine at Millau, also situated near the coast but about 1½ miles west of the Toulon limits.

On 7 September, General Carteaux tried again, advancing in considerable strength down the difficult Gorges d'Ollioules. These were still not defended in depth but were held at the constricted southern end where the defile is flanked by the mass of Sainte-Barbe. Here, some 400 National Guardsmen from the Marseille area, led by a retired captain from the Touraine, held the Revolutionaries for five hours, suffering in the process over seventy casualties, two-thirds of them dead or missing.

Admiral Gravina reacted quickly, despatching to the scene a mobile reserve under Brigadier Izquierdo. Their approach attracted heavy artillery fire from the republicans. This killed the horses drawing the Spanish guns, which were unable to get into action. Unsupported, the Spanish infantry, too, had to fight hard, also taking about seventy casualties. Once again, Carteaux's probing was checked but, in leaving Ollioules for the moment more strongly garrisoned, the allies significantly diminished their strength elsewhere.

The western defences of Toulon had been less well developed because any threat against the town, as earlier envisaged, would likely have originated from Italy, about 100 miles to the east. Any foreign amphibious assault from the west would have been unlikely because it would have had Marseille to its rear.

Well alive to his deficiencies in troop numbers, Hood charged Elphinstone with thoroughly surveying both the western defences and the likely threats to them. Immediately to the north of the town was a valley separating the western end of the Faron Ridge from its neighbouring height, that of Le Croupatier. Although wide, this valley is constricted by a confused series of spurs at its northern end. These spurs command the minor road which follows the course of a small river and which runs through the village of Les Moulins. A mile from the village, Fort Pomets crowned the southernmost spur. Its location was not particularly well suited to command the routes from the north, and the later Redoute Saint-André had been added to cover both Pomets and the nearby road junction. As the route was an obvious weakness in Toulon's defences, further strongpoints had been added: Saint-Antoine and its satellite, Petit Saint-Antoine; Fort Rouge; and Fort Blanc. While these were, for the most part, no more than earth and rock, they were improved and garrisoned by the allies.

On the comparatively flat ground to the west of Toulon, and little more than a mile distant, stood Fort Malbousquet. Half a mile to its rear, it was covered by a battery sited on the rise at Missiessy. Although these defences were vital to the prevention of any advance from the direction of Ollioules, they were sufficiently isolated to be vulnerable to an outflanking manoeuvre.

The western promontory, covering the Petite Rade and facing Toulon directly from about 2 miles, terminates in the twin headlands upon which were located the powerful forts of L'Aiguillette and Balaguier. These strongpoints dominated the navigable channel linking the Petite and Grande Rades, and were within range of both the town and any shipping using its facilities. It was absolutely vital that these did not fall to the enemy so, to protect their rears, work was quickly initiated on a 300-foot eminence known as the Hauteur de la Grasse, or La Caire. This quickly developed into a complex series of positions, known to the British as Fort Mulgrave but to the French as 'le petit Gibraltar'.

Work seems to have begun on removing the threat of L'Aiguillette and Balaguier for, as early as 30 August, the log of the *Windsor Castle* noted: 'At 9 the Captain with a party of men went on shore to dismount the guns on Fort Ballargue [sic] and the Captain of the *Britannia* with a party to [deal similarly with those at] Fort Lagallete [sic].'

Whereas the extremity of the western promontory was thus rendered reasonably secure, its base and the shoreline of the Petite Rade, round to the magazine at Millau, a distance of better than 2 miles, was not protected by any fixed works.

Projecting from the west into the Grande Rade, the Saint-Mandrier peninsula was a naturally strong position, its high ground dominating the low and narrow isthmus that connected it to the mainland at Les Sablettes. To cover the landward approach, the allies here constructed a battery.

Where the strategically important Fort Faron was overlooked by the eastern end of the Mont Faron Ridge, some 500 feet higher, a new strongpoint was erected, carrying the name Fort de la Croix Faron. This stood 1,850 feet above sea level, a fair average figure for the whole ridge, from which every detail of the town below was exposed.

In the midst of all this activity, Captain Nelson, whose *Agamemnon* was, for the most part, engaged in duties other than at Toulon, noted perceptively that, where the French navy could not but be severely damaged by unfolding events, he wondered how this great, combined fleet could see its task through without the assistance of many more troops. All ships' logs are studded with references to parties being sent ashore, not only for working details but for garrisoning and fighting. It is an ironic twist of history that, a short time in the future, Nelson would see fit to ignore instructions from Elphinstone (now Lord Keith and commander-in-chief in turn) and put seamen ashore to fight, earning a rebuke from Their Lordships who, correctly, pointed out the folly of thus exposing ships' crews to the risk of capture or death, thereby reducing or preventing the Royal Navy from discharging in designated tasks.

At Toulon, this rang true particularly in the case of Fort Pomets, which was well inland and poorly located, so that any enemy force moving down the pass would inevitably cut it off. The *Windsor Castle* appears to have been given the early task of this fort's garrisoning and, on 25 September, her log would record the mortal wounding there of Lieutenant Newenham.*

The question of further troops was likely to be a thorny one, for it has already been related how the prime minister, only the year before, had greatly reduced the strength of the army in order to release funds to pursue more politically popular social projects. British troops were now urgently required to reinforce garrisons in the West Indies and for duty at home, where the government had real fear that the virus of revolution might cross the Channel on the back of popular discontent. It was apparent that any military enhancement to Hood's force would need to include a high proportion of hired mercenaries or contributions from allies whose fighting qualities were, at best, suspect.

---

*An interesting, if somewhat irrelevant, side issue is the way in which ships' logs, without further comment, record normal ship routine in parallel with events ashore. For instance, the French isolation hospital, or Lazaret, was quickly put to use, the *Windsor Castle* noting on 7 September 'Punished John McEvoy, Edward Griffiths, William Smith, James Dadd and John Dixon for breaking out of the Hospital on Cape Sepet [sic].' History is silent as to the reasons why!

THE 'IMMENSE but unforeseen opportunity' offered by the occupation of Toulon by the allies was neither universally recognized nor treated as such. At a regional level, Francis Drake, the British minister at Genoa, wrote to Lord Grenville at the Foreign Office extolling the fact that 'no event of the war has so much tended to bring about a safe and honourable peace'.

A 'safe and honourable peace', however, meant different things to different people. King George III and his chief ministers, Pitt, Dundas and Grenville, were engaged in a war that posed little direct or imminent threat to British soil and, lacking the overriding imperative of home defence, they failed to develop a clear war strategy. There were obvious opportunities to injure the traditional enemy, but the means to do so were deficient. There were also chances to acquire French foreign territories, possibly through the diversion of those resources already allocated to the safeguard of Britain's own interests. At the highest level, there was a detestation of the course of the Revolution in France, a visceral urge to stamp out both it and its excesses, both as a moral duty and to excise the very real threat of its spreading.

Was, however, a reversal of the Revolution synonymous with the restoration of the French monarchy? The large-scale dissent in Brittany and the Vendée had resulted in many influential French leaders taking refuge in the British Channel Islands, which became a conduit for contact with counter-revolutionaries and the means of providing them with material support. Lower echelons of French royalty, the *émigré* princes, were also active in seeking help from their adopted homes beyond the French borders. They, of course, were able to bargain with some authority, being able to promise reward for support in the event that that support was successful in returning them to power.

Active among these was the comte d'Artois, brother of the murdered Louis XVI and now resident in Turin. He felt able to offer the islands of Ile de France (Mauritius) and Ile de Bourbon (Réunion) to the British as compensation for their 'guaranteeing the integrity of the other possessions of the French Crown'. The circle represented by d'Artois was not, however, recognized as having the necessary authority to thus negotiate, which was something of a convenience to Pitt and Grenville, who had every intention of profiting by France's disarray to extend British interests in the West Indies. There appeared to be a genuine wish among British ministers that France should not be dismembered by a triumphant coalition but, on the other hand, they were keen to see some advantage accruing from an expensive war. Pitt assured the House that his main interest lay in British national security but 'with a little mixture of indemnification'.

Despite representations to the government by such powerful voices as those of Burke, Portland, Spencer and Windham, the Cabinet refused to give direct support for 'King Louis XVII'. The French duc d'Harcourt had argued to the British foreign minister that a degree of formal British recognition of the 'King' would give massive assurance to those who were waging a counter-revolutionary war in north-west France. Their overtly pro-royalist aims, however, were not those which Britain wished to adopt.

Heartening noises were not sufficient and the French were deeply suspicious of British intentions. They assumed, as had the Spanish in connection with their fleet, that enough British support would be rendered to maintain counter-revolutionary operations without it ever being sufficient to guarantee a decisive result. Indeed, many French intellectuals were convinced that Britain was fomenting further disorder on the back of the Revolution in order to weaken France the more.

Britain's attitudes were certainly inconsistent. As late as November 1793 King George himself would make a formal declaration to the *Deputation du Comité Général des Sections de Toulon*, stating it as his desire to see France return to a state of order. In his opinion, the best course would be to re-establish the monarchy 'in the person of Louis XVII and the legitimate heirs to the crown'. Yet he went on to avoid appearing to favour any particular form of government, stipulating only that it be 'regular' and 'solidly established'.

A major dilemma persisted in deciding priorities for troop allocation. The Duke of York was already leading an expeditionary force in Flanders, pronouncing it inadequate to meet its objectives. Following a build-up of cash, supplies and provisions in the Channel Islands to further the efforts of royalist forces, the British felt sufficiently sure of their ultimate success to commit a military force. Lord Moira, appointed to command it, demanded an impossible 10,000 to 12,000 troops. About 5,000 were eventually assembled, but without full equipment. It mattered not, for negotiations with the relevant French were conducted at an impossibly leisurely pace.

Security was, to all practical purposes, non-existent and the timetable was then complicated by the new and unexpected events at Toulon. For troops to be sent to Toulon at all, the Duke of York had to be further impoverished. Eight under-strength battalions, earmarked for the reinforcement of West Indies garrisons were, to the king's displeasure, then reallocated to Lord Moira's new venture.

Although this diffusion of the nation's military assets caused the prime minister considerable concern, it could be argued that the all-important West Indies could be threatened seriously only by a considerable French military force transported by sea. At that time French armies were, for the most part, fully stretched on home soil, while about one-quarter of the French fleet lay under allied control at Toulon. It thus behove the British government to accord Toulon at least sufficient priority to keep the transport potential of the French fleet beyond the reach of the National Convention.

This begs the issue of the actual status of the Toulon squadron. Although officially at war with France and the French, Admiral Hood regarded the Toulonnais as allies, albeit of many shades of persuasion. As has been stated, he had made it clear that he held both the city and fleet in trust for a future legitimate government. To be certain that the Revolutionary government could, under no circumstances, regain control of the squadron, the obvious solution would have been to sail it to Minorca or Gibraltar with reduced crews for safekeeping. Britain and Spain, however, remained mutually distrustful to the point that neither port would have been acceptable to the other. Further, the General Committee would have experienced great civil unrest had the ships been removed, for town and fleet co-existed, indivisible.

Worse, the French were no doubt well aware that, where Hood spoke in honourable terms of 'safeguarding' and 'holding in trust', London's attitude was rather less refined. Hood regarded himself and, by extension, the British as being in alliance with the Toulonnais but his government, ever eager to disseminate good news to a cynical populace, insisted in speaking of 'surrender', which term was even employed by Chatham, the First Lord and brother of Pitt who, himself, was no flag bearer for the Bourbon cause. There was even talk that Toulon might be permanently occupied as a 'second Gibraltar', terminology which was not at all helpful to Hood in his dealings with the nervous, proud and volatile French, who were traditionally (and with reason) suspicious of the British and highly sensitive regarding their own defection.

Pitt's views on the subject of the restoration of the French monarchy were conveyed by letter to Dundas who, in turn, complained to Hood that his proclamation appeared to favour it whereas the government, although it did not exclude it if circumstances justified it, viewed intervention as no more than repelling aggression.

A contrite Hood replied that he had found himself in a critical situation. 'I might not be perfectly correct,' he offered, but as 'all might [have been] lost by the delay of a few hours, I submitted to the conditions proposed [by the French Commissioners].' Promising to attend more closely in future to what passed as a policy from London, the admiral resumed the task of coordinating the effort of as polyglot a force as any leader could dread. Now within months of his seventieth birthday, Hood might well have pondered the prospect of a quieter posting.

chapter six

Siege and Reality,
September –November 1793

SUCCESS, IT IS SAID, has many fathers, and there were several that claimed parentage of the master plan to force the allies out of Toulon. Proposals were first advanced by the republican General Michaud d'Arcon, assisted by a civil engineer, Doumet-Revest, but the basic working plan which was forwarded to the Committee of Public Safety, marked 'paru mériter quelque considération' [seems to merit consideration], was the simple but direct scheme developed by one J-J. Brunet, an administrator in the directorate of the neighbouring *département* of Hérault.

It was encapsulated in the uncomplicated principle that 'the division that occupies La Seyne [the village on the western shore of the Petite Rade] will then seize *de vive force* the peninsula [i.e. the western promontory] and the forts named Tour de Balaguier and L'Aiguillette'. General J. C. Dugommier, a later successor of Carteaux, wrote that 'nobody who knew Toulon and its defences [could fail to recognize] its weak side, from which one could approach the combined fleets and direct upon them shells and red-hot shot'.

As early as 10 September the local *représentants en mission* reported to the Committee of Public Safety that 'measures have been taken to burn the English [sic] squadron or to force its retreat'. The common factor in all proposals was to seize the weaker western shore of Toulon's inner harbour and to utilize either existing fortifications or other means to make the waters untenable to shipping, recognized as the key to the allies' occupancy.

For their part, the allies were alive to Toulon's limitations, even if over-confident as to their own prospects. Complications quickly arose. The

British military contingent included neither specialist artillerymen nor engineers. Where the lack of the former resulted in some of the new defensive works being sited less than ideally, the absence of the latter made for much wasted effort and inferior results.

Lord Mulgrave, commander-designate of allied troops in Toulon, was, as we have seen, engaged also on high-level diplomatic missions for Henry Dundas. In addition, he was in the somewhat awkward situation of commanding at the time an Anglo-Spanish military force in which Spanish troops comprised a considerable majority. Fortunately, in Rear Admiral Gravina, who headed the Spanish forces ashore, Mulgrave could report to the prime minister on 15 September that he found 'the most zealous and practicable man with whom I ever had any transaction. He is not jealous of command and has opposed no one proposal I have made to him.'

Mulgrave went on to report that he had reorganized his slender British resources into two battalions, headed respectively by Captain Moncrieff of the 4th Regiment and Captain Brereton of the 30th. To support them in their new responsibilities, each was promoted brevet major. Gravina proposed that, as far as was practicable, British and Spanish officers and troops should share duties. The suggestion was met by Mulgrave with 'great satisfaction and comfort', sentiments that would be sorely tried.

The question of British reinforcement was already being aired, Mulgrave hoping to 'take Marseilles and to keep it'. For the moment, however, he was most solicitous of what were limited assets. 'I fear no enemy', he wrote, 'but the sickness or fatigue of the troops; and I rather delay strengthening our defences than employ soldiers in any labour, for it would be truly [illogical] to break an army by erecting works for them to defend.' Works, however, were precisely what was required.

Concerned at the vulnerability of Balaguier and L'Aiguillette if attacked from landward, Mulgrave concentrated his available effort in fortifying the height of La Grasse at their rear. In creating the strongpoint that would bear his name, he had wide swathes of trees on the slopes felled to give clear fields of fire.

As mobile fire support, Hood had his men improvise two large pontoons, each furnished with four long 24-pounders and two brass mortars. Further inshore firepower was added through the enlistment of one of the immobilized French ships, the *Aurore*, which mounted thirty-two 12- and 6-pounders. Her commanding officer, Jonquier, was relieved by temporary Captain Henry Inman, who brought with him a working complement of about two hundred men.

The major reason for the deployment of these craft was the extreme shallowness of the western end of the Petite Rade, the bay of La Seyne. Operating here, larger and more valuable ships would be confined to the deeper water of the swatchways, reducing their manoeuvrability and increasing the difficulties of extricating them under heavy fire.

ON 16 SEPTEMBER, less than three weeks after Hood entered Toulon, it happened that a French military convoy was transporting a substantial quantity of powder from the magazines at newly recovered Marseille to the Army of Italy, whose main strength was still in the region of Nice. Its escort was commanded by one Captain Buonaparte (as he then spelt it), a 24-year-old artillery specialist and a native of Corsica.

The captain's record to date had been less than spectacular. In adolescence he had been known as *ribulione*, or 'troublemaker', and in uniform tended to insubordination and brushes with authority. In October 1791, two years into the Revolution, he had been allowed to transfer from the regular army to the island's National Guard. This gave him quasi-promotion from lieutenant to lieutenant colonel. It also put him into direct contact with Pasquale Paoli, the popular leader only recently returned from exile.

What was then France's National Assembly had only recently declared Corsica to be a limb of '*la République Française, une et indivisible*', a notion with which many of its sturdily independent citizens were less than pleased. Unrest developed in the major centres of population, including Ajaccio, Buonaparte's own place of birth. In restoring order, Buonaparte acted with what Paoli considered excessive harshness. Paoli, first and foremost, was a Corsican patriot and was particularly offended by Buonaparte's overtly claiming that he acted in his, i.e. Paoli's, name.

In its endless purging of officers of the *ancien régime,* the assembly had damaged the French army as much as it had the navy. Its remedial actions with respect to the military were equally unpredictable. Buonaparte was suddenly ordered, in his substantive rank as an officer of the regular Grenoble Regiment, to attend a muster of its officers at Valence. This was some 130 miles distant and, not for the first time, he ignored instructions and was mortified when informed that he had therefore been struck from the regimental roll.

He had to act and to act quickly, travelling to Paris to plead his case. Such was the assembly's need for qualified officers that he left the capital again in September 1792 promoted to a regular captain of artillery and confirmed as a lieutenant colonel of volunteers. He had thus spent the critical summer months at the heart of Revolutionary France and had witnessed both mob assaults on the Tuileries, the second of which had resulted in the massacre of the Swiss Guard. Himself deeply supportive of the aims of the Revolutionaries, Buonaparte was both revolted and educated by the dreadful exhibitions of mob violence that he saw. He recognized the power of its raw energy but knew that it needed to be channelled and controlled with a similar degree of ruthless severity.

On return to his unit in Corsica, Buonaparte found himself involved in the abortive expedition, mounted primarily from Toulon, against Sardinia. A total fiasco in every respect, the conduct and direction of operations convinced him that Paoli's 'cooperation' was deliberately disruptive. In view of Paoli's later actions, this assessment was probably accurate but his reporting of it to the authorities in Paris resulted in Buonaparte being declared *persona non grata* in Corsica. In actual danger to his life, he resettled his family near Marseille in June 1793.

In the course of his service, Buonaparte had made the acquaintance of two men who would now prove influential. The first, Augustin Robespierre, was the younger brother of one of the all-powerful Committee of Public Safety. The other, Christophe Saliceti, was a fellow Corsican but, like Buonaparte, had been opposed to the island's independence movement. Both, therefore, had been branded *Francisé*, i.e. those who supported the French 'occupiers'.

Both Robespierre and Saliceti were highly political and, in these times of rapid promotion, had been made *représentants du peuple*. Both were attached to the Revolutionary armies in the south, Robespierre with that of General Lapoype and Saliceti with Carteaux. Together with two further *représentants*, Gasparin and the grimly efficient Paul Barras, Saliceti had become a virtual commissar, whose word was law.

Himself attached to Carteaux's army, Buonaparte had idled away some hours in composing a pamphlet which argued, in reasonable terms, why the counter-revolutionaries' case could not be justified in opposing the necessary cleansing of the nation through the current upheaval. This tract had been seen by, and had impressed, both *représentants* and, undoubtedly with an eye to the main chance, Buonaparte decided to pay a brief social call on Saliceti.

Following the rebuff at Ollioules, Carteaux still had his headquarters at Le Beausset, which lay conveniently on the route that Buonaparte's powder convoy was following through the difficult country north of the Faron Ridge. For the general, the arrival of the confident young artillery man was propitious. It will be recalled that his artillery specialist, Major Dommartin, had been severely injured in the course of Elphinstone's assault on Ollioules. The planned operations against Toulon would involve extensive use of cannon in both mobile and siege warfare roles. At the moment, Carteaux lacked both the cannon and a chief of artillery but, with a nod from Saliceti, Buonaparte was replaced as convoy escort commander. Within hours, he found himself at La Seyne, looking across at Toulon, some 4,000 yards distant, and the comings and goings of the powerful allied fleet.

From where he stood, the city was beyond the effective range of what weapons were to hand. Buonaparte set to work to assess the situation and to prepare recommendations. He consulted all available local cartography and covered all accessible ground on foot before coming to the same conclusions as those before. This is a significant point, for many Napoleonic hagiographies have credited him totally with the plan.

Traditionally, the British were content to fight with their backs to the sea, sure in the knowledge that the Royal Navy would reinforce, supply and, if required, evacuate them. This applied also to Toulon, and Buonaparte readily grasped that, if he could prevent free access by sea, the town must eventually capitulate. The keys were the two promontories that enclosed the Petite Rade, both fortified and both covering the only deep-water channel. The eastern promontory was powerfully held, had Fort la Malgue at its back, and formed one end of the mutually supportive eastern defence chain. His interest therefore settled on the more vulnerable western promontory, particularly on the intense allied activity creating the new defences of Fort Mulgrave.

Well aware of the superior firepower of the allies, both ashore and afloat,

Buonaparte badly needed to increase his own resources, which amounted to only eight 24-pounders, three 16-pounders and two mortars. Typical of his kind, over-promoted, having been advanced three ranks in as many months, Carteaux was a man still unsure of his abilities. Like his colleague Lapoype, he planned to take Toulon by conventional siege warfare. The brash new artilleryman, however, had the ear of the *représentants*, with whom even generals did not dissent.

As his seniors grudgingly accepted the inevitable, Buonaparte took effective action. Backed by the necessary authority within six weeks he had assembled over 100 pieces of artillery, mostly of the useful, medium-calibre, 24-pounder long cannon and heavy mortars. In the meantime, working parties prepared two sites for batteries in the village of Brégaillon, just north of La Seyne. These had clear arcs down the Petite Rade and, in Revolutionary fashion, were named Sans-culottes and La Montagne. Anticipating the need of many more gunners, Buonaparte further exploited his influence to organize the enforced mobilization of all retired artillery men in the region and to initiate large-scale training.

ON THE DATE of Hood's entry, the General Committee of Toulon had, in all confidence, fairly thrown down the gauntlet to General Carteaux in the open letter which, provocatively, was dated '28th August, Year One of the reign of Louis XVII'. It read:

> A mass of honest Marseillais, victims of their great devotion to [living in] peace with their fellow citizens are, at this moment, detained at your order; they groan in your shackles; and, after having wiped clean [the effects] of all the outrages from which their recognized probity should absolve them, await in horrible confinement the death reserved for blackguards.
>
> Is it you, General, who has authorized this iniquitous abuse of power? And are you able to accept that these atrocities are committed on your orders? ... We cannot believe that you do not have it within your power to cease these bloody actions of despotic authority, but if these hideous executions continue to soil the walls of Marseille, the General Committee of the Sections warns you of the indignation that has gripped the people of Toulon, who carry [the desire] to exact exemplary vengeance.
>
> We retain here two *députés* of the Convention, and the parents of two

others, whom we reserve as hostages; and we declare to you that they will
be subjected to the same [punishment] as you have inflicted on innocent
victims, of whom you claim to be protectors.

The letter continued with the underlying justification for this bold front:
'The English, already one with us, and our friends, have brought about
our security. Thirty thousand men, whether English or Spanish, will soon be
ready to assist in our vengeance; our city and Marseille are under their protection.'

The growling response from *représentants* Gasparin, Escudier and
Saliceti was, in contrast, dated *'du Bausset, le 14 séptembre, l'an second de
la république française'*. It was addressed to those who had gathered in
Toulon to oppose the principles that had 'raised the banner of revolution,
[participating in] a terrible treason which had delivered that city into the
hands of the enemies of the republic'. It charged the directory of the *départ-
mente* of the Var to arrest, according to law, all those not domiciled in the
town, and regarded as *émigrés*.

The *représentants* with the Army of Italy, the much-feared Barras and
Fréron, also wrote in response to a similar missive, urging not only the
arrest of *'une infinité de mauvais citoyens ... se sont réfugiés à Toulon'* ('a
huge number of renegade citizens ... [who] have taken refuge in Toulon')
but also the sequestration of the estates 'furnished or unfurnished' of all
those of the town's citizens who remained 'uncommunicative'.

There continued a war of words, much of it plain rhetoric but some of
it more specific and of ominous portent. The *Moniteur* gazette of 11
September published the National Convention's latest decree. Of its ten
articles, the first stated that: *'Trogoff, contre-amiral, commandant l'escadre
de Toulon; Chaussegros, capitaine des armes, et Puissant, ordonnateur de la
marine du même port, sont déclarés traîtres à la patrie.'* As traitors, their
estates were forfeit to the state.

Rear Admiral Saint-Julien, by contrast, was given honourable mention,
more for his stand against the great treason than for any particular skills
shown by him in opposing it. His lack of foresight had been condemned
in detail by Puissant, who claimed that in the days prior to Hood's entry,
a time when much of the French squadron was minded to oppose the
British, Saint-Julien not only failed to issue the appropriate instructions

but also gave no positive leadership and, for much of the time, was the worse for drink.

Like the two outlawed with him, Puissant had been a stout supporter of the new republic until overtaken by events. He had certainly made every effort to keep the arsenal free of the effects of local upheavals. His vitriolic outbursts were now directed at those contemporaries, such as Saint-Julien, who were being promoted to the lower order of heroes in the Revolutionary pantheon.

It is possible, indeed, that Puissant was not the committed traitor that the National Convention had branded him for, on 9 September, the very date of his condemnation, he was also the subject of a despatch from Elphinstone to Hood. 'Two men of credit' had declared Puissant to be a 'commis' (agent) of the Paris Jacobins and acting under their direction. 'He obeys orders', it was stated, 'with the utmost dilatoriness.' It was probable that he greatly disliked the idea of collaboration but, in making his sentiments obvious, earned the suspicion of both sides.

That the ensuing struggle would be personal and bloody was hinted at in Article IV of the same decree. All English [sic] personnel captured on French soil were to be regarded as hostages for the actions of Admiral Hood and the Toulon *sections* toward the imprisoned *représentants* Baille and Beauvais, the wife and child of General Lapoype and '*et des autres patriots opprimés et incarérés à Toulon*' ('other patriots oppressed and incarcerated in Toulon').

Even as both sides squared up for a final decision at Toulon, as threats and insults, decrees and proclamations flew back and forth, the Convention in Paris received more stunningly bad news. The Brest fleet had mutinied on 13 September.

It has already been related how, since the previous May, Vice Admiral Morard de Galles had been slowly assembling a fleet in the anchorage in the lee of the Quiberon peninsula. Troubled by the extent of the counter-revolution in the Vendée and in Brittany, the Convention reasonably assumed that the British would take advantage of the situation to land an expeditionary force. Morard de Galles's growing strength was intended as what, today, would be termed a 'rapid reaction force', charged with the disruption and defeat of any such landing during its vulnerable initial phase.

His crews had settled to a new disciplinary regime where protestations of patriotism and endless political meetings were deemed more beneficial than the constant exercise of the fleet. Only through the latter, however, could the fleet be welded into an efficient entity, capable of meeting the British on equal terms. The British, indeed, were expected imminently, as conditions for their involvement were very favourable, with the whole of the local coastline outside the main centres being under rebel control and abounding in good anchorages.

Morard de Galles had been ordered to patrol especially the waters between the Ile de Groix (off Lorient) and Belle Ile (off the Quiberon peninsula). This he did, but the poor seamanship thus displayed only served to emphasize the level of inefficiency to which the French navy had been allowed to sink. As offshore incarceration extended from weeks to months, the insubordination of the lower deck grew worse. A secondary purpose in keeping the crews at sea was to deny them the opportunity to desert, and to isolate them from the counter-revolutionary influences that the suspicious, even paranoid, minds of the Convention and local *sections* were convinced permeated the city of Brest. Because of hostility elsewhere ashore, crews could not be landed for recreational purposes, and corrosive inactivity took its inevitable toll. Within a mile of their own shores, personnel were suffering from scurvy and the effects of contaminated drinking water.

Despite the admiral's increasingly gloomy reports to Paris, his orders stood. When, on 10 August, news came of the acceptance by the republic of its new constitution, celebration was in order and Morard de Galles summoned his commanding officers to a reception aboard the flagship. Discussion turned to criticism of the fleet's situation. Autumn was fast approaching and seasonal south-westerly gales could be expected. From this quarter the anchorage enjoyed only limited cover from the peninsula and offshore islands. As the mainland would, in those circumstances, become one long lee shore, the fleet required either a better anchorage or more searoom.

The seamen were not adequately clothed for colder weather and their need for shore leave was obvious, leading the senior officers to propose that the fleet should move 100 miles up the coast to its base in Brest. The admiral duly contacted the minister of marine and, for once, was rewarded with a prompt and unequivocal response. It was, however, unfavourable. He was reminded that, as commander-in-chief, the responsibility for the fleet was his. His instructions he received from Paris and had nothing to do with any council of subordinate officers. The importance of his mission was stressed and existing instructions were to be observed until the end of the month.

Evidence of growing unrest abounded in the generally surly mood of the men, and there were reported cases of minor sabotage. Early in September came orders to form and detach a squadron to intercept a large allied convoy, known to be on its way to Spain and the Mediterranean from Dutch ports. Morard de Galles protested that his fleet and crews were no longer in a condition to mount such an operation while, tactically, it made no sense to divide his forces if the British were to be expected at any time.

Before this problem could be resolved, news came through of the defection at Toulon. Rumour then abounded until, on 12 September, commanding officers were able to muster their crews, to read them the Convention's official announcement of that event. The result was a general disaffection that, virtually simultaneously, affected the whole fleet. It was not, however, either the republic or the Convention against which the seamen directed their anger but those they saw as directly responsible for the appalling conditions under which they existed. Deputations visited the flagship, and senior officers addressed the crews of each private ship. None the less, the admiral was obliged to inform Paris that, should he order the fleet, or any part of it, to sea, his instruction would simply be ignored.

On 15 September the fleet remained under Quiberon in a state of barely contained fury as it awaited the arrival of a *représentant en mission*, the outcome of whose visit could have dire consequences for the principals involved. He, Bernard-Thomas Tréhouart, arrived five days later and, observing the state of things, immediately ordered a return to Brest.

Here, the fleet was divided into groups, classed according to their degree of non-cooperation. Each ship was separately quarantined as depositions were taken to identify the main agitators. Several had already been put in custody before 7 October, on which date arrived Jeanbon Saint-André with unlimited authority to crush the rebellion. Jeanbon was convinced that a 'federalist' plot was afloat to destroy the fighting abilities of the French republic's fleet. This, he maintained, had succeeded temporarily in Toulon but, although he detected adequate evidence of it in Brest, resolute action would prevent a repetition. Once again, the popular response was to blame the officer corps which, despite its tribulations to date, still contained many of aristocratic origin. Many of these were popular with their crews and of uncontested professional ability.

The overall result of Jeanbon's investigations was not the mass punishment that might have been expected. Once again, the lower deck and junior officers were able to convince their interrogators that they represented that undefined force, the will of the people, and were acting against repressive elements that still existed in the service. Commanding officers, when pressed, declared that their crews were not in a state of mutiny but merely expressing their rights as free citizens.

Montagnard dogma might well have agreed with such nonsense but Jeanbon was faced with a fleet which, quite simply, could not do its job. One way or another, it had to be brought back into a state of effectiveness. Once again, the easiest course was to blame the officers. Jeanbon's report recommended a final 'purification' of the navy, with the 'full, complete, absolute dismissal of all the ex-nobles'. The 'eternal plots of [this] caste', he went on, 'condemns it irrevocably to political non-existence.'

Morard de Galles was, to his own relief, dismissed from his troublesome command but, in all truth, could be accused of nothing worse than being ineffective. Imprisoned briefly, he suffered no more than having his naval career put 'on hold' for some years. A few lesser officers were tried and executed to give the illusion of effective action but the main outcome was a policy of retaining the 'Bleus', sacking all who were of aristocratic background or of the old *Grand Corps*, and replacing them with officers from the merchant service, many of them patriotic firebrands known, popularly, as 'pistols'.

The French navy thus continued in its cycle of regular upheaval. Under yet more men promoted beyond their experience or ability, there re-emerged a sort of order. This, however, was not synonymous with efficiency.

LORD MULGRAVE ARRIVED in Toulon on 7 September from Turin in order to reassume his duties as colonel of the 31st Regiment. Admiral Hood, who had a high opinion of him, requested London to promote him brigadier in order to improve his ranking relative to allied officers, but Dundas preferred to transfer Major General O'Hara from Gibraltar and to appoint him governor of Toulon in place of Rear Admiral Goodall.

Among the multiplicity of problems that beset Admiral Hood was the presence of about 5,000 French seamen who had remained loyal to Saint-Julien and the Revolution and who had been promised repatriation. Mostly from Brittany, they were known to the local French as '*Ponentais*' or 'Westerners'. Having disarmed their ships under varying degrees of sufferance, they now took to roaming the streets. Emboldened by the comparatively slight presence of allied troops, they quickly became a threatening nuisance, unsettling an already apprehensive populace and the large number of refugees. Hood could not afford to redeploy further troops to patrol the town. He was also aware of strongly republican elements in the town, currently laying low. Given time, these would inevitably collude with the leaders of the seamen to create a major problem.

On 13 September, Hood voiced his fears in a letter to the Secretary of the Admiralty, stating that 'although kept in constant alarm by Carteaux's army in the West and that of Piedmont in the East ... I am more afraid of the enemy within'. He had been assured by the General Committee on 22 August that what he described as 'these turbulent, disaffected Seamen' would be repatriated but, failing any action, he now took the initiative.

Hood requested Admiral Trogoff to identify the four least battleworthy 74s in his squadron for use as transports. The choice fell upon the *Apollon, Entreprenant, Orion* and *Patriote*. These have since often been written-off as barely seaworthy hulks but, in fact, were still perfectly sound warships, the newest being the 5-year-old *Apollon* and the oldest the 9-year-old *Orion*. Hood greatly regretted having to make a gift of these to the republican navy but, as he again confided to Stephens, it would have made no difference if they had been in a perfect state, for 'our security demands it'. Except for a pair of 8-pounders for signalling purposes, all armament, including small arms, was transferred ashore, into the arsenal.

The ships readied, Admiral Goodall, in his capacity as governor, had posted and proclaimed about the town the following declaration, with immediate effect: 'It is ordered that all Officers, Seamen and Others comprising the crews of the KING's vessels *Apollon, Entreprenant, Orion* and *Patriote* to repair on board their respective ships before midday today, the 15th, on pain, in case of contravention, of being regarded as Prisoners and punished very severely.' Goodall further observed royalist sensitivities in dating the notice '*À Toulon ce 15 Septembre* [sic] *1793 l'an premier du règne de Louis XVII*'.

Threat was unnecessary, for every last man was almost certainly pleased to be given the chance to leave what was, by any standard, a potentially dangerous situation. All sailed on 17 September, ships and personnel issued with passports to guarantee free passage, unhindered by allied warships. To their number had been added a fifth ship, the little brig-corvette *Pluvier,* late of sixteen guns. Although returning loyally to the flag, the personnel on their eventual arrival were received very differently to how they might reasonably have expected.

Carrying a reported 1,420 deportees, the *Apollon* was accompanied to Rochefort by the *Pluvier,* with a further 300. Peremptorily, the ships were ordered to anchor in the Aix roads under the guns and fortifications of the Ile d'Oléron, and flanked by other warships. No communication was permitted with the shore, nor would the local *représentants* allow the crowded ships to be cleared until all aboard had been interrogated. All ratings were adjudged innocent but a Revolutionary Tribunal was set up to try thirty-four officers and sailing masters against the charge that they were involved in an agreement with the Toulon *sections* to similarly deliver Rochefort to the British.

The *Pluvier* was unfortunate in first calling at Bordeaux, where she was detained by contrary winds. Because this city had previously supported a high degree of federalist sympathies, the tribunal seized upon this as proof that her officers were involved in counter-revolutionary activities. Eventually, six naval and two infantry officers, together with a surgeon, were sentenced to death. There had been offered no proof of any complicity on the part of any of them other than their unavoidable contact with the British. For the *représentants,* it was sufficient to make an example, and to remind any waverers in the local population of the power of the state, exercised through them. The executions were public and carried out before a 'frenzied' gathering of townsfolk. Two others were sentenced to deportation, and eight of them to six months' imprisonment.

As a matter of principle, both of the ships were quickly refurbished to prime condition by the yard at Rochefort. To exorcise any remaining taint of defection, both were renamed, the *Apollon* becoming the *Gasparin,* and the *Pluvier* the *Commission.*

The experience of the other repatriation ships was broadly similar. Each carrying 1,400 personnel, the *Entreprenant* and *Patriote* arrived at Brest on 14 October. Following isolation and interrogation, officers were incarcerated for months within the château, whose grim walls flanked the entrance to the Penfeld, where lay the arsenal. Generally, the mood here was less excitable, although six officers were sent to Paris where, following further investigation, they were executed for complicity with the dissident Toulon *sections*.

The National Assembly, obviously curious as to the general experience, summoned a representative party to the capital, accompanied by the Brest *députés*. Individuals were able to plead their case successfully and, following release on licence, were eventually fully reinstated in their ranks and grades.

The final ship of the squadron, *Orion*, anchored inside the Ile de Groix on 15 October. She had aboard 1,447 personnel and was actually welcomed by the commandant at Lorient who declared that, through their successful evasion of the enemy, they should be regarded 'as brothers'. As, however, there were almost certainly 'agents of the coalition powers' among them, he summoned the regional *représentant* while detaining all on board for 'reasons of public health'.

A search of the ship brought to light the journal of a junior officer which detailed how, on Hood's squadron approaching Toulon on 28 August, the *Orion* had been moored so as to obstruct the fairway and how, throughout the ensuing night, her gunners had remained on duty, awaiting orders to resist. Later, the journal stated, the crew had refused to declaim '*Vive le roi*' when so exhorted by Toulon's civic representatives.

On such flimsy evidence did one's fortunes depend during these tumultuous times. Now treated as heroes, all were released except a group of men who, for some reason unspecified, were packed off to the neighbouring Vendée to assist in the fight against insurgency. As for the *Orion*, she too was refitted and renamed *Mucius Scévola*, after another of the classical models so favoured by Montagnard idealism.

Overall, the treatment meted out to those repatriated appeared to be totally arbitrary, directed mainly at impressing upon the public conscience that any counter-revolutionary infection would be cured swiftly with unpleasant remedies. Contemporary French accounts fail to explain any logic or lines of consistency. Typically: '*C'est ainsi qu'obéissant à l'instinct aveugle qui*

*la poussoit à répandre le sang, la Convention frappoit indistinctment les
ennemis de la révolution et ses partisans les plus zélés.'* ('In following its blind
instinct to spill blood, the Convention hits indiscriminately at the enemies
of the revolution and its most zealous supporters.')

AS THOSE REPATRIATED sailed to their various destinies, Napoleone
Buonaparte, Captain of Artillery and future Emperor of France, busied
himself with annoying the coalition fleet in the Petite Rade. As further guns
arrived, he established a third battery (Rade) adjacent to the hamlet of Brégaillon.

There was nothing elaborate about these works. A contemporary sketch
clearly depicts that of Sans-culottes. Three cannon on carriages, grouped
almost as closely as on a third rate's gun-deck, point through gaps in a low
protective wall. This is apparently of broken masonry, roughly stabilized
with stakes and, in places, backed by spare wooden barrels, probably packed
with earth. To one side, behind the dubious cover of an earth bank, are
casually stacked further large barrels, almost certainly containing the battery's
powder. A rude, existing stone building, the Chapelle de Brégaillon, provides
a measure of shelter to the battery personnel while, outside, a Revolutionary
banner flies provocatively from an improvised pole. In the distance, surprisingly close, is the high ground, crowned by a *sémaphore,* behind the key
allied positions of L'Aiguillette and Balaguier. Somewhere on that high
ground, allied troops are labouring, unseen, to elaborate Fort Mulgrave,
a position which quite clearly enfilades those of Buonaparte and which
should have been resolutely neutralized by Carteaux before it became firmly
established. Ahead, and surprisingly close, the masts of allied ships spike
the skyline.

Buonaparte's prize gun, discovered in Marseille, was a 44-pounder
culverin. Such weapons typically had barrels of length some twenty-five to
thirty times their bore, compared with perhaps eighteen on standard cannon.
This extra length conferred greater accuracy, range and consistency of aim,
and the gun was quickly put to work.

As early as the night of 17/18 September, one of the navy's improvised pontoons came under fire from the *conventionnels'* batteries and was
obliged to haul off. The allies were clearly concerned from the outset at
this form of attack, and the fact that they did not put troops ashore to raid

in force or to control the western shoreline is evidence of the dearth of fighting men. It was already too late, for Carteaux held the area strongly and had mounted several sharp attacks against those engaged on constructing outworks. Buonaparte's batteries near Brégaillon were just within range of Fort Malbousquet, and the *Princess Royal* records the despatch of a party to improve the latter's defences, for it was not well supported by flanking works.

On the 25th the British deployed the 98-gun *St George*, Rear Admiral Gell's flagship, in support of the ex-French *Aurore* (now British-manned) and two pontoons. Not for the first time, the navy learned that naval gunfire can rarely dominate land-based artillery. British naval gunners were trained to fire rapid broadsides at close range, so that precision aiming was rarely an issue. Thus, a broadside from the *St George's* lower deck 32-pounders could throw up an impressive curtain of sand or soft earth, but this same soft ground would absorb all of its energy. The heavy balls had negligible effect, injuring the enemy only through a direct hit on an embrasure.

Accuracy of naval guns was affected also by a ship's ranging at her anchor while, even in average conditions, there existed sufficient roll movement to affect the correct angle of elevation for a given range. Such problems did not affect the French artillery. Though far fewer, their guns were absolutely steady, and warships made targets that, with practice, became almost unmissable. To increase the navy's discomfiture, the enemy also began to use red-hot shot, a favoured weapon known as *boulets-rouges*. In order to prevent the batteries annoying the anchorage at long range, it was necessary to engage them almost daily and for hours on end. A pontoon was lost and larger ships were often obliged to shift their berths.

For an interesting sidelight on this occupation, we can again thank Captain Nelson, writing to his wife.

Some of our Ships have been pegged pretty handsomely; yet such is the force of habit, that we seem to feel no danger ... The other day we sat at a Court Martial on board Admiral Hotham, when *Princess Royal*, a French 74, our friend, three Frigates and four Mortar boats, were firing at a battery for four hours, the shot and shells going over us; which, extraordinary as it may seem, made no difference ... The *Ardent*, Captain Robert Manners Sutton, brother to the Bishop [of Norwich], was much cut up, after behaving with the greatest gallantry and good conduct; near thirty of his men were either killed, or are since dead of the[ir] wounds …

The key defence work of Fort Malbousquet now also became the object of a steady pounding from the French batteries. Ollioules, too remote to be held permanently by allied forces, became the location of Carteaux's headquarters, and new contingents of troops from the interior were joining him almost daily. They were billeted mainly in two large encampments at the foot of the heights behind the village. Those not required to garrison forward positions were set to work and, with the general high level of motivation typical of the republicans, showed rapid result.

From their 'front line' on the flats to the east of the little River Neuve, allied personnel looked across to a series of minor heights which each soon became capped by its own masked battery: the *Rédoute de la Convention* on the hill of Les Arènes, the *Farinière* on La Goubran, and the *Poudrière* on the Hauteur des Gaux.

To the east and north, General Lapoype was content to close and tighten his grip on the Toulon perimeter. His resident *députés*, Barras and Fréron, had enforced a 'loan' of 4 million livres from the hapless city of Marseille, which greatly facilitated victualling and general procurement for their army. The third force, from the Army of Italy, had to date made little impact and, during September, General Brunet was arrested for lack of zeal and replaced. Taken to Paris and accused by a tribunal of vaguely defined sympathies with the Toulonnais, he was executed in the November.

The village of Le Beausset, where Carteaux had earlier established his headquarters, was typical of those which declared themselves enthusiastically pro-Convention. It raised its own company of 500 *Sans-culottes,* which proved to be a nucleus which continuously attracted workers and seamen displaced by events in the city, now branded *la ville infâme* by Paris. By now, however, throughout the *départemente* of the Var, mobilization orders had gone out to every able-bodied male between the ages of 16 and 60.

ADMIRAL HOOD WAS considerably troubled by French activities along the western shore of the harbour. Buonaparte, despite being on somewhat distant terms with General Carteaux, who clearly regarded him as an over-confident upstart (and, possibly, a threat), had established here a virtual mastery. Allied garrisons on the western promontory and the Saint-Mandrier peninsula, although powerfully entrenched, were isolated, and now depended upon communication by water. The Corsican's intention to capture or neutralize these positions was an ambition well understood by Hood, who equally well appreciated the implications. Buonaparte's plan, powerfully backed by the *députés*, was favoured above those of the generals. Their task now was to keep allied forces stretched around the eastern and northern sides of the perimeter while, behind the relentless pounding of an increasing number of batteries, the main thrust would be readied from the west.

From the outset, Hood's need was for more troops or, better, more *British* troops, over which he would have undisputed control. Unfortunately, these were simply unavailable in any number for reasons already stated. King George III, still exercising his right of input to what passed for a War Cabinet, was of the opinion that the main British strategic aim should be 'to humble France, for nothing but her being disabled from disturbing other countries, whatever government [she may have], will keep her quiet'. In the process of achieving this aim, he informed Dundas, 'steady attention [should be paid] to obtaining our own advantages'.

Having made a plaything of the defence budget in a desire to be all things to all people, the prime minister, Pitt, now found himself, with Grenville and Dundas, embroiled in squaring the circle of spreading inadequate military strength over a superfluity of hotspots. Into a mish-mash of uncoordinated and conflicting enterprises had suddenly appeared the great opportunity of the defection of Toulon. Hood was promised 5,000 troops but, due mainly to strong representations by the over-stretched Duke of York, these never materialized. British forces could simply be stretched no further, and any successful exploitation of Toulon would require not only a major contribution from coalition contingents but also from the French themselves, drawn from the ranks of regular troops and those National Guardsmen who, already within the perimeter, could be judged reliable.

Standards of discipline and fighting ability would be found to vary greatly, leading an exasperated Admiral Hood at one stage to describe the Spanish and Neapolitan troops as 'dastardly trash'. The Spanish, in fact, generally cooperated well at a tactical level but their government remained deeply suspicious of British intentions, convinced that they, all too often their enemy, would turn the campaign to their own interest, particularly where the French Toulon fleet was concerned.

Some coalition governments were unhappy at the idea of allowing their troops to be commanded by leaders from other states with which relations were less than cordial. From Naples, for instance, Sir William Hamilton wrote to Hood as early as 1 September, assuring him of his Sicilian majesty's every intention of fulfilling his agreed commitments. The letter stated, however:

> Whatever Y. Lp. [Your Lordship] shall please to direct, HSM's Officers have orders to obey. It wou'd not be so with the Spaniards (as Y.Lp. may perhaps know) that the harmony between the Courts of Madrid and Naples is not yet perfect. This Court looks upon our late Treaty as merely between Great Britain and the Two Sicilies.

All efforts by British diplomacy failed, however, to persuade Austria to honour her commitment to the Treaty of 30 August, and to send 5,000 troops. Having already despatched over 8,000 to Piedmont, the emperor was ill-disposed to incur further expense. Lord Mulgrave reinforced diplomatic pressure by travelling personally to Vienna in order to plead 'the distress of [Austria's] allies', returning with an assurance from the foreign minister that he would pursue the matter. Nothing happened. During the whole period of the struggle for Toulon all further requests were met with what Mulgrave described as 'delaying demands, excuses, pretty equivocal words and ambiguous promises'. But no troops.

On 14 September Grenville promised that 5,000 Hessians would be transferred from Flanders by the end of the month, but this never came about as Austria was still expected to stand by her word. The constant expectation of substantial reinforcement, coupled with the relative inactivity of Carteaux's army, went far toward generating an attitude of complacency in Toulon, an assumption that the threat was slight.

Lord Mulgrave, the seasoned professional soldier, was least prepared to take chances, having been appointed commander-designate of British troops in the perimeter. At the outset, when Spanish forces greatly outnumbered the British, it was appropriate that Rear Admiral Gravina be placed in command of all troops, but large contingents were expected from the kingdoms of Sardinia and Naples. These were heavily subsidised by Britain and totally under British control. The appointment of a British commanding officer was thus appropriate. Spanish personnel would, however, remain under Gravina's control and, although he proved to be personally cooperative and reliable, there would be sharp disagreements at lower levels, where the garrisons and combat units were mixed.

Mulgrave had his eye on the British military garrison at Gibraltar, which currently faced no threat. Following his initial inspection of the Toulon perimeter, he reported on 8 September to Hood that 'the line of defence is now contracted as much as it can be, consistently [sic] with the security of the place'. He was, none the less, critical of the enemy's occupation of Ollioules the day before 'when the advanced Corps (which I had requested the Spanish Gen … to withdraw) were driven in. Y. Lp. will feel the absolute necessity of a reinforcement of *British* troops'. He went on:

> I beg leave, therefore, to submit to Y. Lp. the necessity of making an urgent
> requisition to Sir Robt. Boyd [Governor of Gibraltar] for a reinforcement
> of two battalions of infantry, with as large a detachment of artillerymen
> as he can spare from the necessary duties of his garrison (for we have not
> one Artilleryman in the Garrison except a few Gunners from the Spanish
> ships).

Recognizing the other specialist weakness, he added hopefully, 'I wish also to have an officer of Engineers'.

The Admiralty responded quickly to Hood's forwarding of Mulgrave's appraisal. Within the week a letter had been despatched to Boyd (copied to Hood) informing the governor that the admiral 'may find it necessary to have recourse to that garrison for the assistance of troops in the present emergency'.

In the knowledge that Gibraltar's spare military strength would, nevertheless, be insufficient, the Lords Commissioners signalled on 25 September that the government was to lose no time in assembling a 'respectable' military force. This would be headed by Major General O'Hara, who would command not only the contingent from Gibraltar but also 'all other forces collected for the defence of Toulon'. The letter enclosed the commission appointing O'Hara governor of Toulon.

Considerable reliance had been placed on the Kingdom of Sardinia as a source of fighting men. For a British subsidy of £5 million and promise of the recovery and restitution of Nice and Savoy, Sardinia had contracted to raise an army of 50,000, of which 20,000 would be placed at British disposal.

As the Sardinians lacked suitable transport, Hood despatched the *Colossus* to Cagliari. She returned on 24 September with just 350 troops. Meanwhile, the *Bedford* and *Leviathan* had been sent to Oneglia for the same purpose. Between them, they returned with about 800. Over the following month a further 800 were ferried in, but that was it. Of 20,000 promised, 2,000 thus materialized. Much, therefore, depended upon the Neapolitans, the first substantial numbers of whom were not expected before the end of September.

COMMODORE ROBERT LINZEE and Admiral Hood were brothers-in-law, the latter having married Linzee's sister, Susannah, daughter of the Lord Mayor of Portsmouth. On 8 September, early in the campaign, Hood sent Linzee on a mission of some importance.

Paoli's Corsican patriots had already cleared the *campagne* (interior) of what the population viewed as French occupation forces. These had retreated into the three main townships of Bastia, Calvi and San Fiorenzo. As already related, Britain viewed the island as a well-situated forward base for operations against the French in the Mediterranean, although any occupancy of Toulon on a permanent basis would have negated its value. The rebels, in insufficient strength to eject the French from their strongholds, made a strong appeal to the British for assistance, approaching their envoys in Turin and Genoa as well as Hood in Toulon.

Presented with the prospect of a second easy success, Hood could hardly refuse to act. At a time when all his ships were stretched to provide the manpower necessary to improve Toulon's defences, therefore, the admiral gave Linzee a small squadron. The newly promoted commodore broke his broad pendant in the *Alcide* 74, having under his command the *Courageux* 74 (herself taken from the French and already 40 years old, having spent most of her life in British service), the *Ardent* 64 and two frigates, the *Lowestoffe* 32 and *Nemesis* 28. Linzee's orders were to induce the French garrisons to capitulate.

Considering the significance of this mission, it appears strange with hindsight that Hood complicated matters by directing Linzee to make a risky detour. At Villefranche, near Nice, were anchored two French frigates, *Badine* and *Vestale*. Under a flag of truce, a sealed letter was to be taken ashore for delivery to the senior French captain.

Two of the *Nemesis*'s officers were nominated for this rather dangerous errand while Linzee, as ordered, waited offshore for twenty-four hours for a response. Discussions were in progress ashore when a messenger arrived with news that the local *représentants* in Nice required the officers be brought to their presence. Blindfolded, they were duly conducted to where Barras, Fréron, Ricord and the younger Robespierre awaited them. Their despatches were confiscated and examined, proving to be offers of amnesty from Hood, a proclamation from Langara addressed to the Army of Italy and a letter from Trogoff inviting the two frigates to join him in Toulon.

Hood had here made a total miscalculation in handing the republicans a propaganda coup. The *représentants* gathered the civil and military authorities, together with an excited crowd, in a public square. Before the assembled throng the emissaries' despatches were burned with ceremony and a short, defiant address read:

> *Perisse à jamais la royauté! Tel est le cri de vingt cinq millions de républicains français. Cette Nation libre et puissante ne peut avoir rien de commun avec les despotes et les esclaves: elle ne doit et ne veut communiquer avec eux qu'a coups de canon. Elle n'a pas besoin, pour combattre et vaincre ses ennemis, d'avoir, comme eux, recours à la trahison, à la perfidie et à la scélératesse.*

> (Let royalty be dead for ever! Such is the cry of the 25 million French republicans. This free and powerful nation can never have anything in common with despots and slaves. She must not nor wishes to communicate with those who are nothing but noise. She has no need to fight and vanquish her enemies or to have, like them, recourse to treason, treachery and villainy.)

To complete their humiliation, the pair were marched back to their boat accompanied by a large crowd, '*en chantant des airs patriotiques*'. Linzee's subsequent actions are not relevant to events at Toulon other than that they kept his squadron away at a time when the extra manpower would have been useful. It is worth mentioning, however, that he enjoyed no success in Corsica. Local partisans failed to support his shows of strength before the fortified towns, leading Hood to lose patience, labelling Paoli 'a composition of art and deceit'.

The affair caused the commander-in-chief considerable embarrassment in having to admit to Dundas that he had 'received no one Instruction about Corsica, and my sending a squadron there was a spontaneous action of my own'.

Given sea superiority, however, Hood was very inclined to use it, so Linzee's was not the only expedition launched. As related, the British frigate *Aigle*, on entering neutral Genoa with despatches, was impeded there by the French frigate *Modeste*, whose crew behaved in a manner designed to insult the British. This vessel and her smaller consorts were in port in order to escort a pending grain convoy, sent coastwise for the benefit of the Army of Italy.

Diplomatic representations having failed to dissuade the Genoese merchants from persisting in what was, for them, a lucrative trade, Hood resolved to kill two birds with one stone. On 14 September he wrote to Francis Drake, the British minister at Genoa, of that republic's showing 'a glaring and highly unbecoming partiality in favour of French regicides, to the prejudice of our most gracious sovereign and country'. His letter continued:

> [I] have therefore sent R. Adm. Gell with a squadron to Genoa and communicate with Y. Ex. [Your Excellency]; and I must request Y. Ex. … make known to the Doge and Senate that unless Mr. Tilly [the Chargé d'Affaires, described elsewhere as the 'agent from the Convention at Paris'] is ordered to depart the Genoese territories within twelve hours, the port of Genoa shall be blockaded, and not a ship or vessel suffered to go in or out …

Hood then referred to the 'numberless instances' in which the Genoese had departed from 'a fair and honourable neutrality' and demanded that their government make an 'instant, candid and explicit declaration' of its attitude to Britain, for 'avowed enemies are infinitely more sufferable than false friends'. Almost as an afterthought the admiral added that: 'R. Adm. Gell has my orders to seize the *Modeste* French frigate, the moment he arrives.' A most un-neutral action! On 26 September Gell duly sailed with a powerful squadron, his flagship *St George* being accompanied by three 74s (*Bedford, Captain* and the royalist French *Scipion*), five smaller craft and two fireships.

The French account has the *St George* and *Bedford* entering harbour at Genoa at 11 a.m. on 5 October, the latter ship ranging alongside the *Modeste* as her crew were having a meal. The British demanded that she follow the example of the *Scipion* and raise the *pavillon royal*, the royal ensign. Not surprisingly, runs the account, this requirement was met with what was described as a *'refus énergique'*, whereupon a volley was laid upon her deck by marines stationed in the *Bedford's* tops. A light brow, or bridge, was thrown across and the Frenchman rapidly boarded. All who resisted were cut down; all who sought escape overboard were shot. According to which French version is believed, their casualties were either forty to fifty dead, or five dead and thirty injured. British sloops, meanwhile, over-whelmed the two accompanying French *tartanes*.

As might have been anticipated, this precipitate action promoted a furious exchange of diplomatic notes between London and Genoa. Still more impressed by the nearby French army than by the British fleet, the Genoese bowed to French demands and expelled all foreigners except for the French. Genoa was immediately blockaded, so was unavailable for the transit of the 5,000 Austrian troops then imminently expected for the reinforcement of Toulon.

The alternative port for this urgent operation was Leghorn (Livorno), although the Austrians quickly used the rupture with Genoa as an excuse for their troops now having to be deployed to safeguard Lombardy. Leghorn was within the territory of the Grand Duchy of Tuscany whose authorities, intimidated by a powerful French presence close by, had detained shipments of grain bound for the British at Toulon. There lay in the port the loaded British merchantman *Captain* and the Spanish *Bahama*, guarded by the fine French 44-gun frigate *Impérieuse*.

To emphasize British displeasure, Gell detached his three 74s to Leghorn, which action was sufficient to persuade the Grand Duke to eject the French entirely. Tilly had already issued orders that the *Impérieuse* should be destroyed rather than captured. She had, therefore, been trans-ferred to the naval facility at Fezzano, where her armament had been landed prior to her scuttling. A joint Anglo-Spanish force was, however, able to temporarily take over the base, rearm the frigate, remove her from her mud berth and sail her to Toulon.

The French 74, *Scipion*, was left at Leghorn under orders to assist a squadron of British ships under Vice Admiral Cosby in lifting and transporting the 5,000 still-expected Austrians. The wait was, of course, protracted and, in the November, the ship suddenly caught fire. Hastily towed from the harbour, she blew up with the loss of 150 of her crew. The disaster was ascribed to sabotage on the part of members of the crew of the *Modeste* who had elected to serve aboard the two-decker.

In the *Modeste* and the *Impérieuse* (later renamed *Unité*) the Royal Navy acquired two excellent frigates. Representations were made by Langara to Hood, and by the Spanish ambassador in London to Grenville, that the two ships, as the remainder of the French ships at Toulon, should be held in trust in the name of Louis XVII. The Admiralty's more robust view, however, was that both ships had been taken elsewhere, and away from hostile crews. They remained British prizes.

IN AN AGE WHEN the process of ship design was still more art than science, the British freely acknowledged that the French had the advantage. Captured vessels were prized for their sailing qualities and were, invariably, stemmed in dock to have their lines 'taken off'. The chance to acquire an immense quantity of knowledge about both the French ships and Toulon arsenal was not lost on Vice Admiral Sir Charles Middleton (later Lord Barham) who, until recently, had held the post of comptroller of the navy and who retained a keen interest in its material welfare. In a long letter, dated 13 October 1793, he brought to the attention of the Earl of Chatham, First Lord of the Admiralty, the 'many articles of information which it may be desirable to procure while Toulon is in our possession'.

Canny and careful, Middleton proposed sending out a party of experts, including 'a shipwright, a draftsman [sic], a storehouse clerk, a blacksmith, a caulker, a mastmaker and a ropemaker'. Significantly, none of these was senior staff and Middleton made the point that, to use their expertise would be 'without any considerable expense to government'.

He posed, in total, about one hundred questions, the range of which reflects his great experience. With respect to Toulon itself, the procurement of accurate plans of the arsenal and anchorages was obvious. He was also interested in storehouses and magazines: how many were there and how arranged for the best handling of their contents, and how far were they from the wharves? As to the stores – what was laid apart for decommissioned ships? What was earmarked and what for general use? The decommissioned ships: were they laid up in tiers or alongside? Masts in or out? Stored? Covered? How coppered, etc.? Masts and yards, dimensions? Of what materials? Where procured? How constructed, etc.? Docks and slips: how many? Dimensions? Covered? Height of any roof? Building? Sources of timber? Is it supplied rough or ready framed? What proportion? What is the construction time for a 74 from keel-laying to launch? What types of machine have been introduced? How many? Size and purpose?

Middleton's curiosity appeared limitless. If the French enjoyed any superiority or advantage over the Royal Navy then this, surely, was the chance to discover how and why. So detailed were his requirements, however, that his operatives could never have completed their task in the time available.

SEVERAL DAYS OF CONSTANT attention from Buonaparte's batteries were sufficient to convince Hood of the French intention to take the western promontory. He warned Mulgrave that such a move would prevent the use of the inner roads by the fleet but, although the latter fully appreciated the implications, he could not react immediately as his forces were already stretched in the improvement of vital defensive positions.

Hood, greatly concerned, fortunately insisted on action and, during the night of 21/22 September, ferried about 600 British and Spanish troops from Toulon. His instincts, or intelligence, were correct for on the following day this force was able to inflict a sharp reverse on the republicans. Carteaux was keen on measuring the strength of the defence, but there were subsequent allegations by the French that he was so angry that the *représentants* had backed Buonaparte's strategy against his own that he deliberately committed an under-strength force. For whatever reason, the action provided the defenders with a considerable fillip. They suffered two dead and ten injured, but the French assessment of their casualties was simply '*ne nous sont pas connus*'.

The 23rd saw a concentrated effort by the fleets to suppress the batteries. For this, the British divisional flagship *St George* was joined by two Spanish ships (*San Juan Nepomucena* and *San Ildefonso*) and the British-crewed French frigate *Iphigénie*, supported by one of the improvised floating batteries. In eleven hours of bombardment the senior Spanish ship alone fired near 1,700 rounds, suffering considerable damage in return, resulting in one dead and ten wounded. The inhabitants of the neighbouring village of La Seyne had pledged neutrality but, being observed to be actively assisting the republicans, they too were bombarded, obliging the place's evacuation.

Ships regularly reported batteries silenced but, each night, they were rehabilitated by the French. Only by following up a close bombardment with a landing party, to spike the cannon and to blow up powder stores, could the allies fully succeed. The shore, however, was too strongly held.

On 27 September one of the *St George*'s 32-pounders burst with damaging results. One large piece of the shattered weapon was driven upward through two decks, dismounting a 24-pounder on the way. The number of casualties is, however, variously reported.

The French 74 *Puissant* was allotted the task of covering the floating batteries. This she did admirably, having eventually to be withdrawn owing to accumulated damage. Her royalist commanding officer, the 49-year-old Pierre-Jacques Féraud, who had fought against Hood in the West Indies, was now warmly commended by him.

As the navies strove to suppress the growing ring of enemy batteries, the allied command was greatly heartened by the arrival at the end of September of the first contingent of Neapolitans, from the only allied state to honour its treaty commitments fully. Its final contribution would be three 74s, four frigates and four smaller vessels, together with over 6,000 troops. On 27 September the first 2,000 arrived, a battalion of grenadiers and two of fusiliers under the overall command of Prince Pignatelli-Cerchiara. They were enthusiastically received by the populace and Toulon's General Committee when they were reviewed on the town's Champ de Bataille by Mulgrave and Gravina. Their arrival cheered the defenders, too, and resulted in such an optimistic change in Hood's despatches that London was pleased to accept that all was well. Which was never the case.

THE LACONIC ENTRIES in the 'lieutenant's logs' of the various ships involved provide an interesting mix of ship's routine and daily happenings. The *Britannia* noted the Neapolitans' arrival, together with routine fleet comings and goings: 'His Majesty's ship[s] *Fortitude, le Clair, Camel* and *Vulcan*, a Spanish line-of-battleship, a Frigate and a Brig, also a Neapolitan Squadron (with a rear admiral) consisting of two Line of Battle Ships and four Frigates with 2000 troops for the Garrison.'

As with most vessels, the *Britannia* provided landing parties and fire cover for activities ashore: '9 September. Unmoored and carried small Bower anchor farther inshore to guard the pass to the Hospital [i.e. the neck of the Saint-Mandrier peninsula].' On the same day: 'Sent a Lieutenant, two Midshipmen and 30 Seamen to guard the pass on shore.' Then, with a detached view of events: '19 September … sailed a french Ship with Democrats. *St. George* and floating batteries Cannonading the Enemy.'

Ordinary ship's business was also duly noted. Amid more warlike activities the entry for 16 September includes 'Employed painting the Ship'. On the 23rd: 'At 1 fired 21 Guns in commemoration of His Majesty's Coronation, at 15mp[t] [i.e. 15 minutes past] the Spanish Fleet sailed.'

On 9 October: '[A] Court Martial was assembled on board and tried Richard Batty, Surgeon's Mate of the *Illustrious* for Cruelty, of which charge he was fully acquitted. Also, John Williams belonging to the said ship for Mutiny and Desertion, of which Charge he was fully Convicted and Condemned to Suffer Death.'

BEYOND THE REACH of the Toulon garrison, General Carteaux had not been entirely idle. Probing eastward, beyond the Mont Faron Ridge, he contacted forward elements of General Lapoype's army, thus closing the landward ring around the city. In the process, he occupied the château at Dardennes, through whose estate flowed the small river Las. By diverting its waters (today it is dammed at Le Revest-les-Eaux, just to the north) he succeeded in halting most of the mills upon which Toulon depended for its flour. Despite this success, however, the general opinion (including, rather precociously, that of Buonaparte) was that Carteaux was moving too slowly and cautiously. Known for his pretentious uniforms rather than for his military expertise, he attracted a measure of ridicule, but was senior to Lapoype.

The latter, with 6,000 men under orders, had already relieved la Barre and entertained ambitions of taking over Carteaux's command in addition. For the moment, he was ordered by Carteaux to make every effort to take the allied strongpoint at Cap Brun. Situated a mile or more to the east of La Malgue, this battery looked directly across to the Saint-Mandrier peninsula.

This lay well beyond effective cannon shot, and it is unlikely that Cap Brun could have seriously hindered allied ships passing close to the peninsula where, indeed, lies the deepest water. On the other hand, possession would have denied the allied fleets a considerable proportion of their accustomed anchorage in the Grande Rade. To the allies, Cap Brun was the anchor of the eastern defence line, strongly positioned with its back to the sea and a useful outlying support for La Malgue.

Lapoype's interest for the minute was, however, elsewhere. It was known that the allies intended to use 1 October as the date for the proclamation of Louis XVII as King of France. With every intention of spoiling the party, the general had assembled strong groups at points along the foot of the length of the northern face of Mont Faron, from La Vallette in the east, via the Château de Touris and Revest, to the neighbourhood of Fort Pomets at the western end. His plan was in direct contravention of Carteaux's instructions, but there is every indication that the *représentants* Barras and Fréron encouraged him in this, possibly hinting at his taking Carteaux's command should he decide the course of the campaign.

On 1 October the *Britannia's* log noted the morning's events: 'At daylight, saw the enemy in possession of the Heights over Toulon ... at ½ past 10 the White [i.e. Bourbon] Flag was displayed by the French Fleet and Forts with a general discharge of artillery ... at 11 saw Allied Troops march up the Mountains to attack the Enemy.' Lapoype had succeeded only too well.

The allied garrisons atop the Faron Ridge had probably felt secure for, even today, no real track exists up the northern face of the massif which, near its summit, becomes precipitous. Key positions were manned at its east and west extremities and in its centre.

In the west, the Tour de l'Ubac looked across the valley of the Las towards Fort Pomets, some 900 feet lower. The ridge here is approachable via valleys rising steeply from the south. Although these are covered by Fort Saint-Antoine, this is the more accessible end. In the centre is a small spur known as Pas de la Masque. An established military post, it also precariously supports a small barracks, the Caserne du Centre. The approach from the north is up a 45-degree slope which steepens further toward the summit. The going is treacherous, over loose, friable rock. At the allies' right the Fort de la Croix Faron was located at the eastern extremity of the ridge, dominating the larger Fort Faron, situated 600 yards to the south-west but over 500 feet lower.

Starting at about 2 a.m., Lapoype himself led a silent column up difficult tracks to bypass Saint-Antoine and surprise the Tour de l'Ubac position. As an achievement, however, this paled beside that of the centre column. While the allies were distracted by an armed demonstration on the French left, guides led an advance guard of the centre force up a vertiginous goat track. It completely surprised the sixty-man Spanish garrison which, according to Mulgrave, retired 'without a shot being fired' along the ridge, eastward toward La Croix Faron. This capitulation was later to reinforce suspicions of collusion between the French and their late allies.

Spanish naval signallers were based at both Fort Faron and on the naval hospital within the arsenal. At daybreak, urgent signals from the fort caused Elphinstone to react immediately, despatching ninety men of the 30th Regiment from La Malgue. At the same time, a council of war was quickly convened. It was attended by Rear Admiral Gravina, Brigadiers Mulgrave and the Spanish Izquierdo, Prince Pignatelli and Captain Elphinstone. Mulgrave's proposals were adopted, despite some objections from the Spanish.

With a small additional force of fifty men, Elphinstone was to reinforce rapidly those at the vital Fort Faron. They would then create a diversion while the main allied thrust was directed from the western end. This would comprise just over 1,200 troops, advancing in two columns. Climbing from Fort Saint-Antoine was an Anglo-Piedmontese force, some 550 strong, commanded by Mulgrave personally, with Piedmontese as his lieutenants. To their right, labouring up the steep Val Bourdin, were the remainder under Gravina. This column included 180 Spanish, 400 Neapolitan grenadiers and a few Sardinians and French royalists. Gravina's lieutenants were Pignatelli and Izquierdo. Down in Toulon, where the white Bourbon banner was everywhere to be seen in recognition of the day, an anxious Hood awaited the outcome. He had replaced the absent troops with seamen drawn from the fleets.

Having demonstrated considerable elan in the seizure of the Faron Ridge, the republicans were now lacklustre in its defence. Some 200 self-styled *conventionnels* were located on the flattish ground of the western summit, where the memorial now stands. They were of indifferent quality and, having sprayed a brief and long-range fusillade at Mulgrave's column as it breasted the ridge to their west, they retired in the opposite direction along the undulating track that linked the various summits of the main ridge. Captain Moncrieff's advance guard harried their retreat and, without trouble, reoccupied the Pas de la Masque position.

Having yielded so much ground, the enemy was now in something of a predicament. The length of the ridge being precipitous in the direction of friendly territory, the French troops were denied an easy line of retreat. Slowly increasing in numbers as it collected outposts, the citizen army had to keep falling back, its exposed tail under constant harassing fire. About 1,800 strong, it finally arrived at the locality of La Croix Faron, where there was sufficient flattish ground to make a stand. Without artillery, it formed up to meet Mulgrave's advance.

As the *conventionnels* peered into the gloom to the west they were apprehensive regarding activity to their left, where Elphinstone was launching a feint from Fort Faron with about 500 men.

Gravina's column, meanwhile, had advanced below the ridge line, on Mulgrave's right. Out of sight of the republicans to this point, it now appeared before them '*à portée de pistolet*' (at pistol range), their volleys raking the French ranks. Assailed seemingly from front and flank, the republicans broke in panic. Their only direction for retreat was to the north-east, down the steep, rocky slope. Only the lack of light prevented a massacre, for as Hood later remarked in his report to the Secretary of the Admiralty: 'What did not fall by the bullet or the bayonet broke their necks in tumbling headlong over the precipices in their flight.' Although enemy losses were exaggerated in British reports, the French admitted variously to suffering between 500 and 700 dead. Only seventy-five bodies were recovered from the summit. About sixty were made prisoner.

Allied casualties amounted to only eleven dead and about seventy wounded, the majority of whom were from the grenadiers, who had performed admirably. One injury, however, was to Gravina, shot in the leg as he led his men. He was wounded badly enough to remove him from active participation in the defence, where his energies, wise advice and ready cooperation were greatly missed. Day-to-day liaison with Mulgrave now devolved on Brigadier Izquierdo, whose very different nature immediately brought about a rift with the British commander, who retreated into aristocratic hauteur.

AS WITH MANY CAMPAIGNS, before or since, the siege of Toulon brought into near contact young officers still making their mark yet later to become famous. We have already encountered Captain Horatio Nelson of HMS *Agamemnon* who, because his admiral kept him occupied on detached duties, spent little time at Toulon and who, therefore, probably did not become a direct target for Captain Napoleone Buonaparte, the republicans' artillery specialist.

A closer encounter, however, occurred during the battle atop the Faron Ridge. The French republican centre column, which had initially surprised and seized the Pas de la Masque, had been led by Claude-Victor Perrin who, as the Duke of Belluno, would eventually be created one of Napoleon's trusted Marshals of the Empire. Among those leading the allied charge along the ridge on the later date was the Scot, Thomas Graham of Balgowan, who became colonel of his regiment, the 90th Foot and, eventually, General Graham, Baron Lynedoch, a greatly valued subordinate of Napoleon's nemesis, the Duke of Wellington.

BOTH HOOD AND MULGRAVE, in their reports of the action, praised the fighting qualities of the Neapolitans above those of the Sardinians and Piedmontese. The two leaders were also in unison with their adverse opinion of the Spanish, whose troops in general responded poorly to good leadership by their NCOs and some, at least, of their more senior ranks. Neither were the French proving as cooperative as had been hoped, many having unadvertized sympathies other than simply pro-royalist. Overall, weakness in the command structure of the allies and the varying reliability of their troops were making themselves felt.

During September, when Elphinstone was still consolidating the key position of La Malgue he found, as he complained to Hood, 'a Committee of Safety in it who meddled in all things, and was so oddly composed that I sent them all out'. He appealed to the admiral to send 'one or two respectable men who know the character of the national troops, they would be of use to furnish me with the necessary information respecting the description of soldiers I ought to admit into the garrison'.

Even once appointed as governor, Elphinstone's authority was on occasion ignored by the French. Two deserters from the Army of Italy had, for instance, arrived with their horses and had promptly been imprisoned by them. Elphinstone was furious, feeling that it would discourage further desertions. He protested that 'it is customary on such occasions to pay the deserter the value of his horse and accoutrements and to give him all the indulgence consistent with the general idea of prudence and safety'. An interesting sideline on the past customs of war.

On 30 September, the day before Victor's republicans had put to flight the Spanish garrison at the centre of the Faron Ridge, Elphinstone had written to Governor Goodall that undisciplined Spanish 'bandits' were causing trouble on 'Pharon' [sic] and had actually fired cannon at La Malgue. He went on that 'a Captain Dexter states that the men who work at the Pas de la Masque are spies'. Dexter wanted them changed, a view 'of which I approve much'. On this same date, Elphinstone also made a first and specific complaint against the sending of orders to forts 'under my government', a practice which they had to discontinue 'for it is impossible for the Commandant to obey them'.

A fortnight later, an obviously enraged Elphinstone was moved to complain directly to Rear Admiral Gravina, who was still hospitalized with his wound: he began,

> I am much surprised to hear from the Fort Major that Brigadier General Izquierdo came into the garrison where I was and, without taking any notice of me, ordered the troops of His Most Catholic Majesty under arms – he further addressed himself to the Fort Major saying that he was Commander-in-Chief of all the troops and that he had cause to complain of me for having given orders derogatory to the troops of Spain. In the first place, I am Governor of this place and the dependent Forts and am alone answerable for the orders given therein.

It seems that either Gravina had not made clear to what extent Izquierdo could act in his name or that Elphinstone refused to accept his authority (or, indeed, recognize his seniority), for he went on:

> [I]n the second place I am happy to inform your Excellency that I have never given any order but in common to the troops of all nations in the garrisons, and of which I am sure you will fully approve. I have been led to look up to your Excellency as Commander-in-Chief of the troops and I shall be very sorry to discover that I am wrong ...

Humility spent, Elphinstone's anger reasserted itself: 'If in future any officer in this garrison shall presume to complain – excepting in the regular manner – I shall be obliged to put them under arrest and request a Council of War on their conduct…'

French intelligence reports noted well the undercurrent of antipathy that existed between the British and the Spanish, at best reluctant allies. The Spanish complained, with some reason, at what the French described as '*la morgue britannique*', i.e. haughtiness, while between the two forces there persisted 'a continual mistrust'.

About 1,600 trained Frenchmen were formed into the battalions of the Royal Louis and Royal Provence regiments. The force included, and was complemented by, varying numbers of National Guard but, owing to deep and justified suspicions over the loyalties of many of them, these formations were, where possible, not employed in front-line duties.

On 5 October a further Neapolitan 74 arrived at Toulon, escorting transports with 2,000 more of their troops. Again, there was a cause for celebration although at lower levels of command confusion was evident. A major with the Spanish army wrote: 'One does not know who commands, for each pulls in his own direction.' More descriptively, a Neapolitan stated that 'between the English, Spanish, Swiss, Piedmontese, Neapolitans and French Royalists, all is in disorder, nothing concerted. If they don't soon send a military general to this place it will be impossible to recognize in all this [chaos] the hand of God.'

Municipally speaking, the celebrations attending the proclamation of the king, and the general readoption of the Bourbon flag, had greatly assisted the return to something like normality. The once all-powerful civic officers again went about their proper business, being restyled *commissaires municipaux* and wearing a white distinguishing sash.

'Thinking it better that they should be sunk or beat to pieces than my own', Hood had activated several frigates from the French squadron for use against Buonaparte's proliferating batteries. The French ships of the line remained generally inactive but a further contribution to normality occurred on 8 October when Rear Admiral Trogoff transferred his flag from the frigate that had worn it since the handover to the more appropriate 110-gun *Commerce de Marseille*.

IN THE REPUBLICAN CAMP all was not well. General Carteaux was furious at Lapoype's independent operations and even more so at their subsequent failure. He gave Lapoype's command to la Barre and denounced the former to the Committee of Public Safety. Matters deteriorated further, however, for Lapoype had retained the confidence of the three *représentants* attached to his army: these were able to defend him successfully through his previous record and, eventually, to have him reinstated.

Carteaux's anger stemmed mainly from the fact that, at the point of his initial success on Mont Faron, Lapoype had scribbled a hasty despatch (reputedly in pencil on the back of an *assignat* for ten livres), stating without qualification: '*Les troupes de la république viennent d'enlever la montagne de Faron, les retranchements et les rédoutes.*' ('The republican troops have just captured the Faron Ridge, its defences and its redoubts.') Carteaux delightedly informed his *représentants*, Saliceti and Gasparin who in turn rushed the good news directly to the Convention. It was immediately put into circulation in the official organ, the *Moniteur Universel,* with the added certainty that the success would lead to the subsequent reduction of the strategically important forts of Pomets and Faron. The communique (dated quirkily '*le 20me jour du 1er mois de l'an 2 de la république*') was signed by both *représentants*. By the time of its appearance, the success had already been bloodily reversed, and great was the collective embarrassment.

ENCOURAGED BY EVENTS, Mulgrave determined to take direct military action against the gun batteries that now continuously worried the fortifications that bore his name. To the south of La Seyne village, one was located at Quatre Moulins and two on elevated ground at Reynier.

On the night of 8/9 October, therefore, a powerful little force sortied from the fort. Commanded overall by the Irish Lieutenant Colonel Edward Nugent, it comprised 300 British troops, led by Captain Brereton, and about fifty each of Spanish, Neapolitans and Piedmontese. En route the column was joined by fifty British marines and a further fifty Piedmontese, all under Lieutenant Walter Serecold, Royal Navy.

The advance party was accompanied by royalist French, who hailed the battery sentinels. These, apparently easily deceived, were silently killed and the first battery taken at bayonet point. Hotly pursued, the survivors tried to go to ground in the neighbouring works but were flushed out and similarly dealt with.

Considerable numbers of Carteaux's troops were in the neighbourhood and these, helped by the difficult terrain, militated against the recovery of the enemy guns. All were therefore spiked, to a reported total of one 4-, one 6-, two 16- and three 24-pounders, together with several 13-inch mortars.

The raiders then deployed to resist any counter-attack as specialists used the batteries' own powder to destroy their emplacements and stores. Still unmolested, the column retired to Fort Mulgrave with about two dozen prisoners. A very successful night's work cost the allies four dead and seven wounded. French accounts again do not agree except to state that between twenty-five and sixty personnel were lost from a total garrison of about 300.

On 14 October the besieged of Toulon became aware of a general hullabaloo stemming from the republicans' positions and accompanied by a continuous discharge of weapons. At Fort Malbousquet the defenders were convinced that an all-out assault was imminent and, on Mulgrave's order, an offensive patrol was sent out. In crossing the flat land between the little rivers Neuve and Las, the patrol, under Captain Wemyss, was attacked by French sallying quickly from the high ground of Les Arènes. Accounts again vary, but the situation was apparently saved by the timely arrival of fifty Piedmontese *chasseurs*. All were then compelled to retire smartly on Malbousquet as larger numbers of *conventionnels* issued from the neighbouring height of Les Français. The final phase of the withdrawal had, in turn, to be supported by the deployment of even more of the fort's garrison.

What could have developed into a pitched battle on terrain unfavourable to the allies was, with difficulty, restricted to no more than a hot skirmish. As a first military success for his troops, however, Carteaux over-stated its significance. Mulgrave's report blamed it on 'the affectionate Emulation [i.e. rivalry] of the British and Piedmontese'.

The reason for all the initial jubilation had been the news of the fall of the royalist stronghold of Lyon following another protracted siege. An inland city, Lyon's only hope had lain in a relief column that never materialized. Toulon had its back to the sea and, at least for the moment, could be fully supported by the allied fleets, and there appeared no cause for alarm.

Success at Lyon, however, gave the republicans a great boost in morale and, more materially, released considerable numbers of seasoned fighting troops to strengthen further the grip on Toulon. The republicans were also faring well in Piedmont, so any further reinforcement from this source for the Toulon garrison was unlikely.

General Carteaux's success encouraged Lapoype to make an effort against the Cap Brun position. This strongpoint, which was the object of considerable allied effort would, when completed, accommodate a battery that could command much of the Grande Rade. Its garrison would also be able to assist in any defence of Fort la Malgue. As they were separated by a long cannon shot, however, General Lapoype considered that, in its unfinished state, the position could be seized before decisive assistance could arrive from La Malgue.

Thus, at first light on 15 October, 2,000 republicans successfully surprised about 250 men of the French Royal Louis regiment who garrisoned the works. The unit was formed mainly from various line regiments that had acted as marine detachments aboard the ships of Trogoff's squadron. They were seasoned regulars and strongly resisted their undisciplined attackers. Numbers inevitably told, none the less, and, overwhelmed, the defenders were driven to retreat, leaving about fifty dead. A small column sent from La Malgue ensured the survival of the remainder but Lapoype's men were now apparently firmly installed on Cap Brun.

Mulgrave had other ideas: his forces at La Malgue were powerful, and he reacted quickly and in strength. The weakness of the enemy at Cap Brun was that they were located far in advance of their established lines. In addition, their line of retreat, along the road through La Garde, was flanked by the high ground of Thouar.

An allied column was directed straight at Cap Brun, therefore, while others departed Toulon for Thouar and the village of La Vallette. The latter location, at the foot of the eastern end of the Faron Ridge, was something of a republican stronghold.

Bearing in mind that the latter columns had farther to travel, the movements were poorly coordinated for maximum effect. The news of that marching from La Malgue was sufficient to put the republicans at Cap Brun to flight, and their retreat took them past Thouar long before it was occupied by an advancing Spanish force. Although the Cap Brun position had been regained, therefore, its late conquerors successfully eluded the trap that should have closed on them. The thrust at La Vallette also led to a precipitate withdrawal on the part of its garrison. For the allies, this settlement was too exposed to be held and, having left their mark, they pulled back.

Mulgrave was later emboldened to make a further punishment raid, however. A Neapolitan battery was, therefore, sited temporarily atop the Thouar heights and, using the distant outwork of Sainte-Marguerite as an anchor on its left, covered a large patrol which cleared the village of La Garde. This, abandoned and slighted, was also then left for the enemy to reoccupy at leisure.

With Cap Brun recovered, the allied command had good reason to feel confident, based on its success to date. The enemy, although everywhere superior in numbers, appeared to be unable to cope with the cool discipline of regular troops. Mulgrave, none the less, raged to Hood about this 'unfortunate skirmish [which] has cost us three most valuable officers'. Politically, it was always necessary to give equal opportunity to British and Spanish, and he referred to 'the unfortunate circumstances of the Spanish having the turn of being upon the right [and] by the sloth of their movements prevent[ing] our occupation of both [Thouar and La Garde]'. He concluded: 'I much fear till we have absolute command in English hands, and good troops entirely at British disposal, that no real good effects can be produced by efforts of sortie.'

Lord Mulgrave, unfortunately, had inadvertently done great damage with his earlier and over-optimistic reports to the British government. Desperate to find troops for at least four major hotspots, ministers looked carefully at the forces allocated to Admiral Hood and decided that, as all was apparently still progressing so well, he could actually be robbed of some of his strength. This was at a time when the existing dearth of British line troops in Toulon was causing major problems in the organization of an effective defence. It also coincided with something of a silent power struggle between the British and the Spanish. This came about because, at any particular time, a considerable proportion of Hood's naval strength was absent on detached duties. Not so affected, Admiral Langara could keep his fleet concentrated at Toulon, invariably outnumbering the British.

Hood's first setback had resulted from his request for reinforcement from Gibraltar. With Spain currently an ally, this stronghold was in no way under threat yet, because the British government directed him to spare Hood 'as many troops as possible', the aged governor, Sir Robert Boyd, cautiously despatched 750, just half of what Hood had requested and including few of the much-needed artillery specialists. This contingent would arrive, together with General O'Hara, on 27 October.

Their arrival came as little relief to the now-weary Hood who, just the day previously, had received a despatch from the Admiralty. In a lesser man this would have induced despair, for it was an order that Rear Admiral Gell and his squadron were to embark the men of the 30th Regiment, transport them to (of all places) Gibraltar, whence they would be shipped to the West Indies. The move had been precipitated by an approach to the British government from royalist administrations in the French islands, also proposing to defect. Once again, Pitt's men sought to rob Peter in order to pay Paul.

With the extremely slow communications of the day, Hood and Mulgrave could only write of their dismay at the directive and, belatedly, attempt to paint a less rosy picture of the situation at Toulon. 'There are not two hundred British troops in the town', wrote Mulgrave, 'Officers' Servants and Musicians included.' Fortunately, it was possible to delay the move inasmuch as the Admiralty had specified the use of Gell's squadron, obviously overlooking that it was absent on its mission to Genoa.

In the meantime, Hood 'humbly' appraised Their Lordships of the fact that there were already 'upwards of a thousand Seamen doing duty on Shore'. Including these, three-quarters of all British personnel were manning outposts 'which would be in great danger ... were they with drawn'. Rather boldly, he went on to inform Dundas that Gell's squadron would sail for Gibraltar 'without a Soldier or Marine' unless General O'Hara consented.

WITH THE ONSET of autumn came the Mediterranean rainy season, making life miserable for besiegers and besieged alike. Mulgrave complained to Hood that isolated garrisons were being poorly provisioned: Malbousquet had received nothing for two days while outposts on the Faron Ridge, being supplied from the town, enjoyed meat that was 'stinking' and bread 'full of maggots'. Hood noted widespread dissatisfaction among the troops and stated that, if things did not improve, he feared 'very considerable desertion'.

With the republicans having cut off much of the water flow to Toulon's flour mills, the admiral 'was obliged to send to every port in the Italian and other States for provisions, as the town … has no flour and but a few days' biscuits'. The sad fact was that, while the least useful personnel remained in the town, comparatively well-provisioned and billeted, the best were manning the exposed perimeter works, where their health was deteriorating and the sick lists lengthening by the day.

Major Generals O'Hara and Dundas* arrived on the same day, the first from Gibraltar, the other from Genoa.

Charles O'Hara, much to Hood's dismay, came as a replacement for Lord Mulgrave. Being the senior and also a Spanish speaker, he had been given a specific commission as 'Governor of Toulon and its Dependencies, and Commander of the Combined Forces'. This was in accordance with the continuing power struggle with the Spanish.

On 23 October Hood was informed by Admiral Langara that the Spanish king had been pleased to promote Gravina

> to the rank of Lieutenant General of his fleet and to confirm him in the general command of the allied forces in the possession of which he has been, by the agreement between your Excellency and me. And by the same royal order, Major General Raphael Valdés is to remain with the command of the Spanish troops.

Hood responded on the following day, diplomatic phraseology masking much of his exasperation:

> No one can more sincerely rejoice than myself at my much esteemed friend's promotion, but His Sardinian and Sicilian Majesty [sic] having been graciously pleased to confide their respective troops entirely to my disposal, or to act under such British officer as I may judge fit to put them, I am very much at a loss to conceive upon what ground admiral Gravina can take upon him the title of commander-in-chief of the combined forces at Toulon … [I] feel it my duty to put the Sardinian and Sicilian troops, together with the British, under the command of major general O'Hara, the moment he arrives.

---

* General David Dundas should not be confused with the minister, Henry Dundas, to whom he was distantly related.

More such genteel verbal swordplay failed to resolve the situation, which the Spanish worsened with a note from their ambassador in London to Lord Grenville. The latter replied through Lord St Helens, the British ambassador in Madrid. His note pointed out that Toulon had, in the first instance, been surrendered to the British alone, 'the Spanish admiral having expressly declined to concur in the original enterprise'. It followed that joint military government in the unique circumstances of Toulon 'would inevitably endanger the possession of the place itself'. Military government could be vested only in that power to whom the surrender had been made and which, subsequently, had mustered the greater force and incurred the greater expense. Finally, it stated that the Sardinian and Sicilian troops had been entrusted by their respective rulers to officers of King George III and that this monarch was not empowered to place them at the disposal of a further party.

Such diplomatic wrangling would have rumbled on interminably had not events on the ground progressed such as to relegate it to a side issue. At local level, however, it resulted in some quite unpleasant incidents. Hood's fleet, for instance, had been so reduced by detached commitments that its strength at Toulon was barely half that of the Spanish. Langara decided to resort to crude intimidation. Having three first rates at his disposal (his own and two divisional flagships), he placed his own close aboard, and parallel to, Hood's *Victory*, the others on her bow and stern quarters. Allowing the *Victory* barely space to swing at her anchor, Langara conveyed the clear message to the old enemy that he could blow him out of the water at will. The British admiral was, however, no hothead and, with enviable *sang froid*, ignored the Spanish until they eventually tired of it and again shifted berth.

One vitally important and unresolved question was what Admiral Hood intended to do with the French Toulon squadron should the defences of the town suddenly crumble, allowing the enemy to break in. As already noted, a small number of ships had been permitted to be armed and manned by royalist seamen under Rear Admiral Trogoff. A few non-line ships had also been given British crews to undertake local tasking. The remainder, and the bulk of the French strength, lay in the inner harbour and the basins without armament or crew and, in many cases, without masts.

Hood, of course, had every honourable intention to hold the squadron, its arsenal and infrastructure in trust for eventual return to a France ruled by

Louis XVII. But, beset as his defenders were, and with the knowledge that General Kellermann was marching south with the army that had just taken and punished Lyon, he must surely have entertained some reservations with regard to his mission's eventual outcome. It is far from clear, however, exactly what contingency plan, if any, he had in mind in the face of sudden collapse.

This was not the case with the Spanish. During October their foreign minister informed both Lord St Helens and Admiral Langara of the action that should be taken.

> As the case, tho' remote, may possibly occur in which the Spanish and English squadrons may be obliged to abandon the anchorage of Toulon ... His Majesty's pleasure ... has been signified to Admiral Langara ... to settle and resolve, in concert with Lord Hood, whatever may, according to the existing circumstances, be found most advisable.

In the meantime, however, '[it] is enjoined to him ... to have all French ships ...which are fit for navigation, armed and brought into the road, in order to put to sea, when necessary.' They would be manned by the minimum necessary complement of Spanish and British seamen commanded, as in garrisons ashore, by an officer from the predominant nationality. In emergency, their crews would be brought up to strength by the addition of loyal French seamen and if

> the unexpected event of abandoning the port should occur, Admiral Langara should sail, with all the French ships that can be put to sea, to the islands of Hieres [i.e. Hyères], or whatever other place he may appoint in concert with Lord Hood ... carrying in them all artillery, ammunition, arms and stores which they can bring.

A full inventory and notification of the place of refuge would be delivered 'at a proper opportunity, to their lawful sovereign'.

Those French ships that were unfit for sea should, it was proposed, be used as floating batteries for the defence of the port, 'stationing those of the combined squadron where they cannot be damaged'. In the event of the port's enforced abandonment, all vessels that could not be removed would be scuttled or burned to deny them to the enemy, '*for which purpose, preparations shall be made before hand*' [author's italics].

The document concluded with the instruction that, if abandoned, all fortifications should be destroyed and all artillery spiked, 'particularly in all batteries that command the port'. Admiral Langara was charged to communicate all this to Lord Hood 'in order that they may proceed in concert in this business which the two Monarchs have taken under their joint care and direction'.

Although the Spanish proposals were prudent, unequivocal and suggestive of a degree of urgency, Hood's priorities appeared to lie elsewhere. Whether it was through over-confidence, or a simmering hostility and lack of trust between the two admirals, or Hood's over-developed sense of honour and his wishing not to cause the Toulonnais concern about ulterior motives, no action appears to have been taken.

That this was the case was evident a month later when Lord Mulgrave had returned to London and reported to Henry Dundas. His opinion regarding the ability of the garrison to withstand a real assault was obviously not what the minister had either expected or wanted to hear. On 23 November he wrote to Hood from London:

> ... I am sure I need scarcely remind Y. Lp. of the propriety (in case of any disaster happening) of having the French ships captured at Toulon so situated that if you was obliged to abandon the place, none of the ships or arsenals ... should be permitted to fall into the hands of the enemy ...the ships [should be] burnt if they cannot be carried with you. I hope they may be brought away, and in such circumstances ...this would be perfectly justifiable under the nicest and strictest interpretation of the terms of the agreement entered into by Y. Lp. with the people of Toulon.

With letters often taking a month and more between despatch and delivery, there is every possibility that Admiral Hood never received the above reminder in time for it to be acted upon. Unfortunately, neither could he have seen that sent from the Admiralty on 20 December. Marked 'secret', it took the earlier Spanish proposals as its starting point and clearly instructed Hood on the extent to which he should comply with them.

IN ORDER TO PRESERVE equality of rank, the British government was obliged to promote Charles O'Hara to lieutenant general, as which he arrived at Toulon. Of the Irish aristocracy, he had already accumulated over forty years experience in the army, which he had joined at the age of just 12. A brigadier during the American War of Independence, he was captured with Cornwallis's capitulation at Yorktown, but returned to Britain on exchange. He became colonel of the 22nd Foot but, commonly for the time, his financial affairs were in such a disastrous state that he was obliged to live abroad to escape his creditors. Despite this, his cultivation of influential friends, including Horace Walpole, saw him reinstated in society and his being made governor of Gibraltar in 1792.

O'Hara's manner with his peers was liable to be short and bad-tempered, but he was personally courageous, looked every inch the soldier and was very popular with his troops, to whom he was known as the 'Old Cock of the Rock'. In Toulon, his demeanour and appearance brooked absolutely no nonsense from the Spanish.

A final significant detachment of Neapolitans, over 1,500 of them, arrived at Toulon at the end of October. With so many sympathisers in the allied camp, the republicans' intelligence was consistently updated. The following, accurate, appreciation of allied dispositions was produced at the end of October:

ETAT DES FORCES DES ALLIÉS EN ARTILLERIE ET EN HOMMES

A la rédoute anglaise appellée le Petit-Gibraltar, vingt-six pièces de canon et trois mortiers	1,000
Aux deux camps attendant	600
Bivouacs aux deux postes	200
Autres rédoutes visant le Petit Gibraltar, six pièces de canon	250
A la gorge des Sablettes, six pièces de canon	500
Au Lazaret	100
Au Fort Saint-Louis	200
A la Grosse-Tour	200
Au Cap Brun, quatre canons et deux mortiers	600
Entre la redoute du Cap Brun et le Fort Lamalgue, un camp de	1,500

A reporter ci-contre	*5,150*
Report	*5,150 hommes*

Au Fort Lamalgue	2,000
A la hauteur de l'Eigoutier, un camp de	500
A la rédoute de Sainte-Catherine	500
Au Fort d'Artigues	200
Au Fort Faron	300
A la rédoute de Faron	200
A Malbousquet, seize canons, deux mortiers, deux obusiers, etc	800
Au Petit Saint-Antoine, six canons	200
Au Grand Saint-Antoine, un mortier, sept canons	300
Au Petit Saint-André, deux canons	100
Au Fort des Pomets	200
Total de la force en hommes	10,450
Dans la ville	5,000
Outre les forces ci-dessus énoncées les alliés faisoient débarquer journellement de leurs vaisseaux environ	4,000
Total hommes	19,450

References to 'Petit-Gibraltar' were to Fort Mulgrave; 'Gorges des Sablettes' to the isthmus of the Saint-Mandrier peninsula. The western end of the inner roads remained occupied by the republicans, whose increasing number of batteries and attached camps isolated allied strongpoints, which were still accessible only by water.

Interestingly, the above listing credits Fort Malbousquet with two *obusiers,* or shell guns. Although the techniques of firing explosive-filled balls near-horizontally (as opposed to the high-trajectory 'bombs' lobbed by mortars) had been a matter of experiment with both the British and the French for a decade or more, such weapons were still very much experimental.

The French estimate of allied strength is very close to the true figure of 16,900 troops on the muster rolls at the end of October, bearing in mind that the final figure in the above table represents the number of seamen estimated to be put ashore on a daily basis. While this boosted available field strength, it very much depleted the complements of the ships. Hood lamented that third rates (i.e. 74s) were proceeding to sea up to 200 men below establishment. What with the adverse autumn weather and the generally poor standards of hygiene and medical care the allies, at this stage, could muster no more than 12,000 fit men at any one time.

Admiral Hood greatly missed the positive attitude of Lord Mulgrave, as General O'Hara made no secret of what he thought of this new posting. He did, however, firmly admonish Governor Boyd at Gibraltar by letter on 1 November: 'Tried Veteran Troops we wanted, one Regiment of such would have been infinitely more Valuable than six times the number of what we have got ...' Although the overall total defending Toulon he described as 'respectable', he added, pithily, that they were 'unreliable'.

Hood was able to report at the same time to Henry Dundas that, despite the difficulties due to Spanish *amour propre*, General O'Hara had established a rapport with the ever-reliable Admiral Gravina, who was recovering well. Hood's resolute confidence contrasted with O'Hara's gloom.

In a comprehensive assessment of the situation, the new governor highlighted the major weaknesses of the allied defence. Firstly, he was concerned at the length of the perimeter required to defend both the town and the anchorages, a perimeter which, even then, did not prevent the enemy siege batteries from being a real and persistent nuisance. Secondly, for want of qualified engineers, allied outposts were often poorly located, designed and constructed. Up to 7,000 men were continuously engaged in manning them, and the bleakness of their situation contributed much to fatigue and sickness. Thirdly, the vital Allied positions at 'Cepet' (i.e. the Saint-Mandrier peninsula) could be supported only by water which, O'Hara considered, might be impossible 'through a rigorous winter'.

The general's conclusion, fully supported by Major General Dundas, was that only through dislodging the republicans from the surrounding territory could Toulon's security be preserved. He pointed out, however, that the nature of the terrain ('mountainous, laid out into terraces, covered with timber, intersected by deep, rocky ravines and offering no roads for artillery'), afforded the enemy the greater advantage. What, simply, was required by the allies was 'an army in the field, amply prepared for that service and necessarily covering a very considerable district of country'.

He also commented on the reality of the situation where 'the quality and discipline of the greatest part of our present numbers give no very encouraging prospects in any attempts we may make'. With the ever-continuing expectation of the arrival of 5,000 Austrians and further

Sardinians to a total of over 10,000, O'Hara recommended delaying any assumption of the offensive, particularly as, with the exception of the Neapolitans and 'a few of the British', none of the various units was equipped for field operations in deep winter.

Hood's latest despatches (28–31 October) were brought to London by the returning Mulgrave. The admiral reported that 'Gen. O'Hara has just been with me and alarmed me much ... and what is very unpleasant is the conduct of the Spaniards, who are striving for power here'. Then later: 'Our situation here ... from what Gen. O'Hara has reported to me is not a very pleasant one; but yet I do not despair of overcoming every difficulty.'

In the face of such pessimism from a competent military commander, one can only wonder at the continuing resilience of Admiral Hood who, not a young man, was also faced with dealing diplomatically with a number of senior officers of allied contingents who could prove every bit as sensitive as the Spanish.

Causing current problems was Marshal Forteguerri, who commanded the second tranche of Neapolitans. Described as 'proud and susceptible', yet never having seen action, the marshal appeared to have received instructions at variance with those agreed between the two sovereigns, i.e. that he and his force were fully at British disposal.

Obviously near the end of his patience, Hood railed about Forteguerri in a letter to Sir William Hamilton, the British ambassador at Naples.

> He is undoubtedly the proudest, most empty and self-sufficient man I ever had anything to do with, and totally ignorant of the rudiments of Service ... If the King of Naples intended, ... by sending his Fleet ... to the good of the common Cause [it is] entrusted to me and not to gratify the pride and vanity of Commodore Fortiguerri [sic] (who is fond of having as many Neapolitan Flags daily to look at as he can).

By the end of October, Toulon had been in allied hands for two months. In Paris, the Committee of Public Safety was growing impatient that, like Avignon, Marseille and Lyon, the town should be recovered and suitably punished. If Carteaux's slow progress was irritating, adverse reports regarding his military skills were disturbing. Buonaparte, whose plans he only grudgingly supported, was most vocal in his criticism, openly informing Gasparin, one of the army's *représentants en mission*, that he would no longer serve under an officer to whom he referred as 'the old painter', a man who did not possess 'the least notions of the military art'.

The brash young *parvenu* was speaking from a favoured situation, for his obvious expertise and powers of personal leadership had already been rewarded by promotion to *chef de bataillon,* or major. His clear view as to the way ahead would also soon result in his being given the staff rank of *adjudant-général,* the equivalent of lieutenant colonel and divisional chief-of-staff.

The committee continued by ordering Carteaux to move to the command of the Army of Italy. This order he ignored, keeping his replacement waiting until 21 October, when a formal directive arrived in language that brooked no further intransigence. Despite this, he still contrived to delay his departure until 7 November, a level of defiance which, in a location less remote from the capital, might well have proved fatal.

In Carteaux's place was the elderly General Doppet who, with the Army of the Alps, had recently assisted in taking Lyon but, it was said, 'without really knowing how'. Until comparatively recently he had been a physician, enjoying rapid elevation mainly because of his extreme Jacobin beliefs.

Arriving soon afterward, and giving a great boost to Buonaparte, was baron du Teil, a career artilleryman, who had instructed the former at the military academy at Auxonne. His health now having greatly deteriorated, du Teil gave his protégé a very free hand and, by his very acquiescence to each proposal, added greatly to Buonaparte's stature.

THE TAIL-END of Carteaux's stewardship was marked by little more activity than offensive patrolling. Indeed, by the time Doppet formally took over, there had passed nearly a month with no more than the ceaseless annoyance of allied ships and strongpoints by Buonaparte's batteries.

Obviously given a firm brief for decisive action, Doppet moved quickly. At 6 a.m. on 15 November, Fort Malbousquet found itself under attack. It proved to be a feint. An offensive reconnaissance was then mounted against Fort Mulgrave, withdrawing after an exchange of fire. During the afternoon the allies were further lightly tested by minor probes against the widely spaced objectives of Fort Pomets, Fort Saint-Antoine and the battery at Cap Brun. Only when the winter afternoon was well advanced did the true objective emerge.

A second sharp thrust against the Fort Mulgrave outposts was sufficient to make their Spanish defenders fall back, reportedly firing their weapons into the air. A follow-up wave, more powerful, then passed through the gap, closely followed by a third. The whole defence was mobilized, for this was a serious attempt to seize the western promontory.

General O'Hara happened to be aboard the *Victory*, conferring with Hood and awaiting the arrival of Sir Gilbert Elliot. Hearing the commotion, he had himself hastily transferred ashore. His eventual arrival at the fort rallied a dour defence and, supported by flanking fire from a frigate and *chaloupes canonnières* (as the French termed the gunboats), the garrison went onto the offensive. This was something of a bluff for, according to French accounts, between 3,000 and 4,000 republicans were involved and, in three columns, had advanced almost to the allied ramparts.

Supported by a heavy barrage from the fort's artillery, the Royals charged and broke the enemy centre, though losing their senior officer, Captain Duncan Campbell. Doppet's nerve failed him, reportedly when a trusted aide at his side was decapitated by a ball. The retreat was sounded.

Though brief, the confrontation had been bloody. Differing estimates put the allied casualties at between sixty and ninety, including Lieutenant Lemoine of the Royal Artillery, one of the few invaluable specialists. The French speak of 500 to 600 republican casualties, although most are listed as 'lost in action' which in most cases meant that they had simply deserted to return to their farms.

The capture of Fort Mulgrave was central to Buonaparte's overall plan and, disappointed at Doppet's failure, he complained loudly. Over the head of his superior, du Teil, he wrote directly to the Committee of Public Safety, alleging that Doppet's staff were not facilitating his urgent demands for artillery, of which he knew there to be an abundance at Marseille. Separately, he contacted the Convention's war minister to present an exact list of what he required if, as he intended, the artillery was to perform the lion's share of defeating the allies. Infantry, he expected, would be required only to complete the task.

Scarcely, then, had General Doppet assumed command than a single failure saw his removal, at last in favour of a career soldier. General Jacques Coquille, known as Dugommier, had seen over forty years of campaigning, although he had now been moved from his appointment as the Windward Islands representative of the Legislative Assembly. Of proven ability, he was personally courageous and well respected by his troops. Appreciating that, in Buonaparte, he had an unusually competent, if forthright, artillery specialist, Dugommier allowed him complete freedom in his area.

Republican reinforcements continued to flood in, to an eventual total of about 35,000 effectives. As the 'big push' could only be a matter of time, the prospects for the defenders of Toulon looked bleak.

WITH SO MANY of their crews ashore, Hood's ships remained dangerously undermanned. The admiral therefore took the unusual course of approaching the Grand Master of the Knights of St John in a nominally still independent Malta for the hire of a thousand or so trained seamen. Their purpose was to assist in sailing his ships, not fighting them. Having agreed to pay the Maltese the same rates as British sailors, a much-relieved Hood could report that 'His Eminence immediately and in the handsomest manner [consented]'.

On 10 November Hood despatched the *Captain* 74 but, although she returned with 400, no further volunteers were forthcoming, despite Hood's sending down three further ships that he could ill spare. This was just the latest in the series of disappointments that marked the progress of this ill-starred affair.

AS A SHARP REMINDER of the nature of those with whom they were dealing, the allies belatedly learned of the execution of the late king's consort, Marie Antoinette, an event which had occurred on 16 October. Sir William Hamilton wrote to Hood on 8 November, describing how the court at Naples had declared four months of official mourning and expressing anxiety for the continuing survival of the young Louis XVII. Genuinely shocked, Hood expressed his 'real and unfeigned Grief'. Declaring his contempt for the 'truly Diabolical Wretches [that] these Conventional Jacobins are', he ordered his own officers into three weeks of mourning.

chapter seven

Confrontation and Evacuation, November–December 1793

IN ADDITION TO HIS responsibilities as commander-in-chief, Mediterranean, Admiral Hood shouldered those involved with the overall administrative and military aspects of running and safeguarding Toulon. Each day he was faced with complexities and complaints from the courts or senior military personnel of the allied states. Everything, none the less, was handled with promptitude and rare good humour, but it was plainly overwhelming him.

London, therefore, decided to spread the burden by the appointment of a senior administrator to oversee municipal affairs. The choice fell upon Sir Gilbert Elliot, who duly arrived on 19 November, via Genoa, bearing instructions that he, Hood and O'Hara had been designated royal commissioners for 'Toulon and its dependencies'. Elliot's assumption of duty also released Rear Admiral Goodall for more appropriate employment.

Elliot was not pleased at what he encountered. Having come from a Whitehall resonant with optimism at the possibilities of so great an opportunity, he found that the general tenor of despatches sent by Hood and Mulgrave had greatly understated the problems. He now discovered a Hood depressed by the flow of adverse reports from O'Hara, whose nature was the very antithesis of Mulgrave's. Elliot noted that, even allowing for considerable causes for despondency, he had never met a man 'half so nervous or half so blind to every side but the black one [while] Lord Hood … is perhaps over-confident, and will never admit the slightest doubt of keeping the place'.

The British government's policy was now to formalize the situation, both with respect to the governance of the Toulonnais and to relationships with the allies. A firm grip on the town was seen to be the best way of maximizing its possible value as a bargaining chip at the eventual peace table, a means of obliging a future French administration to indemnify the British both for declaring war on them and for causing the considerable expense of resulting hostilities.

A further and substantial complication had arisen in the person of Lewis Stanislaus Xavier, comte de Provence who, in the previous January and on the execution of the king, had made a proclamation that the dauphin, Louis-Charles, was now, as Louis XVII, the rightful king of France and Navarre. By French law he, as uncle of the new king, then but 7 years of age, would 'in consequence of our obligations and duties so to do, take upon ourselves the said charge of regent' during the minority of the king.

As an apparently secure enclave within strife-ridden France, Toulon was considered by the regent a suitable launch pad for a revived monarchy. The proposal aroused great enthusiasm among the Toulon *sections,* but the British were suspicious that much of their optimism was based on behind-the-scenes Spanish support.

London was resolutely opposed to the comte's coming to Toulon, anticipating complications in administration and in the conduct of the defence. Worse, he would almost certainly attract a hard core of senior French *émigrés*, whose presence was plainly undesirable. The new constitution of 1791 was thus conveniently invoked to claim that the comte's right to declare himself regent was invalid and, therefore, not recognized. A second, and suddenly useful, point was in the wording of Hood's original declaration, which had included the unequivocal statement that he was holding Toulon 'in trust only for Louis XVII'.

In case the new commissioners failed to get the point, it was underlined in a letter from Grenville:

> The measures which ... have been taken for conveying to the Comte de Provence His Majesty's sentiments in respect to his going to Toulon will, His Majesty trusts, prevent his proceeding thither ... The consideration which is due to the rank and situation of the Comte will naturally induce you to communicate this determination in terms of proper civility and respect ... [but neither] acknowledge any authority he may attempt to exercise ... nor admit him, under the present circumstances, to come within the town or forts of Toulon.

A potentially ticklish situation did, in fact, resolve itself as the comte travelled leisurely from the place of his enforced Westphalian exile to Genoa. So leisurely that events at Toulon overtook him.

A further problem which troubled the British commissioners was the actual extent of collusion that existed between the Spanish defenders and the republican besiegers. At the highest levels, of course, the Spanish were dedicated to supporting a pact between members of the royal Bourbon families. On the basis that 'their enemies are our friends', the Spanish had thus become reluctant allies of the British. With almost the singular exception of Admiral Gravina, however, the alliance was here observed with bad grace. The British, being very much in the minority at Toulon, were obliged to woo Spanish cooperation. For their part, the Spanish were in a position to parade attitudes conditioned by centuries of intermittent hostilities. Officers would do their duty, but invariably in a manner that illustrated the maximum contempt for those who, although outnumbered by more than three to one by the Spanish alone, still contrived to exercise overall command. At the level of the average foot soldier it was a case of cultural similarity. The Spaniard had much in common with his French Revolutionary counterpart but very little with the British 'squaddie' fighting at his shoulder.

The *représentants en mission* with the French armies had little difficulty in passing their agents in and out of the allied perimeter for, in appearance and language, a Toulonnais Revolutionary was interchangeable with a Toulonnais royalist. Not only did agents make known every allied move to Fréron and his colleagues but they were active also in subversion. Spanish troops themselves were not far removed from the soil and their people suffered much the same inequalities as did the French. Revolutionary ideals were in the air all over Europe and were highly contagious, ordinary working folk being the most susceptible to their blandishments.

Years of battle against them had taught the British that the Spanish were, militarily, as able as any. Yet here, on the Toulon perimeter, were occurring too many instances of Spanish units pulling out of a confrontation following a token resistance. At the outset it was of little consequence for, as Sir Gilbert Elliot observed on his arrival, there were 'little battles and the music of cannonades and musketry all round ... as these Battles are pretty bloodless, one may look at them as fire-works'. As republican strength and resolve grew, however, this assessment changed, the popular opinion growing that smaller

British units would, in real adversity, be abandoned to their fate by the Spanish. The actual incidence of such behaviour cannot be quantified: it might have been very low, but it engendered a deep feeling of distrust.

The rapid build up in the strength of the besiegers following the fall of Lyon brought its own problems. Over 30,000 (and still increasing) troops were billeted in the same miserable conditions as those within the perimeter. Even under normal circumstances the region's poor communications would have been strained to provide for such a number but, now that allied ships were blockading the coast, shipments of grain were sparse and even more was demanded of the inadequate road and transport system. Discontent was rife.

Republican reinforcements, none the less, continued to pour in from all points. Seven battalions from Lyon were followed by no less than seventeen from the Army of the Alps, its operations being scaled down with the approach of winter. Two thousand men arrived from the Lozère, 4,000 more from Toulouse. From that same region in the south-west there then came a further 6,000. General Lapoype's Army of Italy reported a very precise 12,347 along the eastern and northern sides of the perimeter.

In some desperation, the *représentants* appealed to the Committee of Public Safety for the means to support this multitude. The committee, in turn, invited the Army of the Pyrenees to share its provisions. Its commissars responded that, far from being able to assist, they would be faced with revolt should *their* rations be further reduced. This refusal reached the committee at the same time as a letter, reputedly from Barras and Fréron at Toulon. It contained the surprising proposal that current operations against the town be suspended and that the besieging forces be allowed to fall back beyond the line of the Durance, wintering in the Vaucluse, a more fertile area where it would be the easier to quarter and supply them. This implied a retreat of over 40 miles and no further direct action until the spring.

What happened next is not too certain but, although the letter was later verified by Buonaparte himself, the two *représentants* apparently disassociated themselves from it, attributing it to counter-revolutionaries or, naturally, to the British. The provenance was, none the less, vigorously debated by the Convention, which concluded that the phraseology had an English 'feel' to it and that the document was, indeed, a forgery. Operations continued.

On 17 November the Committee of Public Safety issued the interesting order that *boulets incendaires* of a large calibre should be prepared for use aboard a considerable number of *tartanes*. These were single-masted lateen-rigged Mediterranean traders of no great size which could, at most, be armed with one or two cannon. As it would appear impracticable to heat solid balls to red heat aboard such small craft, it is probable that the *boulets incendaires* were explosive-filled, hollow shot (known as 'bombs' to the British) and that their associated cannon would actually be mortars.

The project was to prove surprisingly effective for, although the resulting flotilla failed in its objective '*pour bloquer Toulon et brûler la flotte ennemie*' ('besiege Toulon and burn the enemy fleet'), it certainly proved a nuisance in its ability to employ innocent-looking craft to appear intermittently to lob missiles into the sprawling works of Fort Mulgrave.

With communications by land being so uncertain, most of the powder and ammunition for Buonaparte's endlessly energetic batteries came by sea. It may be assumed that the offshore waters in these times were alive with fishermen and small traders, for the Royal Navy's patrols admitted to being unable to intercept all of what were described as the enemy's 'polaccas and luggers'. Small craft such as these were also of considerable service to the allies, near a dozen being converted in the Toulon arsenal and, described variously as armed zebeque (xebec), schooner, tartan or galley, used for patrols or 'special duties'.

One larger ship, the 32-gun frigate *Lutine* (eventually wrecked in the North Sea and whose bell hangs to this day in Lloyds of London), was converted to a bomb vessel whose high-trajectory missiles could be used for indirect fire against Buonaparte's masked batteries. Such acquired vessels, sailing under their original names, made excellent first commands for enterprising lieutenants, of which the fleet was not short.

The duelling between allied warships and enemy batteries continued every day, the rumble of their gunnery being the distant background to events elsewhere. Unable to put parties ashore on this heavily protected coastline, the ships could only hope to keep the batteries suppressed. Even if one were silenced, it was only temporarily, for a gun could be destroyed only by a direct hit, broken carriages could be repaired or improvised and smashed earthworks rebuilt.

As the necklace of batteries closed ever more tightly around Fort

Mulgrave, the need for counter-battery fire became more urgent. The *Princess Royal*'s log shows her to have been allocated to this duty more often than most, it becoming almost a daily routine. From entries taken at random:

October 13th … At 8.30am began our fire on the enemy as before and continued at intervals all day … [The French fired] both shot and shell … One of the shells struck the ship just below the water line, but did no mischief. Many others fell near us all round. Some of the running rigging was cut by shot.'

[The bombardment continued for nine hours on this date.]

October 15th … Received a large shot just abaft the larboard cathead.

October 19th … 5.30pm. Enemy began their fire at us with shot and shell [it] being a very fine moonlight evening. Immediately returned their fire from our lower deck guns till 7 when we ceased firing; the enemy continued throwing shells … one broke nearly over our heads but did no mischief. The Spanish bomb vessel throwing shells at the Battery till nearly 11 o'clock.

October 23rd … [One] of the lower deck guns burst, four men killed, two lieutenants and 29 men wounded, many of them very badly.

October 26th … Received several of the enemy's shot, some of which weighed 44 pounds.

November 3rd … [A] red hot shot came in at one of the lower deck ports, disabled the gun by knocking off the trunnion, wounded five men and went through the mid gun deck where it was taken up in a bucket and thrown overboard. It was perfectly red hot and burned the deck as it rolled about.

November 14th … Enemy with a very long gun they have got fired several shot over our masthead and which went so far beyond us that I am certain it throws at least 3 miles.

As the naval gunners sweated and suffered against particular batteries, Buonaparte sought to improve the overall effectiveness of his forces, by better location as much as by establishing new sites. Although his prized objective remained Fort Mulgrave and the two forts at the tip of the promontory, he recognized, too, both the importance and the relative isolation of Fort Malbousquet, the major impediment to an advance on Toulon from the west. None the less, any pressure exerted on Malbousquet was probably calculated by him to be a suitable means of disguising a decisive push further south, where it mattered.

A first move was to improve the situation of the Batterie de la Convention, which was expanded to comprise six guns and resited behind a screen of olives. Buonaparte wished to keep its new identity secret until he was ready to act with full effect, but he was overridden by the *représentants*, who insisted that it commence firing on the night of 27/28 November, immediately upon completion. On neighbouring heights were the Poudrière and Farinière batteries, with a further fourteen guns. These had also been supplemented, with Dugommier's full support.

The sudden concentrated bombardment from this quarter caused both the allied command and the populace of Toulon considerable disquiet. Although Malbousquet could withstand a battering of limited duration from this direction, it was now clearly within easy range of concealed batteries, the nearest a bare half-mile distant. A further annoyance was that Poudrière included one of Buonaparte's prized long cannon, a weapon which could just reach to Toulon's western ramparts, which he knew would exert considerable moral effect.

Had he intended to provoke an allied response, Buonaparte could have done no better. For the next two days there came a counter-bombardment from warships and from Fort Mulgrave. This was not particularly effective as the shallow water of the north-western corner of the roads prevented the use of the big second rates, while Mulgrave was firing at long range, largely indirect and with no means of correction.

The activity did, however, hold the attention of the *conventionnels* while Major General Dundas assembled his forces for a land attack, comprehensive by standards to date. With Hood further denuding his warships to take their place, troops were ferried over by night and concealed in the wooded areas around the La Grasse heights upon which Fort Mulgrave was situated. The force was quickly built up to a total strength of about 400 British, 700 Spanish, 700 Neapolitan, 300 Piedmontese and 250 French of the Royal Louis battalion. In addition, there was a reserve of 600 each of Spanish and Neapolitans, under the overall command of Brigadier General Izquierdo.

As commissioner, General O'Hara should really have had no input beyond assisting in the formulation of the plan, but he insisted on being with the artillery that had been placed on the right flank of the projected line of advance. These guns directly faced the troublesome enemy batteries across the low depression in which ran the Neuve River.

At 4 a.m. on 29 November the allied troops advanced in three columns. Barely one-sixth of the total, the British were on the left. Silently and rapidly, the force skirted the village of La Seyne, apparently without alerting any of the several enemy batteries in the area, forded the shallow river and progressed in good order up the steeply rising ground below the Poudrière battery. Totally surprised, its sizeable garrison wilted after a few scattered shots and fled, leaving about sixty prisoners.

Dundas's orders had been to take this height and, staying in battle order, to await further instructions. Elated by their early success, however, many of the attackers (including the British) swept on in general chase. Now fragmented, other units carried the Farinière battery and, according to some accounts, the Convention battery itself.

Now in smaller and scattered groups, the allied infantry pursued the enemy over rough, broken ground, while others discovered and pillaged a just abandoned encampment. Dundas's frustration at this breakdown in discipline can well be imagined. As he struggled to get his force back into some semblance of order, he was joined by his superior O'Hara who, on observing the easy dislodgement of the enemy, had ridden over from his vantage point with the artillery.

Once their pursuers had fanned into small groups, the republicans quickly realized that they themselves were in considerably greater strength. In their midst was Dugommier, who was able to rally his men. Now isolated, small bodies of allied troops found themselves suddenly surrounded and cut down. As the French moved back, still in open order, a new rout began.

From the battery position, O'Hara could see disaster looming and, ever the soldier, rode down at the head of a detachment to salvage the situation. Encountering an enemy force, this group was involved in a brisk exchange of fire in which O'Hara was wounded in the arm. The injury was not serious but resulted in much loss of blood. As a small battle raged around, the general took cover behind a wall to attend to his wound. The action moved on and he was lost to sight. Inevitably, he was captured.

At the batteries, meanwhile, the race was now on to disable the guns before the republicans fully regrouped and came flooding back. Here were Spanish troops under the comte de Puerto, none of whom had brought the studs or tools needed to spike the weapons. Urently, men were sent to Fort Malbousquet to obtain the required items, but it was too late.

Some reports put Dugommier's available strength at 6,000 but, whatever the true figure, it swept the allies back off the heights. What had been the right-hand column, of Sardinians under Thaon de Revel, remained in good order and now deployed along the course of the Neuve as an improvised line of defence. The initiative was timely and rescued a difficult situation, for the line screened the allied artillery on the far bank and formed a barrier through which their disorganized and beaten colleagues could pass to the rear and the rallying point of Malbousquet.

As the mass of victorious French swooped down from the high ground to complete the rout, it was the turn of the British gunners to draw blood. Three times the republicans tried to carry their momentum on to Malbousquet, on one occasion advancing as far as the *chevaux de frise* that fronted it. Each time the artillery, the Sardinians and, finally, the fort's Spanish garrison, threw them back. A republican enveloping movement along the shoreline to the south was broken up by naval gunfire.

The allies were, in turn, now rallying, being joined by a detachment from the Moulins strongpoint, which had advanced under cover of fire from the Petit Saint-Antoine battery. More significant was the arrival of Izquierdo's reserve force. After seven hours of fierce and sustained combat, both sides fell back to their original positions.

For the coalition forces, the British in particular, the affair had been disastrous, with General O'Hara among their 148 casualties – dead, wounded or missing. For once the British could not fault the Spanish, who incurred 119 casualties of their own. When, to these totals, are added 65 Neapolitans and the same number of Sardinians, one has a debacle, an ambitious raid which, starting well, failed expensively. Materially and morally it was a victory for Dugommier, whose division had sustained considerably fewer casualties – reportedly 179 dead, 68 wounded and 23 taken prisoner – and remained in control of the heights. This general, too, was well forward, being wounded in the shoulder. His adjutant general, Cervoni, also took a hit.

In his report, Dugommier praised both his adjutants general and also his *commandant d'artillerie*, 'Citoyen Bonnaparte [sic]'. The general was justifiably cock-a-hoop for, besides O'Hara, seventeen other allied officers were captured. They included Major Archibald Campbell of the 69th Regiment, Captain Reeves of the 1st Regiment and Lieutenant Colonel Echavuru, aide de camp to Admiral Gravina.

An interesting sidelight on the story of O'Hara's capture is that his French captors agreed with an earlier opinion of Thaon de Revel that the general was actually seeking to die in combat. Beforehand, he had become increasingly depressed, even demoralized, his dark assessments, as expressed to Hood, becoming even more pessimistic. 'The governor promised not to go out himself', complained Hood to Henry Dundas, 'but unfortunately did not keep his word.'

The French, too, were mystified at their capture: '*[Un] exemple peut-être unique d'un gouverneur fait prisonnier dans une sortie, exemple d'autant plus extraordinaire que l'objet de la sortie avait été parfaitement rempli. Est-ce imprudence, ineptie ou quelque chose de pis?*' ('Perhaps a unique example of a Governor made prisoner during a sortie, an example even more extraordinary in that the object of the sortie had been perfectly achieved. Is it imprudence, ineptitude or something worse?')

O'Hara certainly did nothing to ingratiate himself either with his fellow captives or with his captors, demanding the free passage of his surgeon, Dr Graham, to attend his wound, accompanied by a servant and his effects. Dugommier, to his credit, sent an emissary to Fort Malbousquet with letters from both O'Hara and other prisoners.

Accounts, mostly apocryphal, later abounded regarding attempts by both sides to capitalize on the situation by making extravagant demands for exchange of prisoners. In particular, these involved the wife and daughter of General Lapoype, who had, from the outset, been detained in Toulon. In view of the general's long spells of comparative inactivity, one may indeed speculate that this factor weighed heavily upon him; that resolute action on his part might result in reprisal. He was, however, not replaced.

In the event, the terms of capacity for each of these celebrities were not particularly long. Madame Lapoype and daughter were confined with other women detainees in the Saint-Ésprit hospital, in the charge of the National Guard. Probably through the connivance of a republican sympathiser, a group of fourteen disappeared late on 7 December. These included the mother and daughter, who were lodged in a safe house until the 18th, when they were able to slip out of the town in the midst of the general confusion then obtaining.

General O'Hara was moved to Paris where, following a lengthy interrogation, he was confined in the Luxembourg. Subjected to no worse than a few indignities, he spent about three years here until repatriated in a direct exchange for the French General Rochambeau.

THE AFFAIR OF 30 November marked a definite watershed in the fortunes of the allies at Toulon. Until then, the republicans had been on the back foot for, having arrived flushed with victory at Marseille, Avignon and Lyon, they had, for the first time, encountered regular army units and had discovered that sheer numbers and Revolutionary fervour were no match for discipline and good military practice. Now, with professional generalship and artillery support, they had worsted the allies in open battle. And still their reinforcements flowed in.

For the allies, despondency was in the air. General Dundas took over from O'Hara but the overall strength of his forces was little augmented. A final batch of Neapolitans, 566 men of the Messapia Battalion, arrived at Toulon on 26 November, their passage from Gaeta having taken twelve days. Hood, however, remained indignant at London's intransigence regarding the 300 men of the 30th Regiment, now lost to him by virtue of their departure in service as marines aboard the *St George* and three 74s.

The public mood in the town no longer reflected confidence in the allied cause and hope for the future. There was considerable resentment that the comte de Provence had not been given permission to come. It was seen as inconsistent that the town was being held in trust for the imprisoned Louis XVII yet his rightful representative, the regent, should be denied access. This called into question the true British motives.

In the town, the population had been roughly doubled by the influx of refugees, creating friction over accommodation and priorities. The situation was not helped by the military having commandeered public buildings for billets and having introduced a variety of illnesses and afflictions for which there was little available medication. A general apathy prevailed, the people now being dependent upon the occupying forces for both their protection and their subsistence. Normal life had been suspended and matters had been largely removed from the control of individuals.

Thanks to allied sea control, the quantity of foodstuffs was sufficient, but it was difficult to control prices in the absence of adequate hard currency. *Assignats* were still in circulation but had now lost most of their value. Public employees benefited by having a guaranteed proportion of their wages being paid in coin. The General Committee, in fairness, was obliged to impose price controls but it was found in practice that only those on bread, meat and fish could be enforced. Even this proved to be impossible in the case of bread for, once the republicans cut off the flow to most of the town's flour mills during October, the supply of basics was intermittent. Employees of the arsenal could be paid partly in bread supplied by the navy's bakers but, for the populace, prices rose simply because the town's suppliers refused to accept any further paper money.

Suspicion of who favoured whom was rife, and with some reason, for the republicans were becoming more obviously active in trying to establish a form of resistance movement. This began in a small way, as instanced by the arrest of a young fruit seller, one Marie Coste, who had been searched on entering the town, proving to have letters and copies of the new constitution concealed in her basket. To dissuade any other would-be collaborator, the General Committee acted rapidly, publicly and severely, the hapless girl being despatched on the gallows that had replaced the hated guillotine.

The shadowy head of this embryonic movement was named Adet, who later became a French diplomat in the United States. His efforts were much hampered because many on his recommended list of contacts were either already detained or inaccessible, the latter either serving aboard French-manned ships or in distant outposts on the perimeter.

Intercepted correspondence, intended for those engaged in the importation of Genoese grain, requested information on the number of troops being shipped in, and on long-term allied plans, specifically whether the intention was to defend the place indefinitely, to abandon it or to destroy it. The letters referred to an imminent general assault on the town by the republican armies and of a simultaneous insurrection, commencing in the arsenal.

A letter from the *représentants* with Dugommier's army, addressed to the

Committee of Public Safety, enumerated ways in which the seeds of disquiet were being sown throughout the town. It forecast that future correspondence would be '*datée des ruines de Toulon*'.

Previously anxious to encourage life to return to a sort of normality, the military authorities now had to tighten and enforce security. Citizens were checked randomly for their identity and details of their business. House searches were initiated on the basis of information received. All weapons in private hands had to be handed in. Gunsmiths had to submit inventories of their stock and, although they were apparently permitted to retain it, were prohibited from making any further sales. Movement, in and out of the city gates, was tightly controlled and military patrols were stepped up. Cumulatively, these measures served to create a general feeling of alarm in the populace, placated little by the General Committee's assurances that they were temporary, and were being imposed only until the situation was stabilized.

ON ARRIVAL IN LONDON, Lord Mulgrave reported immediately to the secretary of state, Henry Dundas. His assessment of the situation at Toulon was no longer optimistic and, for the first time, alerted the government to the possibility of defeat. Dundas immediately (23 November) wrote to Hood (date of reception not known), detailing the measures that should be taken in the event of disaster. They echoed clearly those already despatched to Admiral Langara by the Spanish government.

> I need scarcely remind Y.Lp. of the propriety ... of having the French ships captured at Toulon so situated that if you was [sic] obliged to abandon the place none of the ships or arsenals ... should be permitted to fall into the hands of the enemy. The arsenals must be destroyed and the ships burnt if they cannot be carried with you. I hope they may be brought away, and in such circumstances as I have referred to this would be perfectly justifiable under the nicest and strictest interpretation of the terms of the agreement entered into by Y.Lp. with the people of Toulon.

The admiral probably did not need to be reminded of his obligations, and would certainly have baulked at London's continued use of such words as 'captured'. A phrase such as 'the nicest and strictest interpretation' also suggests a wavering about the borderline of legality.

ONCE THE ELATION OF action cooled, more mature consideration by either side of the battle of 30 November resulted in more qualified conclusions. The French had to accept that, in the opening phase, a considerably inferior allied force had routed the republicans in an established location. Had the allies then maintained their cohesion, there was nothing between them and Dugommier's headquarters at Ollioules, less than 3 miles distant. Even when they had gained the initiative, the republicans were still unable to break the narrow line of defence that the Sardinians established before Malbousquet. Dugommier expressed himself extremely dissatisfied with the performance and conduct of his troops, even through a difficult situation had been resolved favourably.

To those of the allied high command, General O'Hara, with his nervous excited manner and his enduring pessimism, represented little loss. Thaon de Revel, no mean soldier himself, praised O'Hara faintly, crediting him with all the necessary martial qualities except those essential for a commander-in-chief. Sir Gilbert Elliot had been far from impressed by him but, regrettably, thought little more of David Dundas, his successor. Although he rated him as relatively sensible and steady, he thought that his age and state of health were against him. Also, like O'Hara, Dundas did not believe in the success of the allied mission (and, indeed, lost no time in advising Hood to pull out while it could still be done in an orderly fashion).

The importance of Fort Malbousquet to the defence of the western approaches to Toulon cannot be overestimated and, although it had been defeated, the enemy thrust on 30 November caused considerable concern. Open at its back, the strongpoint was vulnerable to an encircling movement and, to frustrate such an occurrence, the allies reactivated and improved an old fortification on the small rise of Missiessy. This was situated some 750 yards south-east of Malbousquet but, being within the comfortable range of the French batteries on Les Arènes, suffered intermittent bombardment.

Food supplies began to be a major preoccupation for both sides. Letters from the *représentants* to their colleagues in neighbouring provinces reflect the problems of feeding their armies in a region already stripped of supplies. By early December it was apparent that Dugommier and Lapoype must soon resolve the issue or begin to disperse their hungry forces, now estimated by them to be nearing 40,000 strong. Within the perimeter, the British commissioners were still hoping that substantial reinforcement might yet materialize from Austria, although the provision of adequate rations for those already present was obviously causing some strain on available shipping capacity.

Elliot, in a late November letter to Dundas, sought to make a virtue out of a necessity while, simultaneously, alluding to the tight fiscal constraint exerted by London. 'There are, in this town', he wrote,

> many thousands of young men consuming provisions, without any advantage to the common cause, although perfectly capable of service ... The expence [sic] must, it is true, be borne by England in the first instance but, if they prove useful, they will certainly be the cheapest troops His Majesty can employ at Toulon. The charge of raising them would be very inconsiderable, there will be no expence [sic] for transporting them from distant places, and there will be neither half-pay nor subsidy.

To command this proposed body of extra fighting troops, Elliot received approval to recruit 'about twenty or thirty emigrant officers of known merit ... now in Italy'. This initiative was, however, offset by the necessity to disarm much of the deeply infiltrated and unreliable National Guard.

Elliot's own assessments of the situation soon echoed the underlying gloom: 'I cannot help ... confessing that the possession of this place seems to be precarious, and that every day is critical. The quality of a great majority of the troops is such, that they cannot possibly be depended on; and yet, the most important posts must, of necessity, be entrusted in a great measure to them.' Then, with respect to the enemy: 'Their numbers are encreasing [sic] and their preparations of every kind advancing ... and if our force should not increase proportionably in much less time than at present seems possible, the event cannot be answered for.'

Small parties of allied reinforcement still materialized, the very last group of Neapolitans arriving on 5 December. Lacking battle experience, they were accompanied by the Franco-German Marshal de Gambs, who had been sent as their senior officer and to instil a coherent sense of discipline into the Neapolitan force as a whole. His military reputation preceded him but he was never able to produce any noticeable effect on his troops, who were widely scattered around the perimeter.

If a mobile reserve needed to be committed to reinforce any threatened sector of the defences, it remained Hood's practice to land seamen in numbers sufficient to police the town in the absence of the military. He therefore regretted the loss of Linzee's squadron, sent to Tunis in the vain hope of overawing the pro-French Bey. Once again, other vessels idled in the ports of Liguria in the anticipation that, even now, the promised Austrian troops might arrive, a force which was hoped would prove to be Toulon's salvation. With the prolonged absence of so many ships, the demands on those remaining were increasingly onerous.

As Sir Gilbert Elliot had observed, the enemy's preparations were indeed being advanced. Buonaparte, it seems, never lost an opportunity to lobby Dugommier, the Committee of Public Safety, or Carnot, the Convention's minister of war, as to the definitive plan for defeating the allies in Toulon. He forecast that, subjected to sustained and general attack, the coalition would cut its losses and settle for inflicting what damage it could before evacuating by sea. Dugommier himself was keen to bring the campaign to a close, having been advised by the committee to 'take l'Aiguillette or merit our disappointment'. As many before, the general knew that the committee's 'disappointment' was not to be lightly courted.

Buonaparte's plan had been developed somewhat further in that, while he still proposed to make his major thrust at the primary objective, the western promontory, a simultaneous all-out attack by Lapoype should be directed at the Faron massif. The seizure of Fort Mulgrave was still central to the plan and, importantly, Dugommier's strength was now sufficient to simultaneously pin down the garrison at Malbousquet, preventing any sally designed to relieve Mulgrave. As we have already seen, however, there still existed several variations on this main theme. It was necessary to have a major review to decide on the definitive version, to define which would be primary thrusts and which would be feints and distractions in their support.

Just five days before the abortive allied attack on the batteries on Les Arènes, therefore, Dugommier had called a full council of war, attended by all commanders and senior staff officers. Those present included Lapoype, la Barre, Garnier, du Teil and Mouret, Buonaparte (now adjutant general), Brûlé, Flayelle, la Mothe and Sugny. The final agreed plan reflected the enormous strength that Dugommier, in overall command, had at his disposal. As Buonaparte had demanded, the main attack would be launched against Fort Mulgrave, with a coordinated move against Malbousquet as a distraction. Simultaneously, the Faron Ridge would be seized. Malbousquet would be muzzled sufficiently to allow the establishment nearby of a battery of *mortiers à longue portée*, effectively howitzers, which would be within range of the town, where panic would ensue from a steady hail of bombs. As a final gesture toward the creation of total confusion, the Cap Brun battery would also be bombarded from a long range. Subsequent meetings on 5 and 11 December further refined the plan as *conventionnels* laboured to complete the three major batteries, Convention, Poudrière and Farinière atop Les Arènes. This work was finished on the 6th.

To the south of Fort Mulgrave, Buonaparte energetically established three further batteries. These stood virtually shoulder to shoulder and, being within mortar range, were in considerable danger from the fort's heavy artillery. As was customary, they were named: Jacobins (predictably); Chasse-Coquins* (with grim humour); and, thanks to its particularly dangerous situation, Hommes sans Peur.

Sprawled over the high ground known to the French variously as Le Caire or La Grasse, Fort Mulgrave looked more formidable than it actually was. It had been improved and extended piecemeal under the direction of Brigadier Izquierdo, whose artillery specialist was fully employed at Malbousquet and who lacked also the support of a qualified military engineer. Overall, the fort was described as having three main redoubts, which could support each other with crossfire.

The republicans had a useful informant, referred to in documents as 'l'Ingénieur Sardou'. He had already reported on Admiral Trogoff's recent public announcement which, designed to lift the public mood, stated that 10,000 more allied troops were only awaiting a fair wind. Sardou described Mulgrave in some detail, stating that the redoubts had their banks revetted in earth and timber. Up to 15 feet in height, they were surrounded by deep ditches. The ground between the redoubts was also covered by fire from outworks, or redans. Faced by protective walls and firing through embrasures were a total of twenty-five guns, a mix of 32-, 12- and 8-pounders. Some were stated to be *obusiers*, or shell guns, and there were mortars in support. The whole was fronted with a deep ditch, either edge of which was protected by *chevaux de frise*.

* 'Nail the buggers!'

Typical of any report on an enemy, the detail was greatly overstated, for Fort Mulgrave's defences were far from mutually supportive. The position was particularly weak on the enemy's right. Of its garrison of some 700, about 250 were British, the remainder Spanish and Sardinian. Beyond the fort, located between it and the fortifications at the end of the promontory, was a camp accommodating an estimated 3,000 further troops.

Until the republican armies were positioned and poised for the great assault, it was Buonaparte's task to soften up Mulgrave. To this end, his batteries worked ceaselessly, despite the attentions of allied warships. So intense was the fire that reports speak of several mortar bombs being occasionally visible simultaneously while in flight.

CAPTAIN HORATIO NELSON in the *Agamemnon* spent little time in Toulon during the period of occupation and his letters betray a certain ambivalence regarding the eventual outcome. Writing on 1 December to William Locker, the lieutenant-governor of Greenwich Hospital, he noted:

> At Toulon, I think that they will have plenty of fighting this winter … Shot and shells are very plentiful all over the Harbour. I wonder more damage has not been done … not that I think Toulon is in the smallest danger. At all events, we can destroy the French Fleet and Arsenal in a very short time; one Fire-ship will burn the Fleet and Arsenal. They are some of them the finest Ships I ever saw …

On the following day, he wrote one of his many letters to his close friend and confidant, the Duke of Clarence, son of George III. It was addressed as from '*Agamemnon*. Off Corsica, Dec[r] 2nd 1793'. In it he reiterated his belief that the threat to Toulon was slight and that 'whatever may happen' the French fleet and arsenal could be quickly destroyed. He made the further observation that '… unless we can have an army in the field we cannot prevent the enemy possessing some of the heights which will annoy the harbour and posts near it …'

Good news arrived at Toulon on 16 December with the frigate *Ariadne*. She had on board a small detachment of artillerymen from Gibraltar; even better, her despatches reported that the planned military reinforcement of the West Indies had been deferred and that two whole regiments, possibly more, would be sent to join the coalition forces as soon as possible.

'Urgency', however, was a word imperfectly understood by Gibraltar's governor. The troops duly arrived at the end of the month, too late to be of any possible use.

Further hopes were raised in Hood's command when, at about the same time, the Emperor of Austria finally announced that the long-promised 5,000 troops would be sent 'immediately'. The seemingly endless prevarication had been due not only to a lack of commitment to crushing of revolution but also to less than cordial relations with other coalition partners, notably Prussia and Sardinia. Joint operations with the latter to recover Nice had been brought to a standstill by French opposition. On this front there was now an effective stalemate which, for the Austrians, was a cheaper option than active warfare, but which soaked up available manpower. Winter stalemate also suited the French republicans, for it allowed significant strength to be diverted from the Army of Italy to operate against Toulon.

Continuous diplomatic pressure had finally stirred Austria into making at least a cosmetic start to assembling a force with which to meet its coalition commitment. It, too, would prove to be too late to be of use, but the ultimate blame must lie squarely with the British government which, as ever, had over-committed an over-reduced army, and which preferred to believe over-optimistic reports from Toulon rather than taking no chance and solidly reinforcing the British presence there.

ON THE EVE OF the republican assault, the coalition's military strength stood at an estimated 18,700, comprising 7,000 Spanish, 6,200 Neapolitans, 2,000 British, 2,000 Sardinians and 1,500 royalist French. About 4,000 were reported to be on the sick list yet, according to Major General David Dundas, there remained only about 11,000 effectives who could 'bear a musket'. These were spread around the same long perimeter of about 15 miles, a perimeter which, to give reasonable protection from artillery to both town and anchorage, could not be shortened.

Where considerable forces of seamen could once be put ashore quickly to meet an emergency, this reserve had been greatly reduced as increasing demands on Hood's Mediterranean fleet saw ever more ships absent on detached duty. Of the British fleet, only the *Victory* and the two divisional flagships, together with a pair of frigates, lay off the Grande Rade while, in the inner roads, were three 74s and two more frigates, usually deployed against the enemy batteries. Why Admiral Langara's Spanish fleet, present in force, could not be prevailed upon to act in lieu remains something of a mystery.

At the latest count, the republican French numbered 38,000 effectives, comprising 36,000 infantry, 1,650 artillerymen and a cavalry squadron. A further 3,000 were listed as either sick or absent. Dugommier had to attack soon, for inactivity was resulting in an increasing number of incidents of breakdown in discipline in his largely citizen army, already paid and vict-ualled somewhat haphazardly. The general also claimed that many of his peasant detachments were, as yet, only crudely armed, lacking muskets.

December 1793 in Toulon was dark, wet and windy, depressing for defender and besieger alike. On the 14th Dugommier visited his forward units opposite Fort Mulgrave and received a briefing on the local situation. Satisfied, he gave the order to commence what, today, would be termed a softening-up bombardment. Eleven batteries, in a deadly arc stretching from the *Sans-culottes* near Brégaillon in the north-west, to Faubrégas, located next to the Saint-Mandrier isthmus in the south-west, targeted Mulgrave, Malbousquet and the allied camp at Saint-Elme (covering the isthmus) at ranges from 250 to 2,000 yards. The general's orders were to maintain steady fire throughout the 15th and to double the intensity (*'très vif'*) for the whole of the 16th.

Darkness fell early in the afternoon of 16 December, with a cold, driving rain cloaking the assembly of 7,000 *conventionnels* in and around the village of La Seyne. So violent was the weather that the *représentants*, the prime movers of the operation, were inclined to postpone it. Dugommier, the experienced campaigner, would have none of it, as standing down such an assembly would have lost him the element of surprise. Buonaparte added that it would be a waste of an extended artillery barrage that had already consumed the bulk of available powder and ammunition.

Their arguments prevailed and, at one o'clock in the morning of the 17th, under the tactical control of Captain Muiron, the assault forces moved off in two columns. The left-hand column, under Victor, followed the line of the coast to take Mulgrave from the left and rear, cutting off its commu-nications by water. Simultaneously, Brûlé's column, on the right, advanced along the centreline of the peninsula to attack the fort head on. A third of the total number of troops was held back as a mobile reserve.

With Dugommier in the van, and four *représentants* keeping close watch, sometimes ahead or behind, sometimes on the flank, the columns stumbled through the stormy gloom. Not surprisingly, the leading elements lost their sense of direction and, in a touch of farce, the two groups encountered each other. In the prevailing conditions, each assumed the other to be the enemy. A measure of panic firing ensued, but thanks to robust leadership, the situation was quickly resolved.

Suitably rallied, the republicans were in numbers that simply flowed over the fort's two outposts. One had been held by British troops, the other by Spanish but, almost to a man, they died by the bayonet. Resistance at the fort itself was fierce, one *chef de bataillon* later reporting:

> Our progress was slowed, but not stopped, by the numberless difficulties in our path and the heavy fire from cannons and muskets. [There was] the *chevaux de frise*, obstacles to get over; the cannons to avoid; the parapet to clear; the multiple intersections which formed in effect a second and unexpected enclosure. All slowed us down. The deadly musket fire obliged us to gain entry through the embrasures. Again and again we went in and out. At last a third and final charge gave us victory and the formidable redoubt was ours.

It had been a violent encounter. The first wave had been repulsed by a combined British and Piedmontese defence. A second assault was mounted and this, too, suffered – so badly that Dugommier was heard to express concern that the attack was faltering. He summoned the reserve column, which appeared promptly, led by Buonaparte and Mouret.

The assault was renewed and this time the parapets were successfully scaled and the allied artillerymen cut down at their guns. Sensing victory, the invaders swarmed into the fort, where they were engaged hand to hand. No quarter was given, none asked. The dead were piled in heaps (*'les morts s'entassent par monceaux'*).

On the right, the Spanish defenders were reinforced by further British and Piedmontese but, despite a backs-to-the-wall resistance, were simply overwhelmed. At this stage, the British reserve was committed, led by elements of the 18th (Royal Irish) Regiment. For a while the defence stabilized once again, but the Spanish then broke and fled, leaving the Irish and Piedmontese to hack their way out, and the position was lost.

Sited between Mulgrave and the forts at the tips of the promontory was a camp that accommodated a further Spanish force, commanded by Brigadier Izquierdo. Through his pointedly ignoring a pitched battle only a few hundred yards distant, Izquierdo is often blamed, even by the French republicans, for the loss of the fort. He, in turn, cited problems caused by a mass of Neapolitans who, having retreated down to the shore at the first assault, had to be restored to order.

Into this chaotic scene arrived some 400 men, boated across by Dundas and Gravina, only to find the situation beyond resolution. Commander Cooke, ever in the thick of things, was later scathing in criticism of his allies, speaking of the British twice rallying the Spanish, but to no effect. He reported them as determined to escape and firing at those who sought to stop them. His worse condemnation, however, was for the Neapolitans, whose conduct he described as 'unspeakable', their officers 'the most notable cowards who ever shouldered a gun'. A separate account by Sir Gilbert Elliot speaks of the total breakdown in their morale following the earlier death of four to a mortar bomb. The remainder claimed to be sick and sought to be relieved of their duty. Unsurprisingly, their posts were easily taken by the enemy.

Even allowing for the habitual overstatement of British virtues by native chroniclers of the time, it is evident that the multi-national structure of Fort Mulgrave's garrison was a considerable factor in its loss. On the other hand, it is doubtful if a brigade of guards could have contained the mass of republicans who, fired with Revolutionary enthusiasm, hurled themselves at the defences, regardless of cost. Buonaparte himself had a horse shot from under him, then, fighting on foot within the bastion, took a bayonet thrust into his right calf.

With Fort Mulgrave gone, the situation facing the essential positions of Balaguier and L'Aiguillette was hopeless. Designed to be formidable from seaward, they were protected only weakly from the rear. Again, their mainly Neapolitan garrison was to face allegations that they were more interested in a rapid evacuation than in covering the retreat of those falling back from Mulgrave.

Rather unrealistically, Admiral Hood still deemed it unnecessary to commence full evacuation of the promontory, but he was persuaded by General Dundas that the situation there was irretrievable. Fortunately for the allies, the victorious republicans were content to mill around the scene of their success, for a while, rather than regroup and sweep the disorganized coalition forces into the sea. These were thus given precious time to withdraw in comparatively good order in boats provided by the royalist French flagship *Commerce de Marseille* and the two-decker *Pompée*, supported by three Spanish frigates, the evacuation being from beaches below the Tour de Balaguier.

About 2,500 men were thus successfully taken off by ships which, by the end, were exchanging a lively fire with republican mobile artillery. So hot did this exchange become that the last ship out was obliged to cut her cable.

Much of the artillery in the forts remained unspiked and there is no evidence that any attempt was made to blow the magazines. Such was the general disorder, however, that little could immediately be put to use. Supported by warships, a British force still retained the Croix-de-Signaux position on the Saint-Mandrier peninsula, but this was of little consequence with the vital western promontory now firmly in the enemy hands.

For the few British warships remaining at anchor in the roads, the din and stabbing flashes of battle were necessarily remote, but the uncertainty of it all was the cause of some anxiety for those ashore. With the reluctant and miserable dawn of 17 December, however, the reality of the situation was all too evident, the republicans swarming over the height of La Grasse that frowned above the stone fortifications of Balaguier and L'Aiguillette, whence the sounds of violent confrontation still emanated.

Daylight revealed the presence on the beach of many more allied troops, who had continued to filter down, hoping for rescue. They had done their best and the navy could not desert them. As the log of the *Windsor Castle* recorded laconically:

> … at 5 found the Enemy was in possession of Fort Mulgrave and they began to fire cannon on the ships. Observed the Enemy had also taken possession of the heights of Ferron [sic]. All our Boats employed in bringing off the Troops from Fort Mulgrave. Came out of the inner Harbour the *Terrible, Robust* and *Sincere* [the last-named being the French sloop *Sincère* under British colours].

The number of allied troops lost in the savage fight for Mulgrave is not known with any certainty. About 300 British and 70 Spanish died but casualties to others are not known. Some 250 were listed as missing and the French claimed 400 prisoners. It is possible, however, that this number included those captured on Mont Faron, whose reoccupation had also been noted from the *Windsor Castle*. For the French, Dugommier's report was more precise. As was customary, their commanding officers led from the front and counted among the wounded were General Delaborde, Colonel Buonaparte and Captain Muiron. There were about eighty dead.

Throughout the struggle for Mulgrave, Fort Malbousquet was kept under a continuous bombardment as Mouret and Garnier ostentatiously drew up their forces for attack. It was, of course, no more than a demonstration but it succeeded in its objective of preventing any force being sent to the assistance of Mulgrave.

GENERAL LAPOYPE'S ASSAULT to secure the Faron Ridge for the second time was synchronized with that on Fort Mulgrave and, owing to the elongated nature of the objective, again involved several separate forces. The largest of these, led by the general himself, assembled in the grounds of the Château Baudouvin, near what was then the village of La Vallette. Having fought the wind and rain all the way up the zigzag track from Beaulieu, the troops then formed for an assault on Fort Faron at the ridge's eastern end. This strongpoint is, however, located on a spur and easily defended. The attack was repulsed. Nothing daunted, Lapoype regrouped and tried again, with the same result. A third attempt was ordered but again failed, it being noted that many of the citizen soldiers were by now more concerned with their own safety. Despite the efforts of both Fréron and Barras, the *représentants* accompanying the operation, the force could no longer be rallied, with rain-sodden groups of men finding cover wherever they could.

At the western end of Mont Faron, meanwhile, the fort of Saint-Antoine also held out, barring the main route up from Le Jonquet. Here, however, the massif is incised by deep valleys offering alternative, if more difficult, routes. Following in the tracks of '*une compagnie de pionniers et de 600 travailleurs*' ('a company of pioneers and 600 workers'), a column commanded by Adjudant-Général Micas surprised a Spanish force dug in around the Pas de Leydet and carried the position without much difficulty.

Just to the east is located the higher, and key, point of Pas de la Masque, now held by a British detachment. Already alarmed by events close on its right, this force was attacked by a third republican column, led by Commandant Argod. This had toiled up the north face of the ridge from its assembly point near Le Revest. A British casualty list exceeding 300 was evidence of the stout defence, but the post was eventually overrun and the survivors scattered for their own salvation. The senior British officer succeeded in making his way down to Fort Saint-Antoine, where his request for shelter reportedly gave the Spanish commander considerable satisfaction.

With the centre and western end of the Faron Ridge now secured, the combined French forces moved eastward against the allied garrisons still in control of Fort de la Croix Faron and the lower Fort Faron. The former was also defended robustly but, lacking supporting artillery, the republicans dismantled their small cannon, manhandling the heavy component parts over rock and gully to secure commanding positions. Now under fire seemingly from the front, flanks and above, the defenders wilted, finally giving up when their commanding officer, the Piedmontese Lieutenant Colonel de Germagnan, was killed.

With this position in their hands the elated French looked down on Fort Faron from superior locations. They were in such numbers that the garrison perceived its task as hopeless and capitulated with only token resistance. With daylight, as the watch aboard the *Windsor Castle* had noted, republican forces were signalling their triumph from the length of the Mont Faron Ridge.

In Toulon, confirmation of the loss of the critical forts of Balaguier and L'Aiguillette came at about 4 a.m. on 17 December. Even before hearing of the news from Faron, Admiral Hood called an emergency council of war ('that sure herald of discomfiture'). Meeting that afternoon were Hood, his second-in-command Rear Admiral Sir Hyde Parker, Sir Gilbert Elliot and Admirals Langara and Gravina, together with the senior field commanders, Dundas, Valdés, Forteguerri, Pignatelli and Thaon de Revel.

Sending for their artillery specialists they asked their opinion on whether the further defence of the town was practicable with both the western promontory and the major heights under enemy control. With allied forces falling back, and with reserves of only 1,500 troops in the town, there was no immediate prospect of effective counter-attack. What were the possibilities of controlling the anchorages from new batteries established on the Saint-Mandrier peninsula?

The response of the artillerymen was predictable. Prospects for holding the outer ring of strongpoints – Pomets, Saint-Antoine, Sainte-Marguerite, even Malbousquet – were unattractive. Heavy batteries located on Saint-Mandrier could, supplemented by naval gunfire, dominate the coastline from the Grosse Tour (the present-day Tour Royale), at the eastern entrance to the inner roads, as far east as the Cap Brun position, but the forts on the western promontory could not be thus suppressed and would continue to make it impossible for ships to use either the Petite Rade or the port itself.

Hood still clung to the fiction of the imminent arrival of the Austrian contingent or substantial reinforcement from Gibraltar. The ever-willing Gravina, hardly recovered from his recent wounding, offered to lead a counter-attack with what was available. It was obvious, however, that the one could never be in time and the other could serve no useful purpose on such an extended perimeter. Dundas and Elliot both made it clear that they considered that insufficient numbers of reliable troops remained. The Neapolitans had completely lost heart, while Revel was known to have been against the venture from the outset, having, on more than one occasion, already advised his king to recall his forces.

Hood took a majority decision and the council agreed the following:

◊ That the survivors from the garrisons of the positions on the Faron heights should fall back on the town in light of the impracticability of mounting any attack to recover those positions;

◊ That the forts of Pomets, Les Moulins, Saint-Antoine and Saint-André should be evacuated while it was still possible for this to be done in an orderly fashion;

◊ That the garrisons of Malbousquet, Missiessy, Artigues and Sainte-Catherine should be augmented and ordered to hold on at all costs;

◊ That the inhabitants of Toulon should be informed that, should the occupying powers deem evacuation necessary, those who wished to go could take passage on one of several mercantile auxiliaries present, and that the General Committee would put the necessary arrangements in hand;

◊ That the sick and wounded would be embarked without delay;

◊ That those French ships which were armed and effective would leave with those of the allies and the remainder, along with the magazines and arsenal, should be destroyed. *Preparations for these actions should be put in hand but not carried through until the last moment* [author's italics].

Opinions were invited from the various allied representatives. Admiral Langara reportedly wished to use his frigates to evacuate his troops to the offshore Iles d'Hyères immediately, but was refused. The loyal French, alarmed at the likely fate of the town, wished to continue the fight. Féraud, the commanding officer of the *Puissant*, proposed retaking Fort Mulgrave, using a couple of smaller ships to transport and support the grenadiers of the Royal Louis regiment, under the command of Colonel le Boisgelin.

While Hood no doubt appreciated the fighting spirit of his French allies, he knew that their proposals were born of desperation and they were refused. To implement the council's decisions, the necessary orders were immediately written and despatched. The allied command had reacted to its reverses exactly as Buonaparte had predicted. The republicans now had only to maintain pressure to ensure that retreat became total evacuation.

On the same day, the 17th, the first garrisons to pull out were those of the two Saint-Antoines. While observing closely, the republicans allowed the abandonment to proceed without interference before immediately taking over.

Throughout the day, warships' boats riskily brought off groups of survivors from the western promontory, rearguards and individuals who had gone to ground. Although the boats were closely covered by naval guns, the enemy appeared sated, letting events largely take their course rather than engaging in more bloodshed.

Again, the log of the *Princess Royal* is informative in its summary although, being written almost contemporaneously with events, varies in detail:

December 17. Capture of Fort Mulgrave. The enemy put nearly the whole of the garrison to the sword, very few escaping. The number of the British amount to about 250, the rest Spaniards. The Neapolitan camp, consisting together with the reinforcement from the town of about 1500, kept the enemy at a stand till about 7, when it was determined to withdraw all troops from that Post. All the launches and other craft being ready to embark them received orders with the *Nemesis* and *Ariadne* to cover them, for which purpose got out springs and brought our guns to bear. By 10.30 the whole of the troops were embarked without loss … [At] noon got everything in readiness to move the ship, being within musket shot of the two batterys [sic] now in the enemy's possession.

The Neapolitan command early showed signs of yielding to the now powerful psychological pressure exerted by an imminent and overwhelming menace. The colonel commanding the garrison at the Cap Brun redoubt indicated that he would pull out if attacked. This was echoed by his opposite number at the Cap Cépet battery on the Saint-Mandrier peninsula. In light of what happened next it would appear that the whole Neapolitan contingent to the coalition forces had been issued with prior orders.

Without notice, and without any acquiescence by the allied high command, the Neapolitan garrison of the Missiessy position spiked its guns and marched out. This left Fort Malbousquet vulnerable to attack from the rear and brought about a rapid withdrawal by its apprehensive Spanish garrison. As the enemy had anticipated, the whole allied defence was unravelling.

During the rest of the 17th and over the following night, the Neapolitans systematically abandoned their positions. Cap Brun was not attacked but was deserted anyway, the remaining Piedmontese being obliged to leave. To this was added Cap Cépet and the position controlling the Sablettes isthmus.

The actual timing and sequence of these desertions is rather confused but the disgust felt by Hood at the conduct of some of his allies is clear in his preliminary report to Minister Dundas, written two days later:

Very early in the morning [of the 17th] Don Langara came to me and expressed great impatience for a council of all the principal officers of navy and army to be called, at which, late in the afternoon, it was decided to retire at a fixed time after proper regulations were made for it. But on that very night the whole of the Neapolitans stole off from the town without the consent or knowledge of the governor … The unaccountable panic that has taken hold of the Neapolitan troops made the retreat absolutely necessary to be effected as soon as possible, and prevented the execution of a settled arrangement for destroying the French ships and arsenal …

By the morning of the 18 December the whole population of Toulon was close to panic. Sounds of battle in the small hours of the 17th had been followed by much activity on the part of small craft and ships' boats bringing in the surviving troops from the western promontory. As the day progressed further military detachments arrived in the town following their abandonment of outposts. As if by prior arrangement, the Neapolitans began boarding their own ships for evacuation.

The General Committee did its best to convey to the populace the need for an orderly withdrawal for all those who wished to take passage on the transports but, as the day wore on, the trickle of people became a flood, a multitude pleading for assistance. This was despite General Dundas's considerable efforts to have reassuring proclamations publicly posted, military patrols doubled and instructions given for citizens to remain in their homes and not to form crowds. They were requested to make necessary preparations if desirous of leaving but then to await orders to report for any orderly embarkation.

By midday on the 18th the republicans had taken over the positions at Artigues, Sainte-Catherine, Sablettes and Cap Brun. Fort Pomets was a ruin following the withdrawal of its British naval garrison. Here, its commanding officer, Lieutenant Brisbane of the *Britannia*, blew the magazine containing 500 barrels of powder. All returned safely to their ship. In the various fortifications, hurried departures saw many cannon left in a serviceable condition. These, and others in Malbousquet, were used, where they could be brought to bear, to bombard the town, further increasing the general sense of panic.

The embarkation of the Neapolitans caused more apprehension to the general populace although uninformed service personnel thought that they were either being transported to recover the western promontory or were leaving following a dispute with the British.

Hood's decision to evacuate, however, 'could not be defer'd beyond that Night, as the Enemy commanded the Town and Ships by their Shot and Shells. I ... directed the Boats of the Fleet to assemble by eleven O'Clock near Fort le Malgue'. Although, to avoid the creation of further alarm, these preparations were not made public, the general intentions of the allied military soon became apparent.

Already under intermittent, though not yet fierce, bombardment, those

British warships still in the Petite Rade were ordered to shift their berths to the outer anchorage. Coming alongside in the arsenal, however, were the royalist French warships *Puissant* and *Iphigénie* which, together with gunboats, had been engaged in incessant dueling with Buonaparte's shore batteries. Liberally scarred by their efforts, their duty was now done, their battle lost. Their final service would be to help save that that could be saved. A discouraging sight was the loading of personal effects of Admiral Trogoff and other senior officers. Even more obviously, British cavalry units were to be seen embarking.

A world away, yet separated by only half a mile of water, the warships awaited their orders, their logs noting events as dispassionately as ever. That of the *Britannia*: '... At 9 hove up and Warped to the eastward of Cape Sepet [sic]. The Troops and many of the Inhabitants embarking on board the Fleet.' In view of the warships' yet unfulfilled priority of embarking the fighting troops, it would seem that it was against Hood's intentions to embark civilians at this stage, although the *Britannia's* lieutenant was not specific as to the nationality of the ships involved.

A massive surge toward the quays began when Admiral Gravina, who was known to feel keenly that the ordinary citizens of Toulon had been badly let down by the coalition, let it be known that evacuation was definitely planned. Churches, full of supplicants, emptied as confirmation of the worst quickly spread. Clutching necessities and boxes of items most dear to them, families, couples and single folk, young, old and infant, joined the flood of humanity heading for the ships. Any ship would do, the only hope for evading the fate of their fellows in Marseille, which town, savaged into submission by the forces of the Convention had now, ominously, been renamed by it as '*La Ville sans Nom*'.

As daylight again faded, an estimated 20,000 thronged the quaysides, everywhere encumbered by handcarts, boxes and baggage discarded by those more anxious to save themselves when ships refused to accept their bulky belongings. On the open space of the Champ de Mars a military party, endeavouring to maintain order, fired warning shots over the head of the throng. This promoted near-panic on the nearby quays as it was feared that the republicans were upon them. There were screams of 'Voici Carteaux!' for, while few knew of his supersession for incompetence, all knew of his reputation at Marseille and Avignon.

As the town dissolved into increasingly uncontrollable chaos, it suddenly became Hood's responsibility to destroy the arsenal and those ships of the French Toulon squadron that could not be brought out. Both he and Admiral Langara had received unambiguous orders from their respective governments as to their actions in this event, yet there is no evidence of any prior preparation or plan. Hood's naivety seems to have matched that of the less-experienced Captain Nelson, who was confident that a single fireship would suffice to destroy both the French fleet and an arsenal the size of a small town. As so often throughout history, an unpleasant decision had been deferred to the point at which events took charge, dictating the outcome.

RECENTLY ARRIVED AT Toulon was the 29-year-old Sir Sidney Smith. In a service which abounded in 'characters', Smith still contrived to stand out, becoming one of that band of senior commanders (including Cochrane, Charles Beresford and, dare one say, Nelson) who combined a wayward genius with unbounded personal courage and talent for leadership, yet who were touched by a weakness for self-publicity and a facility for making influential enemies within the establishment.

From a non-naval and not particularly wealthy background – his parents were 'trade' – Smith had been packed off into the Royal Navy at the age of 13. Following two years on the North American station, he returned as midshipman before being posted to the *Sandwich* 98, wearing the flag of Admiral Sir George Rodney. During an eventful commission he then saw considerable action, including the 'Moonlight Battle' off Cape St Vincent and at the Saintes.

Smith's obvious qualities caught the attention of his admiral, who gave him command of the 16-gun sloop *Fury*. This was in the West Indies, then a place to die as easily from disease as by enemy action. Thus, in 1782, the command of the *Alcmene* 32 fell vacant and Rodney, still greatly impressed by Smith, made him post captain. While not unique, it was certainly exceptional to find a frigate commanded by a 19-year-old, but these protracted wars did offer exceptional opportunity to exceptional men.

None the less, the end of the American War of Independence saw an immediate run-down of the fleet and a mass shift of unemployed naval officers, of whom Smith was one, to half-pay. Smith's enquiring mind drove him to spend his time travelling, and it thus happened that he was on the Baltic when, in 1789, hostilities began between Sweden and Russia. Having become acquainted with Swedish society and, as usual, having widely advertised his opinions, Smith was summoned by no less than King Gustav III himself, who invited him to serve as a squadron commander in the Swedish navy.

The Admiralty refused Smith permission to accept the appointment but, as considerable latitude was allowed for half-pay officers to 'keep their hand in', a blind eye was turned to Smith's acting as unofficial naval adviser to the king. As an 'adviser', in the widest possible sense, he was involved in a considerable amount of action and, although the Swedes profited none too well from the war, Gustav knighted Smith for his services. The honour could not be assumed without the acquiescence of the British monarch but, at the specific request of Gustav, George III invested Smith in 1792, from which point he became known in the service, with some irony, as the 'Swedish Knight'.

Still on half-pay, Smith gravitated to the Levant, attracted not only by the war then being waged between Turkey and Russia, but also by the fact that his brother, Charles Spencer Smith, was about to be appointed British ambassador to the Porte. Due to good connections already established he was also apparently engaged on an errand for the British Foreign Office.

On hearing of the French declaration of war on Britain, Smith began to make his way home for re-employment. He set about this in typical Smith style for, happening to be in the port of Smyrna, he noticed many British seamen there, unemployed. At this, he purchased a local craft ('one of the lateen-rigged, fast-sailing craft of the Archipelago'), renamed her the *Swallow Tender* and hired forty men ('truculent fellows') for crew.

Having 'sailed down the Mediterranean in search of the English fleet', Smith and his irregulars turned up at Toulon early in December. He made himself known to Hood, offered his services and (being Smith), proceeded to criticize the general conduct of the campaign. While any addition to his small fund of skilled and willing manpower must have been welcome to the admiral, the fact that Smith and his men were volunteers made their employment difficult. Smith proposed the formation of a light, inshore flotilla to harass the enemy along the coast, but Hood declined.

With the panic of 18 December, however, the admiral discovered the ideal role. As he later reported to Dundas in London:

I ordered the *Vulcan* fireship to be primed, and Sir Sidney Smith, who
joined me from Smyrna about a fortnight ago, having offered his services
to burn the ships, I put Captain Hare [of the Vulcan] under his orders,
with the Lieuts. Tupper and Gore of the *Victory*, Lieut. Pater of the
Britannia and Lieut. R.W. Miller [actually Middleton] of the *Windsor
Castle* ...

Thus, while the half-pay Smith had no official status, he now commanded
commissioned service personnel. To assist this small band with the enormous,
and extremely hazardous, task of destruction Smith was also given a mixed
flotilla of three British and three Spanish-manned 'gunboats' as well as the
Vulcan. The three British craft were crewed by 300 selected men,
commanded by the lieutenants named. Langara's vessels had a further 260
crew and were commanded by Lieutenants Riquelme, Cotiella and Trujillo.
They had in company a second fireship, the *San Luis Gonzago*.

By the time that Smith's force had secured in the arsenal, the day was
well advanced. The governor had ensured that the dockyard's massive gates
had been locked and barred for, despite the general mayhem, many of the
yard workers, having sought some protection in discarding their white
Bourbon cockades, were already trying to force their way in, in order to
prevent the allies destroying their livelihood. No doubt in their intended
action they sought also to re-establish their credentials in the eyes of the
représentants, shortly expected.

A more direct menace to Smith's men was from the crews of the French
fleet's galley flotilla, also secured in the main basin. For the most part the
dregs of the fleet, these men, 500 to 600 in number, would normally have
been confined to their craft but some, at least, appeared to be on the loose.
Taking no chances with this sullen bunch, Smith had them rounded up
and penned again in their flimsy vessels. Encouraged to keep quiet by the
simple expedient of having cannon trained upon them, they were assured
that they would be harmed only if they misbehaved. Although successful,
this measure further drained Smith's resources of both manpower and
time.

Shot and shell were now landing indiscriminately over a wide area,
most of it from the new incumbents of Malbousquet. Despite the resulting
random danger, however, Smith considered the cannonade an asset, helping

to cow the galley crews and encouraging the emerging republicans among the town's citizens to remain under cover.

As daylight faded the enemy could be seen advancing, followed shortly by his opening 'an irregular though quick fire on us from the Boulangerie [facing the west wall of the arsenal from across the tidal moat, empty at low water] and the heights which overlook it'. Worried that the enemy should realize the 'insufficiency' of his force, Smith kept the *convention-nels* at a distance with irregular bursts of grapeshot. He also stationed a gunboat and a couple of discovered field pieces to cover a wicket gate, a weakness and likely point of entry.

Meanwhile, due to 'the steadiness of the few brave seamen that I had under my command', Smith could see preparations slowly advancing with combustible matter of all descriptions being located in storehouses. Ships lying in the Petite Rade were prepared by the British, those in the two dockyard basins by the Spanish.

At about 8 p.m. the *Vulcan* fireship was brought in and secured athwart a tier of French vessels. This, for a while, also allowed her guns to command the galleys. Smith recorded that this silenced the 'tumultuous debates' of their, by now, thoroughly panicked crews, the only sounds now emanating from their craft being that of purloined tools being used to smash their fetters. This he allowed to continue in order that they could better save themselves when the arsenal was fired.

The appointed hour for firing the trains had been fixed for 9 p.m. but, according to some accounts, it had to be advanced due to a fire started prematurely by a French *boulet rouge* aimed at a nearby Sardinian frigate, the *San Vittore*, which was taking no part in the operation.

Once fired, the great storehouses were quickly ablaze. Lieutenant Tupper's men had been charged with the priority destruction of those containing pitch, tar, tallow, oil and hemp. To move things along they had also piled there a large quantity of soft timber ('deals'). The critically important mast house was well fired by Lieutenant Middleton's crew while Lieutenant Pater's worked in squads, moving around to reignite or accelerate those fires that were reluctant to spread.

The conflagration stimulated the republicans to direct a heavy but scattered fire on the arsenal, but the increasing fierceness of the heat, the noise and their concentration on the task in hand, rendered the men well-nigh oblivious to the balls whining around them. It was a calm night, with no wind to encourage a rapid spread of fire, yet Pater's men were successful to the point that Smith had to call them off for fear that they would be isolated.

In firing the *Vulcan*, the priming went off prematurely, blasting Captain Hare and Lieutenant Gore into the harbour, badly burning both. While they were being rescued, Midshipman Eales took charge to ensure that the fireship would do her work effectively, action for which he was warmly praised in Smith's report.

It was the usual practice with fireships to load the guns before firing the ship. These, as they heated, would discharge at irregular intervals. Those of the *Vulcan* must have been more of a hazard to Smith's crews than to the enemy, but were left loaded none the less.

The enemy were now all about, 'their shouts and republican songs' being clearly audible above the general racket. Covering the crews as they went about their work was a force of the Royals under army Lieutenant Iremonger. Their task was to protect the gates and walls from direct attack and, being the rearguard, they would have the dubious distinction of being the last to leave. (As it happened, they were 'saved to a man', being brought off safely by Captain Edge of the *Alert*.)

While the bulk of the Toulon squadron was berthed within the two enclosed dockyard basins, five vessels were anchored along the half-mile or so of coast between the arsenal and the Grosse Tour. Farthest removed were a pair of 32-gun frigates, *Iris* and *Montréal*, which were acting as auxiliary magazines. In them was stored the powder that had been removed from the remainder of the squadron, amounting to '*deux mille quintaux*' or, at that time, roughly 100 tons.

The two ships lay off a shore that was still in allied hands, backed by Fort la Malgue, but were the closest targets to the now republican forts on the western promontory. Fire from L'Aiguillette, only some 1,500 yards distant, persuaded the Spanish team responsible that the task of scuttling wooden ships was too time consuming, so they were fired.

As Hood later reported:

Don Langara undertook to destroy the ships in the Basin, but I am informed found it not practicable; and as the Spanish troops had the guarding [of] the powder vessels ... I requested the Spanish Admiral would be pleased to give orders for their being scuttled and sunk; but, instead of doing that, the officer to whom the duty was entrusted blew them up...

The *Iris* detonated in a cataclysmic explosion (*'un fracas épouvantable'*) that momentarily concussed both sides equally, causing a distinct lull in the otherwise continuous crackle of musketry. British craft were in the vicinity, dealing with other ships that were lying off, and suffered the blast and the initial swathe of fragments followed, for what seemed an age, by a deadly deluge of flaming, falling timber which had been shattered and projected hundreds of feet into the air. As Smith recorded '[it] nearly destroyed the whole of us'. The gunboat *Union* was 'shaken to pieces', with four men killed. Lieutenant Pater with a boat's crew narrowly escaped.

Dazed and battered, Smith and his surviving craft made back for the arsenal where, although the conflagration was extensive, much remained to be done. Nine ships of the line and three frigates were firmly ablaze, most of them in a group at the outer corner of the 'new' basin where the *Vulcan* had effectively done her work.

'I had given it in charge to the Spanish officers to fire the ships in the basin before the town [i.e. the 'old' basin where lay most of those ships 'in ordinary' or under large repair]; but they returned and reported that various obstacles had prevented their entering it', wrote Smith later. As soon as they had 'completed the business in the arsenal', therefore, Smith's weary group tried to rectify the omissions of the Spanish, but were unable to get their craft through the narrow gut that linked the two basins, owing to its being inexplicably barred by a floating boom. Working desperately but unsuccessfully to move this obstacle they came under sustained and direct fire from what Smith described as the 'flagship' and from the Batterie Royale, whose cannon had already been spiked by order of the governor. Implicit in this action is treachery from assumed loyal French personnel.

Having done all it could, the party had now to withdraw, for death stalked the arsenal in many forms and to delay further would have been folly. From beyond the walls, Buonaparte noted the scene almost with appreciation, later writing: 'The whirlpool [*tourbillon*] of flame and smoke that issued from the arsenal resembled the eruption of a volcano, while the thirteen ships that blazed in the roads were thirteen magnificent firework displays. The fire defined their masts and detail; it lasted several hours and presented a unique spectacle.' Thus were destroyed what Nelson had described as 'some of the finest ships he had ever seen'.

Through the eyes of an artist, François-Marius Granet also left his impressions. Viewing from an eminence, he noted that, beyond the sea of flame and smoke ('as red as blood'), he could see on the horizon, clearly illuminated against the black sky, 'the British and Spanish squadron sailing away in good, extended order, their lanterns lit; they had the appearance of a long procession'.

Smith's business was not yet done. As the defending rearguard slipped through the town wall via a postern near the Porte d'Italie, to make its way successfully through the chaos to the *Alert*'s waiting boats, the British demolition flotilla made for three more French ships moored offshore. One, the *Thémistocle* 74, was being used as a prison ship, having aboard a reported 260 detainees. An earlier approach had been met with hostility and Smith had moved on to more urgent business. By now, however, the prisoners had been rendered more amenable by events to which they were all too close.

Having already noted the presence of three local craft manned by republicans, Smith delivered an ultimatum – be ferried ashore or burn with the ship. Assisted by a Spanish gunboat, he was thus able to land the majority, but some preferred to swim, presumably in the direction of known friends. As it was, Lieutenant Miller stayed aboard too long in ensuring the ship's destruction and, at some risk to the others, he had to be rescued 'much scorched'.

With the *Thémistocle* was burned a further 74, *Héros*, and the frigate *Courageux*. As was too common on this frantic night, the fire on the last-named failed to take hold, leaving the ship ultimately repairable.

His work done, Smith drew off under fire in the *Swallow Tender* and three other craft. As they shaped up to rejoin the fleet, the second powder ship, *Montréal*, blew up, 'with a shock even greater than the first'. His exhausted crews again had to find what shelter they could from the awful rain of flaming debris, yet still found sufficient reserves to return ('running the gauntlet under a few ill-directed shot from the forts of Balaguier and Aiguillette') via the evacuation beach, where they embarked as many as they could carry.

Eventually arriving back aboard the *Victory*, Smith presented a startling figure, his rating's uniform badly damaged, hair bristled by heat and 'with the general appearance of an operatic devil'. He was subsequently sent to London with Hood's despatches, being 'enthusiastically received' and being 'caressed at the Admiralty and distinguished at the court of his sovereign'. Following his report and once the initial euphoria had passed, however, Smith found himself widely and unfairly blamed for his having failed to destroy more. In truth, this was much his own fault as he was victim of his own self-publicity.

Much within the arsenal was indeed saved for, once the threat of Smith's gun crews had been removed, the galley crews opened the main gates to a throng of volunteers – *ouvriers*, republican troops and men of the Marine Artillery. Then commenced a long battle with the raging fires, a battle eventually successful in saving several ships that were well ablaze. Others, threatened, were warped to safer berths. The rope-house, hemp and grain stores were rescued, as were a large tar warehouse and a gun store, the latter reputedly saved by a convict who extinguished a lighted fuse with his bare hands and who was awarded a pardon by the Convention and voted the sum of 600 livres. All the other convicts/galley crewmen who assisted in fighting the fires were also granted their freedom.

THE KEY TO THE ALLIED withdrawal was Fort la Malgue, the location of which made the eastern promontory a safe zone. Granet may have witnessed many allied ships offshore, but they were certainly not all in the process of departing. There remained about 9,000 troops to be embarked and, on Hood's orders, as many loyal citizens 'as manifested inclination to come'.

Although some disorder had been threatened by the precipitate withdrawal of the Neapolitans, their panic was not communicated to the remainder of the coalition troops who, from dusk on 18 December, began to concentrate on the beach between La Malgue and Fort Saint-Louis, a little to the west. They were not too troubled by Lapoype's republicans who kept a respectful distance from such a force, contenting themselves with conducting a ragged bombardment from such guns as remained serviceable in forts Sainte-Catherine and Sainte-Marguerite.

Admiral Hood had taken a considerable gamble with the weather, for the stretch of coast selected was open to easterlies. Fortunately, it remained calm. From the very opening of the campaign, nearly four months earlier, Captain Elphinstone of the *Robust* had played a prominent role and now, on this final night, he acted the vital part of senior beachmaster, assisted by Lieutenants Hallowell and Matthews of the *Leviathan* and the (British) *Courageux* respectively.

Ships' boats worked methodically in continuous relay to embark the seemingly endless files of troops who waded out into the dark waters, transferring them to the waiting ships, where they jostled, cheek by jowl, with such of Toulon's populace fortunate enough to have secured a place in local small craft. The *Courageux* would normally have been classed unserviceable at this time for, having touched bottom some time earlier, she had damaged her rudder. Normal procedure would have been to stem the ship in dry dock, both to repair the rudder and to examine the stern post and hanging arrangements. Now, assisted by the quiet weather conditions, the ship was anchored off and, trimmed by the bow, was the scene also of frantic effort to rehang this monster of several tons.

The files of troops gradually thinned, being finally joined by the rearguards. Great credit was attached to the very last party to embark, Sardinians under Major Koehler, who had calmly spiked the remaining guns of La Malgue before leaving. Their boats were covered by the guns of the *Romulus* frigate which, having the privilege of being the last allied ship to weigh, did so under small arms fire from republicans, many of whom had already slipped into La Malgue.

Hood was able to report that, by dawn on 19 December, all troops had been lifted 'without the loss of a man'. On this date, the *Britannia*'s log noted:

> The Boats of the Fleet embarking the Army from la Malgue, at ½ past 9 saw the Arsenal and Men of War on Fire, the Army having evacuated Toulon and retiring to the Fleet. AM at 5 Weighed and made sail, at daylight the fleet working out to sea and taking up the Boats loaded with Troops ...

If the various army contingents had been evacuated in safety and with discipline the same, regrettably, had not been the case with the citizens of Toulon.

As autumn turned to winter in 1793, few Toulonnais could still really have believed the first confident predictions of the British, that their town was the stem from which a whole new, royalist France would bloom. The greater and ever growing military presence was that of the republican armies that invested them. Then, as the slender coalition forces were obviously going nowhere beyond the defensive perimeter, apprehension had taken root, the more strongly as the fate of Avignon, Lyon and Marseille became general knowledge, stories growing with each telling. Around them, however, was every evidence of the allied fleets, which enjoyed undisputed sea control. At least, if the unthinkable occurred, there was this lifeline, a reliable means of escape.

On 18 December, however, the unthinkable *had* occurred. Across the town as the forts were abandoned, republican shot and shell crashed, exploded and burned indiscriminately. Fragments of roofing tiles scythed the streets, themselves increasingly strewn with the rubble and assorted debris of ruined homes. Fires began to spread unattended as people gathered together their essentials and, instinctively, gravitated toward the quays. Proclamations were being posted, and military patrols were occasionally met with, but official control had effectively collapsed in the face of mass fear that increasingly was turning to panic.

As ever, this was the time for opportunists, closet republicans and plain criminals. Except as deliberate shows of defiance, the optimistic white flags had disappeared; the white cockades were increasingly and openly replaced by the tricolor of the enemy as the waverers and the true revolutionary supporters revealed their hands. Old scores and the deep divisions of the past few months could now be resolved with little risk as order broke down. For those who would take advantage of even the most desperate situation, abandoned homes promised easy pickings.

Throughout the night of 18/19 December there was good money to be made by the owners of the large number of *chaloupes*, fishing craft and Leghorn traders that jostled for berthing space. As fear mounted and boatloads departed, terrified heads of families offered ever more exorbitant sums to be taken to safety – to Piedmont, Genoa or even Catalonia. Some skippers may have worked from altruism but, for the most part, the opportunities offered were too attractive to be ignored. Fortunes were both made and lost on that terrible night.

Accounts speak of a mêlée of 200 to 300 craft competing for quay space, the scene lit by the lurid orange glow reflected from the underside of low rain clouds. Mortar bombs and cannon shot added their own horrors, aimed deliberately at what the *représentants* had damned as traitors and enemies of the Revolution.

Small boats, overloaded and fighting to reach craft moored further offshore, capsized, their occupants joining the many struggling and dying in the cold, debris-strewn waters. Several vessels had been hit, themselves becoming microcosms of the general panic as crews fought to keep them afloat until they could be beached. Not all were successful. Scores, maybe hundreds, of dead were now strewn on the quays or were floating silently in the dark waters below.

Among the accusations against the evacuating powers that inevitably followed, those against the British were the most bitter. Little attempt, it was said, was made by their ships to save loyal Toulonnais, only Spanish and Neapolitan vessels being prominent. As noted already, however, only very few of Hood's squadron were actually left at Toulon, and all left well loaded. Doubtless, this was an opportunity to vilify the old enemy further.

The fact that no boats from the fleets reached the quays before 2 a.m. on the 19th was due to their first having to evacuate between 4,000 to 6,000 wounded in addition to the troops, who were the first priority. Such was the urgency that the baggage of both officers and men of several regular units had to be left behind.

At the same time, Hood's claims of up to 15,000 civilian refugees being taken off cannot be substantiated. There was later a hint of remorse as he wrote: 'I most earnestly wish more had done so [i.e. found their way aboard his ships] from the insatiable revenge that has been taken.' None the less, the logs of all his ships speak of taking aboard Toulonnais without any qualification as to number or status.

The log of the *Windsor Castle* may be taken as representative:

[T]he cutter employed in bringing off wounded men from Toulon, all other boats employed towing the *Pinto* fireship into the Arsenal [an indication that Sir Sidney Smith's men were not the only ones engaged in the hazardous task of demolition] and bringing off troops from Fort la Malgue, at 10 [i.e. 10 p.m. on the 18th] all our Troops evacuated the

Town of Toulon ... received a great number of Sardinian and British troops [and] French emigrants, at 4 [i.e. 4 a.m. on the 19th] weighed and came to sail in company with Lord Hood and the Fleet, also Admiral Turgoff [sic] in the *Commerce de Marseille* of 120 guns with the *Pompey* [sic] of 74 guns and the *Puissant* of 74 with several French frigates all the Spanish and Neapolitans fleets and a great number of small craft.

It is likely that the British evacuated about 2,000, a number endorsed by Sir Gilbert Elliot. The Spanish lifted a probable 3,000, the Neapolitans rather less. Royalist French warships and merchantmen claimed a further 2,000. Of an estimated population, therefore, perhaps two-thirds remained. Many of these, however, were sailors and arsenal workers whose support for extreme causes of any sort had always been lukewarm. They had given full-blooded support to neither the Revolution nor any restoration of the monarchy; they knew their value to the national effort and were confident of being found blameless by the avengers yet to come.

With the departure of the fleet and the convoy of overladen commercial craft the plight of the remaining committed population became all too evident. Although the artillery fire tailed off to the occasional delivery and the victorious *conventionnels* were yet to enter the town in any number, the flame, smoke and stench of the many fires, mostly left to burn, created the perfect backdrop for panic, exacerbated by the shouting and chanting from mobs of born-again republicans, rampaging, pillaging and assaulting with none to control them. As the last remaining craft completed and let go, many that were left abandoned self-control, giving way to their abject despair.

Nelson was not present at the evacuation, his *Agamemnon* yet again engaged on detached duties. Nevertheless, he was in close contact with those who were, so that his letter to the Duke of Clarence, one week later, was probably not exaggerated when he wrote:

> On the 19th, in the morning such a scene was displayed as would make the hardest heart feel; the mobs had risen, was [sic] plundering, and committing every excess; many – numbers cannot be estimated – were drowned in trying to get off; boats upset; and many put a period to their existence. One family, of a wife and five children, are just arrived – the husband shot himself. Indeed, Sir, the recital of their miseries is too afflicting to dwell upon ...

Yorke and Stevenson's account, written soon afterward, is critical of Hood who, 'fully sensible' to the plight of the royalists

> had not the means or the opportunity of bringing [them off] in the manner and with the speed he wished: it must be confessed also, that there seem to have been a want of plan and foresight ... and probably the Royalists in their extreme anxiety to get away, created a confusion which was fatal to many of them ... [crowding] to the shores and in all the violence of grief and fear, clamorously demand[ing] that protection which had been promised them on the faith of Britain.

These authors, too, give a vivid snapshot of the conditions endured by even those fortunate enough to secure a berth aboard a man-of-war.

> Scenes on board the British ships were scarcely less dreadful and appalling. In them were crowded in utter confusion and inexpressible agony and apprehensions, aged men and infants as well as women; besides the sick from all the hospitals, and the mangled soldiers from the posts just deserted, with their wounds fresh, bleeding and undressed. These scenes struck the eye on all sides while horrible screams of distraction, pain and apprehension, mixed with the lamentations of those who had lost their fathers, mothers, sisters, brothers, children and friends met the ear in every direction.

French accounts make much of the fact that the English [sic], before departing, restocked and revictualled their ships from the much-depleted reserves of the Toulon arsenal. While one would reasonably expect this to have been the case, Yorke and Stevenson note that 'to increase the distress on board the ships, they were without sufficient provision for this mixed and helpless multitude; and a great part of the provision which they actually had was almost unfit for use'.

And, on that unhappy note, a brief but unique chapter in British maritime history stuttered to its close.

chapter eight

Retribution
and Recrimination

THE PRECIPITATE WITHDRAWAL of the coalition forces from Toulon came as something of a surprise to the besieging republicans. To the west, General Dugommier had caused 4,000 ladders to be manufactured in Marseille for the purpose of a mass storming of the town walls. He had reasoned that the remaining strongpoints held by allied troops could not hold out for long and, as soon as they had been abandoned or taken, he would make his move. When the allies pulled out of these locations voluntarily on 18 December, the general thus readied his army for immediate action. Activity in the town, however, kept the French in a state of curiosity and amazement and, as the enemy was obviously withdrawing of his own accord, there was little purpose to be served in seeking a direct confrontation before he went.

Observers on higher ground could see clearly what was going on. The *livre d'ordre* of General Marescot noted:

> The noise that could be heard from Toulon indicated the disorder and despair that reigned there. The *petite rade* was covered with small craft which came and went with great frequency, embarking in haste English, Spaniards, Neapolitans, nobles, clergy, conspirators, etc. It was very clear from all this that the rebel town had opened its gates.

The hurried demolition programme was punctuated by periodic explosions, mostly a consequence of fires already raging. Those from the two powder hulks, however, and a third, most impressive, detonation as the magazine at Fort Saint-Louis was blown, created a considerable impression on the waiting republicans, who suspected that the allies were mining various points in the town in order to surprise them on their entry.

Dugommier did not endorse the mine theory, but concern was so general that he delayed moving into the town until it had been reconnoitred by a picked advance guard. This, which entered the town late in the evening, comprised 200 of the Légion des Allobroges, commanded by Adjudant-Général Cervoni. Formed only the previous year, the legion was of expatriate Swiss, Piedmontese and Savoyards, and was widely feared, having been closely associated with the 10 August massacres in Paris. They cultivated their fearsome reputation by, among other habits, reportedly removing the ears of their victims to use as hat decorations. Their inspection complete, they signalled the go-ahead for 6,000 waiting troops who began to move in at about 3 a.m. on the 19th, at about the same time as the military embarkation near Fort la Malgue entered its final phase.

General Garnier, nominated by the *représentants* as the town's commandant, made it his first duty to detach 500 men to assist the *galériens* (galley slaves) and *canonniers* (gunners) who were battling the violent fires that now threatened arsenal and town alike.

The artist Granet accompanied some of the first troops to penetrate the town, which he described as presenting a pitiful sight. Nobody was on the narrow, debris-strewn streets except a group of old women who dutifully cried '*Vive la République!*', only to attract the foulest of insults in return. Seeking a rest at one stage of his exploration, the young artist made to enter a church, only to discover, blocking the vestibule door, a heap of new corpses, defiled 'with mud and ordure'. He assumed that he had come upon some of the first victims of Barras and Fréron.

Moving cautiously, the army had reached most points in the town by midday. Preliminary assessments indicated a considerable amount of booty in *matériel* and supplies abandoned by the allies. In the town park were discovered 400 head of cattle, sheep and pigs, with adequate fodder. There were tents, artillery equipment, 100 large-calibre cannon and an estimated 40,000 charges. There were 200 Spanish horses, ready saddled and bridled. In the arsenal, despite the damage, there remained a good supply of timber for masts and spars, a large quantity of English canvas, thirty sets of sail for ships of the line and eighteen for frigates.

An early arrival at the quay was *représentant* Fréron, accompanying

General Dugua and searching for Madame Lapoype who, unknown to them, was safe elsewhere. Among the general carnage here is recorded a ship sunk with 400 aboard and many smaller craft swamped, awash or capsized.

The big effort now over, General Dugommier, the veteran professional, expressed some sympathy for those remaining in their ruined town. 'Do you see the fugitives?', he is reported as saying,

> They are the traitors of Toulon; they are those who are escaping the pun-
> ishment they deserve. Who are the guilty that remain? Women, children, the
> elderly and those men who have already shared the horrors that we inspired
> and which led the rest to flee, and who now stand, unjustly accused.

His intercession, however, counted for little against the grim formality of republican justice as interpreted and dispensed by the *représentants en mission*.

The anger of the Committee of Public Safety at what it viewed as the prolonged betrayal of Toulon could be assuaged only through terrible vengeance. Its original intention was to raze the town totally but, as this made no practical sense, penalty was exacted from its unfortunate remaining inhabitants. To expunge its shame, the town was renamed Port de la Montagne, an allusion both to its geography and to the extreme left wing of the National Convention. Interestingly, the edict announcing this change was dated '5 *nivôse* [the fourth month of the new Revolutionary calendar] *an 2 de la république française*', which date had been Christmas Day.

In the first instance, the soldiers of the republic, ill-nourished and resentful from weeks of uncomfortable siege operations, sought food, booty and any further comforts that could be extorted from the citizenry. Suffering the fate of any town sacked in this era, Toulon saw an unknown number of its people killed casually for resisting robbery or violation. There existed no accountability, for had they not all been branded traitors, Enemies of the Republic?

An early action was to round up as many inhabitants as could be found. These, led by a military band playing jaunty patriotic airs and by bearers of tricolour standards and symbolic laurel wreaths, were marched to the open space of the Place d'Armes. Here, a 'patriotic jury' of the town's Jacobins, suddenly reunited with their true beliefs, selected 200, apparently at random.

Many old scores and outstanding debts died with them as they were summarily shot against the long wall of the Cordérie, the rope house. As a warning to all, their corpses were left where they dropped.

Frustration was quickly evident, however, as the *représentants* reported to Paris that 'all those in charge, all the ringleaders [*meneurs*] and all the Marseille refugees have left, escaping in three of our best ships, under the command of the perfidious Trogoff'.

During the afternoon of 19 December, roving patrols proclaimed that all, without distinction, should congregate on the Champ de Mars, all too recently the scene of parading coalition forces. Each house was visited and any who refused were shot where they stood. Individuals, making their way as required, were hurried and humiliated with blows or by prods with sabres. Surrounded by soldiers, covered by cannon, the considerable throng was then kept waiting, each with his own fears, all expecting the worst. As darkness again gathered, the *représentants* arrived. To widespread relief, all that followed was a harangue which ended with an order for all to return to their homes to await the decision of the Convention as to what should happen next.

On the following day, all were again assembled and, on this occasion, were faced by 'jurors' largely drawn from prisoners released from the *Thémistocle*. These, soured or angered by their confinements, now had the pleasure of tormenting their erstwhile judges. Each, wearing a red Revolutionary cap and bearing a sign with the ironic label *patriotes opprimés* ('oppressed patriots'), passed slowly among the silent crowd, arbitrarily selecting their victims, who had then to move and form a group to one side. There was again a brief preparation by the troops, pleas and tears ignored, and a further crashing volley. Many were only injured and, according to French sources, there came a shouted instruction that those who could still march away would be pardoned by the state. Bloodied, the survivors fought to stand, but all they succeeded in doing was to identify those still worth further attention. A second volley finished the job.

This arbitrary slaughter at the whim of the *patriotes opprimés* was later succeeded by a more ordered fate, judicial execution at the hands of a military commission composed of '*sans-culottes Parisiens*'. Fréron not only gave every indication of relishing his employment but also wished to impress this upon the Committee of Public Safety, to which he wrote regularly. On

28 December he indicated a requirement for no less than 12,000 masons to demolish and to reconstruct the town's public buildings. In passing, he mentioned 200 executions each day to date (or, in his own chilling words: '*Tous les jours, depuis notre entrée, nous faisons tomber deux cents têtes*'), equivalent to an execution every three minutes over a ten-hour day. Then, shortly afterward, he wrote again: 'Fusillades are the Order of the Day here, the mortality being among the friends of Louis XVII … ; fusillades there will be until there are no more traitors …'

As a measure to discourage further indiscriminate pillaging of private property, the *représentants* announced a bounty of 100 livres to every soldier who had taken part in the taking of Toulon. The money, however, was to be raised by a sale of the effects of the inhabitants (though to whom remains a mystery). Each who had lived in the town throughout the rebellion was required to make an inventory of all furniture and valuables, together with their title. Each house would be visited to verify the list, and any person refusing to comply, or who submitted a false list, would be summarily punished ('*sur-le-champ*'), following judgement by the military commission, which sat in continuous session.

As the mass shootings of the first horrific days tailed off, the commission substituted its favoured instrument, the guillotine. The commission was described as comprising six members, of whom three sat in judgement. There was no public prosecutor and no jury. And no appeal. Those detained were brought directly from their cells, their name and profession noted, together with the value of their estate. Sentence was passed and the prisoner sent down to join the cart which was waiting outside the main entrance of the Palais de Justice. With the cart loaded, the commission would appear on the balcony above and publicly announce the list of sentences, whereupon their unhappy subjects would be trundled off to meet the humiliation of a public fate. Records include a 94-year-old man as well as a young mother, 'recently delivered'.

The extent of the seemingly limitless horrors visited upon the hapless citizens of Toulon is difficult to gauge accurately, although studies indicate that it was less severe than in Lyon. Of the four *représentants*, Fréron was dominant. Vindictive and boastful, he wrote continually to the Committee of Public Safety about the scale of the vengeance that he had levied yet, come the later, so-called 'Thermidorian Reaction' and the downfall of the

Jacobins, we find him backtracking vigorously, claiming that his victims numbered no more than 150. Records list about 600 executed by order of the military commission, or without trial. Such documentation is far from complete, however, and anecdotal evidence suggests an overall figure that exceeded 2,000.

For his part, General Dugommier was genuinely appalled by events in Toulon following the town's recovery. Stating that his mission had been completed, he requested that the Committee of Public Safety arrange his relief. Duly recognizing his services, this body appointed him Commander-in-Chief of the Army of the Pyrénées-Orientales and less than a month after his forces' successful assault on Fort Mulgrave he departed.

The main beneficiary of the whole affair was Buonaparte. On 22 December the *députés en mission* promoted him to the temporary rank of brigadier general, confirmed soon afterward by the Committee of Public Safety. It was well deserved for, even if he could not take personal credit for the grand plan, nor for the capture of General O'Hara (both of which he later claimed), he had shown a steadfast resolve to see the plan through and, on a tactical level, had created a chain of well-sited batteries whose continuous activity, like the long jabs of an agile boxer, slowly accumulated damage to their coalition opponents, steadily wearing them down. In creating this decisive element, Buonaparte had personally and energetically laboured against torpor and inertia in others, demonstrating the 'can-do' philosophy that would shortly catapult him into the position of head of state. For the moment, he was a 23-year-old brigadier who had greatly impressed the right people, and who was about to assume the appointment of artillery commander of the Army of Italy.

AS FOR THE TOWN of Toulon, there was a wider war in progress, and it was apparent even to the dogmatic diehards of the Paris Convention that the town, arsenal and skilled workforce comprised a national asset too valuable to squander. The French Mediterranean fleet, although hard hit by recent events, proved not to be beyond the possibility of redemption, given the political will to reconstruct it. This the Revolutionary government had in abundance.

Fréron's grand plan for razing the town centre was thus reduced to the destruction of a few symbolic buildings. The principal villains ('*scélérats*') had, to a man, departed with the allied fleets and there was a limit to how far the remaining populace could be punished for its sins against the new republic, despite the idealistic ranting of the thoroughbred Revolutionary deputies such as Louis-Antoine Saint-Just who, during the siege, had declared,

> We must govern by iron those who cannot be governed by justice ... It is impossible for revolutionary laws to be executed unless the government itself is truly revolutionary. You can hope for no prosperity as long as the last enemy of liberty breathes. You have to punish not only traitors but even those who are neutral...

Toulon and its population were, none the less, needed for the national cause. Reduced to some 15,000 by the troubles, the population began to expand rapidly with the energetic input of Jeanbon Saint-André, lately instrumental in settling the serious mutiny in the Atlantic fleet at Quiberon. Many of the town's bourgeois aristocracy, the principal employers outside the arsenal, had left as fugitives and were now proscribed. Despite this, there existed work in abundance as the Convention, with characteristic vigour, put its weight behind the civic regeneration necessary to rebuild the fleet into a credible force once more.

The French themselves were surprised at the number of their ships which had survived in a repairable condition. Most of those in the old basin, the majority of them unmasted hulls, had come through due to the inadequate attention of the Spanish demolition teams (which further convinced the British of large-scale collusion, Hood writing in his report to Henry Dundas that Admiral Langara had told 'a very respectable person' that it might be for the interest of England to burn the French fleet, but that it 'was by no means the interest of Spain'). In all, there were thirteen ships of the line and five frigates capable of being brought up to a battleworthy standard, while three more ships were under construction. Three further vessels, that had been absent on detached duty, were also now able to return.

As few of the *ouvriers* had been involved actively with the secessionists, few had felt the need to leave and, indeed, few had been punished directly. The arsenal's workforce was, therefore, largely intact and was expanded rapidly, rising to a strength of nearly 10,000 in the following six months. This was due largely to the exertions of Saint-André, who was always ready to import the necessary skills. His own technical appreciation of matters maritime may have been suspect but, as a mainspring for action, he was highly effective. At Brest he had recognized the genius of Jacques-Noël Sané in the areas of both ship design and dockyard management.

As reorganized, the arsenals were now intended to have more specific core roles. That at Brest would be fleet repair and maintenance. Ships of the line would be constructed primarily at Rochefort and frigates at Lorient. Toulon, having been brought back to its previous first-class standard, would retain its multi-purpose capability, due to its comparative isolation and its requirement to support alone the French Mediterranean squadron.

By the autumn of 1794, ten months after Hood's departure, Toulon's workforce had reached 12,000, and four line ships and a frigate were under construction there. Progress was still slow, however, due to a continuing shortage of essential materials. Most keenly felt was the dearth of major structural timber, supplies of which had been most efficiently destroyed.

Although the vengeance of a thwarted republic had been adequately demonstrated, and similar powers remained within the gift of the omnipresent Jeanbon Saint-André, there is no reason to suppose that the workforce toiled in anything other than its normal manner. Certainly, the levels of drunkenness, disobedience and absenteeism caused complaint at high management level, but appeared to indicate a workforce hardly in fear of draconian punishments.

Jeanbon Saint-André, determined to get a grip on this sturdy insouciance, strictly regularized working hours, with rolls being called. Those who worked well now qualified for incentives: those who did not, or absented themselves from their place of work, were liable for a range of punishments. Pilfering, previously viewed as a perquisite, was ruthlessly stamped upon. Had he been in a position to see, Jeanbon Saint-André would have encountered exactly the same problems in any English dockyard.

Superficial study of surviving records of Toulon may give the impression of a town that had fully returned to normal business. Closer examination, however, indicates that the majority of recorded activities, such as births and marriages, concerned individuals from outside the town. So many of Toulon's influential citizens were now in exile, scattered between Elba, mainland Italy, Corsica or Spain, that their town had been essentially repopulated by a new middle class, and also by an influx of workers, mainly from

Provence but including a significant number from other regions of France.

The Revolution continued along its variable and troubled course and, in time, the young republic began to develop a kind of normality. In April 1795 an amnesty was announced for specific classes of *émigré*, but few dared to return to Toulon. Those that did found their homes and estates sequestered, and encountered the lingering, deep divisions that would persist for a generation. The lasting legacy of the affair at Toulon lay in the extent of its permanent repopulation.

WE NOW NEED TO backtrack to the morning of 19 December 1793 when, the evacuation completed, Admiral Hood sailed a few miles down the coast to anchor off the Iles d'Hyères. Accompanying his squadron were those French ships that had been seized, ordered in two divisions under the continuing command of Rear Admiral Trogoff, and each defiantly wearing the white banner now almost eliminated on French soil.

The purpose of the stop was to identify and to redistribute, on an ordered basis, the thousands of troops and refugees, the sick and the wounded. It was also necessary to allocate an armed British party to each French ship to ensure against non-compliance. Several allied store ships, unaware of the loss of Toulon, were intercepted (although even as late as 11 January HM frigate *Juno*, all unsuspecting, entered the Petite Rade, spoke to the French, ran aground, was refloated and escaped with no casualties, some damaged rigging and two 36-pound balls in her hull).

During its stay at Hyères the fleet was struck by a considerable storm which resulted, however, in only one casualty. This was an auxiliary xebec, still laden with injured, which had to be assisted with some urgency. The craft herself was so damaged that she was burned.

Admiral Langara and the Spanish fleet sailed on 21 December, but the weather was so severe that he ordered its return. Four days later he was able to leave again for Port Mahon in Minorca, where he landed about 1,000 refugees. Thence proceeding to his Cartagena base, Langara put ashore the remainder, some 2,000 in number.

The Spanish king graciously allowed all expatriate French naval and military officers to join his own armed services in their equivalent ranks, the significant number of clergy to find employment in the archbishopric of Toledo, the artisans to settle and practice their professions, and all the orphaned children and the sick to be cared for from public funds.

Some contemporary French accounts record falsely that those refugees embarked on British ships were dumped on the Iles de Hyères and left to the eventual mercy of the republicans. This was pure fabrication, as was another story that Hood and Langara quarrelled to the extent that the two fleets were on the verge of combat. Many of the inhabitants of the islands had also declared for the royalist cause, and these were all taken aboard. Sir Gilbert Elliot wrote to his wife that he had become 'the guardian of numerous widows and a number of orphans who have scarcely a friend but me ... I will do my best to ensure that we do all we can for them ...' The assurances that he gave these and the remainder were all honoured by the British government.

Some 400 refugees were landed at Naples by a local merchantmen. They included the ex-governor of Toulon and the previous commander of the National Guard, both of whom were accepted into local society. As reward for their support, the Sardinians had been allocated two French frigates in exchange for their own. These, the *Victoire* and *Alceste*, carried their unhappy *émigré* cargoes to Oneglia and Spezia.

Captain Elphinstone, in the *Robust*, left Hyères on 6 January in company with the French First Division (*Puissant, Pompée* and *Aréthuse*), bound for Gibraltar via Porto Ferraio in Elba. Having thus distributed his refugees, he was to escort a homeward-bound convoy. Besides the Toulonnais, the ships had aboard several hundred royalist French troops, who became most unhappy at the news that they were to be landed at Gibraltar. In the face of open revolt, Elphinstone diverted to Corsica to put them ashore.

More problems, however, waited at Gibraltar, where the small local community viewed with some apprehension a large influx of French refugees. The three French warships had aboard nearly 1,000, although this figure included their greatly under-strength crews. Many were sick, while the women and children required immediate attention.

The French Second Division (*Commerce de Marseille, Topaze, Perle, Poulette,* and *Tarleton*) sailed with Hood's main fleet. The admiral had sent word to Lord Hervey, the British ambassador at Florence, to request the assistance of the Grand Duke of Tuscany. Permission was thus obtained to land refugees at Leghorn (Livorno) and more at Oneglia.

The major warships, except *Victory*, sailed on Christmas Day, Hotham's

Britannia recording: '29th December. Arrived Oneglia ...Hoisted out all the Boats and employed them landing the Sardinian Troops ... Standing off and on the Town of Oneglia, in company with the *Windsor Castle* and *Commerce de Marseille*, landing the troops as before ...'

The squadron then proceeded to Porto Ferraio, where the town of some 2,000 inhabitants was swamped by a similar number of *émigrés*. This local generosity of spirit was underpinned by a British guarantee regarding supplies and support.

Having destroyed the fortifications and magazines on Hyères, Hood also sailed for Elba, where the over-crowded conditions were already resulting in epidemics. One notable victim was Admiral Trogoff, who was interred with considerable ceremony. Never a royalist, the admiral had always fought to preserve the independence of the fleet from Jacobin influence and, could he now have been in Toulon, he would have found a nice irony in Jeanbon Saint-André echoing his own sentiments that 'Discipline must reign'. The difference was that Jeanbon Saint-André enjoyed the necessary backing of the Convention to enforce the demand, assistance that the various ministers of marine could, or would, never render Trogoff.

IF BUONAPARTE HAD been the main career beneficiary among the French, it was Elphinstone who profited most from among the British that were involved. He had demonstrated courage and leadership in the field as well as considerable tact and firmness in his various governorships. Above all, he was totally reliable, thus alleviating the great load shouldered by the commander-in-chief.

Hood rewarded him appropriately, signalling on 4 January (1794): 'With this you will receive an order [to hoist] a distinguishing pendant [i.e. commodore] ... and [I] am very happy in giving you this proof of the regard and esteem with which I have the honour to be most truly, your faithful and humble servant. Hood.'*

With respect to the Toulon operation itself, British objectives had never matched those of the French royalists. Among the nation's military commitments it was regarded by the British government as something of a

---

*Eventually being made 1st Viscount Keith, Elphinstone rose to become Admiral of the White. Although he served in turn as Commander-in-Chief Mediterranean, North Sea and Channel Fleet, he was never fortunate enough to be able to demonstrate his worth in pitched battle with the enemy.

sideshow. By the standards of the day, British casualties were not excessive, while the damage done to the republican cause went a fair way to justify the expenditure in money and *matériel*.

That neither Hood nor the British government really learned any lesson from their defeat at Toulon was demonstrated by the former immediately turning his attention to assisting Paoli's insurrection in Corsica. Operations were again successful to the extent that, in June 1794 , the French administration was again deposed. At the islander's request, King George III accepted its crown, and Lord Hood and Sir Gilbert Elliot again found themselves commissioners.

The British government's military preoccupations were still predominantly elsewhere, however, and Corsica failed to be exploited as a secure base for major operations in the Mediterranean. Buonaparte, as he rose to become France's general, harboured a desire to regain the island of his birth and, in addition to enjoying a string of military successes, found time to organize the underlying forces of rebellion that were ever a feature of the Corsican scene.

Intimidated by developments in Europe, Spain, that unreliable ally, concluded a peace treaty with France in July 1795. Supping with the devil, however, requires a long spoon and, where Spain wanted only to enter a defensive alliance, adopting a neutral stance with respect to the coalition, particularly Britain, the French Directory forced the state into active opposition. Offering in return to cede Louisiana, and to assist in the taking of Gibraltar and Portugal, France succeeded in having the Bourbons declare war on Britain in September 1796.

With the coalition itself showing every sign of disintegration, the British government ordered the new commander-in chief, Admiral Sir John Jervis, to evacuate the western Mediterranean. Corsica and Elba, thus abandoned to the French, became further examples of the general strategic incompetence of the British ministers of the time.

UPON ADMIRAL HOOD'S ability to make clear and correct decisions had rested the conduct of the campaign. He could, of course, do little about the unwillingness of the various coalition governments to provide him with adequate resources. All he could reasonably do was to use what he had in the manner best calculated to achieve his government's objectives. He can be accused of dissipating his naval strength in various expeditions of varying success but, even had he kept its strength concentrated, it would hardly have affected the outcome, which was decided militarily.

Hood suffered from his government's vacillating policies but, if his campaign was thereby continually underrated, he again must shoulder some of the responsibility for writing to Henry Dundas in over-optimistic terms, regarding both the general allied situation and Anglo-Spanish relations. The government certainly needed no further encouragement to sit on its hands. A week before Hood even entered Toulon, a youthful but perceptive Captain Horatio Nelson could observe that 'it seems of no use to send a great fleet here without troops to act with them [sic]'.

Later military historians have argued that, as a leader, the admiral displayed a contemptuous attitude toward the enemy, encouraging his officers to do likewise. This is probably acceptable criticism, but was a feature of attitudes of the time, where overt displays of almost foolhardy indifference to enemy fire were the norm, as was the common display of almost courtly manners toward a beaten enemy. Customs have simply changed.

Fortescue, in his great thirteen-volume history of the British Army, makes a considerable case of Hood's alleged arrogance toward General David Dundas and his successors in the Corsican campaign. This criticism accords ill, however, with David Dundas's own communication with Henry Dundas, immediately after the Toulon evacuation, where he speaks of the 'most perfect harmony and zeal' which had characterized the cooperation between army and navy. He speaks, too, of the efficiency with which seamen compensated for non-existent troops, particularly in the specialist field of artillery and in general, day-to-day labouring. 'It was', he said, 'the constant attention of Lord Hood to relieve our wants and to alleviate our difficulties.'

The military strategist General C. E. Callwell none the less states that General Dundas had few gifts in military leadership and that Hood had no confidence in him. He had, however, a thorough appreciation of matters military and Hood should have respected his opinion (according to Callwell) when he advised a general withdrawal 'some days before this had to be carried out in hot haste under pressure from the Republican army'. This implies that Dundas counselled evacuation at some point between the capture of O'Hara on 30 November and the opening of General Dugommier's offensive on 17 December. As, during this period, the situation was as stable as it had ever been, it is scarcely surprising that Hood chose to ignore his advice, for this would have been to evacuate in the face of just the threat of a French attack. No senior commander could have been expected to act thus, not least because it would have been professional suicide.

Keeping the coalition forces working in reasonable harmony, and worrying about and resolving the endless quibbles and hollow promises of fellow officers and statesmen, certainly took their toll of the 69-year-old Hood although, during October, Nelson was able to record that 'Lord Hood is now quite as he used to be, he is so good an Officer, that every body must respect him. All the Foreigners at Toulon absolutely worship him; were any accident to happen to him, I am sure no person in our Fleet could supply his place ...'

However well he held his forces together during those months at Toulon, Hood failed badly over the matter of the French fleet, the fundamental reason for the Royal Navy being in the Mediterranean in the first place. What appears to have been an over-developed sense of honour, bordering on naivety, resulted in his finally failing to observe the require-ments of his orders from the Admiralty to attempt 'some decisive Blow against the Naval Power of France ... and use [his] best endeavours to seek the French Fleet and bring it to action'. Having had a quarter of the enemy's total naval strength delivered to him without a shot being fired, Hood placed too much import on holding it in trust, ignoring the fact that, should the worst have happened, it should have been beyond the republicans' reach.

The campaign in Corsica soured the last few months of Hood's service with the navy to which he had devoted fifty-four years of his life. Like that at Toulon, the operation was dogged by lack of resources, but was made worse by the army being ravaged by disease. Inter-service disagreement flourished in a situation where, in Fortescue's words:

> A great part of the Navy was constantly ashore ... doing the work of soldiers, and a great part of the Army was on the fleet doing the work of sailors. Such a condition of things rarely fails to bring about friction, since it means that constant placing of seamen under the command of Generals and of soldiers under the command of Admirals.

In September 1794, his health deteriorating, Hood decided to anticipate his recall by the Admiralty and to request his relief in order to retire
from the service. Nelson typified the manner in which the services had
become polarized, writing: 'When Lord Hood quits ... I should be truly
sorry to remain ... what can be said against him, I cannot conceive, it must
be only envy ... But this comes from the Army, who have poisoned some few
of our minds.'

Early in November, having handed over his command to Hotham,
Hood sailed for home in the *Victory*, accompanied by the ex-French frigate
Sibylle, now commanded by the newly promoted Captain Edward Cooke.
They docked on 21 November, seven days after Cosby had arrived at
Spithead with the French Second Division. For Lord Hood it marked the
beginning of twenty years of contented retirement.

Epilogue

THE BRIEF OCCUPATION of Toulon by coalition forces inflicted a severe reverse on the French fleet. It should, however, have been nothing less than a catastrophe, a fact apparent when one examines the number of ships involved.

Anchored in the Grande Rade and fully ready for sea when Lord Hood arrived were seventeen ships of the line (one 120, one 80 and fifteen 74s), five frigates and eleven corvettes. In various stages of refitting in the New Basin were four ships of the line (one 120, one 80 and two 74s) and a frigate. Mainly in the Old Basin and, for the most part, awaiting middling or large repair, were eight ships of the line (one 80 and seven 74s), five frigates and two corvettes.

Of those in the first category, only the *Commerce de Marseille* 120 and *Pompée* 74 were taken by the British. Six of the 74s were totally destroyed by fire, but the *Tonnant* 80 and four 74s, although damaged in various degrees, were later repaired by the French. The remaining four 74s were those used for reparation purposes. Of the five frigates, four were taken into the service of the Royal Navy and one given to the Sardinians. Only two of the corvettes were destroyed at the evacuation. Seven had already been put into British service (of which three were to be lost during the ensuing Corsican campaign). Of the other two, one assumed the Spanish flag, the other the Neapolitan.

Of the group refitting in the New Basin, the 120-gun *Dauphin Royal* was not burned by the Spanish party detailed for the task – was she the 'flagship' mentioned by Smith as having fired upon his demolition party? –

although the 80 and one of the 74s were destroyed. The other 74, *Puissant*, under a French royalist crew, served with distinction throughout the campaign, eventually being taken over by the British. The sole frigate, although damaged by fire, was later repaired by the French.

With respect to the final group, the Spanish appear to have made little effort to carry out their task. Thus of the ships of the line, only the 80 and one 74 were total losses, the remaining six 74s being repaired by the French. From the five frigates, the *Lutine* was commissioned by the British, two were blown up when serving as powder magazines, while the remaining pair was refitted by the enemy, as were the two corvettes.

On the building ways were one 74 and a 40-gun frigate. Only the latter was destroyed.

It will be noted that, while the British commissioned, and eventually acquired, a significant number of the French ships, most of them frigates and corvettes, the Spanish took but one corvette into their service.

Of the British prizes, the huge *Commerce de Marseille* proved to be a white elephant. As was usual with French ships, she was well constructed and sailed well, but her hull form gave her an unacceptably deep draught. Worse, her scantlings proved to be inadequate, so that her hull was quickly strained by hard sailing. She was soon reduced in status, first to a store ship, then to a prison hulk, in which capacity she was broken up in 1802. More valuable was the *Pompée* 80, a Sané-designed ship whose fine characteristics went on to influence British design. She served until 1811 before also being reduced to prison service. As such, she lay in Portsmouth for many years and her name, anglicized to *Pompey*, curiously became the popular name for Portsmouth itself.

The only other line ship retained by the British, the *Puissant* 74, was never commissioned for sea service by the Royal Navy.

THE FRENCH SHIPS spared by the allies' sins of omission went on to cause considerable nuisance in the Mediterranean. It was more than appropriate, therefore, that one of Admiral Hood's most loyal admirers, Horatio Nelson, was able to rectify some of his senior's errors at the Battle of the Nile in August 1798.

Here, in Aboukir Bay, the British fleet all but annihilated the French force that had brought Buonaparte's army to Egypt. Of the enemy ships taken or destroyed, eight (one 120, one 80, five 74s and a frigate) had been among those recovered by the French following the allies' evacuation of Toulon. As they comprised two-thirds of the force that had transported the army, it has to be conceded that General Callwell had a point when he concluded that, had Hood done his job properly, there would probably have been no French invasion of Egypt.

ALTHOUGH NELSON'S GREAT victory at Aboukir was fought nearly five years after the affair at Toulon, it was not quite the last of the reverberations thus created, for there remained the important business of the prize money. The dream of every sailor, an inducement that offset to a degree the rigours and dangers of naval service, prize money was calculated in accordance with arcane rules, made the more mysterious by the government's overriding rights of interpretation. The result often meant that awards were paid a considerable time after the event. So it was with Toulon.

Hood's own proclamation that the French squadron was being held in trust, for eventual return, precluded making any claim for capture. Subsequent events, of course, dictated that such a return was no longer feasible. Good planning, and a timely removal of the ships to a place of safekeeping would, therefore, have benefited Hood as much as the British nation. As it was, some were taken, others destroyed, some only damaged. Prize money as such was not usually paid for enemy ships destroyed; yet there were exceptions, for a delighted and relieved Parliament would be pleased to reward Nelson for ships destroyed at both Aboukir and at Copenhagen. A further exception would be in the award made to Vice Admiral Sir Andrew Mitchell, whose force accepted a surrendered Dutch fleet without a fight in 1799.

Due and eventual deliberation by a Committee of the Privy Council decided that a total award of £265,336 should be made, an amount apparently calculated only on the value of the ships and stores brought away. As commander-in-chief, Lord Hood was entitled to a share of one-eighth. The award was made in 1804, over a decade after the event, and the year in which Hood celebrated his eightieth birthday. None the less, he lived long enough to enjoy it, not dying until 1816, by which time his erstwhile nemesis, now Napoleon Bonaparte, was languishing on St Helena. A task well finished.

Afterword

IT IS A RATHER FUTILE occupation to speculate on the many 'ifs' of history, but it is difficult not to detect the influence of the Toulon affair extending even to the Second World War, a century and a half later.

Following the Dunkirk evacuation in May and June of 1940, Winston Churchill moved up from First Lord to Prime Minister, presiding over a British nation that hourly expected invasion. With the capitulation of France and the entry of Italy into the war, the Royal Navy had lost a powerful ally and gained an equally formidable foe, drastically shifting the balance of naval power. Now immobilized by armistice terms, a large proportion of the French fleet lay in Toulon, still its premier base in the Mediterranean. In various ports of the French colonies in Africa, however, lay further squadrons and units of the French navy. Those at Mers-el-Kebir (Algeria) and at Dakar (Senegal) were particularly powerful.

From a British perspective, there appeared every chance that the Germans would fail to honour the terms of their armistice with France, seizing the Toulon fleet to compensate for the considerable deficiencies in their own. In such an eventuality, an already unfavourable balance of power would shift even more disastrously against the Royal Navy.

Churchill was renowned for his deep sense and understanding of history and its lessons. He undoubtedly knew of the extent to which the French ships allowed to survive by Lord Hood so long before had continued to be a nuisance. He understood that, to minimize risk, the detached French squadrons must at all costs be prevented from joining the main fleet at Toulon. There was no room for half-measures, particularly at Mers-el-Kebir, where the squadron was within a day's steaming of Toulon.

On 3 July 1940, therefore, the Admiralty ordered the heavy ships of Force H, under Admiral Somerville, to proceed to Mers-el-Kebir. Discussion began in an air of great urgency, the French senior officer, Admiral Gensoul, informing the British that under no circumstances would he allow his squadron to fall into enemy hands. The British responded that, while they did not doubt French intentions, they believed that the Germans could not be relied upon to abide by the terms of the armistice. Accordingly, Gensoul was presented with an ultimatum, with the options of joining the British to fight on as allies, to sail to a British port for internment, to sail to a French Caribbean port for supervised demilitarization, or to scuttle his ships where they lay. Failing acceptance of any of these, he would be fired on by the British.

French pride had already been badly hurt by their defeat, and Gensoul almost certainly did not wish to be seen as a latter-day Trogoff, supinely handing over his squadron to the British while under threat. He prevaricated for hours, communicating with Paris as Somerville's capital ships stood off and on, in imminent danger from submarine attack.

Under heavy pressure from his government to resolve the issue, Somerville none the less continued the parley for nearly ten hours before being obliged, as a last resort, to open fire. The action was brief. Within minutes, nearly 1,300 Frenchmen lost their lives. By supreme irony, Somerville was wearing his flag in the battle cruiser HMS *Hood*. It had been a demonstration of ruthless violence, but it served to inform the world that Britain had the will to fight on.

France then lay partitioned and in the unoccupied south the Toulon fleet lay idle for twenty-eight months, except for such activity as it was permitted under the terms of the armistice. Then, in November 1942, the allies landed in North Africa and, on that pretext, Axis forces rolled into the French south. Toulon proved to be the primary objective and, on the 14th, there occurred a near re-enactment of the panic events of 1793, the fleet being scuttled even as the German army stormed into the arsenal.

This action confirmed two things. First, that the French *did* keep their word in doing everything possible to keep their fleet from falling into enemy hands, but second, it showed that the British suspicions had been right in assuming that, given the right circumstances, the enemy would not hesitate to try to seize it. Churchill, despite the enormity of the act at Mers-el-Kebir, had been right.

Select Bibliography

Allerdyce, Alexander, *Memoir of the Hon. George Keith Elphinstone, KB, Viscount Keith, Admiral of the Red* (Edinburgh and London: Wm. Blackwood & Sons, 1882)

Bertaud, Jean-Paul (trans. R. R. Palmer), *The Army of the French Revolution. From Citizen-Soldiers to Instrument of Power* (Princeton: University Press, 1988)

Brenton, Edward Pelham, *The Naval History of Great Britain from 1783 to 1836* (London: Henry Colburn, 1837)

Callwell, General C. E., *Military Operations and Maritime Preponderance: Their Relations and Interdependence* (London: Blackwood, 1905)

Chevalier, Edouard, *Histoire de la marine française sous la première République* (Paris: Hachette, 1886)

Clowes, Sir William Laird, *The Royal Navy. A History* (7 vols.) (London: Sampson Low, Marston & Co., 1897–1903)

Cormack, William S., *Revolution and Political Conflict in the French Navy. 1789–1794* (Cambridge: University Press, 1995)

Cottin, Paul, *Toulon et les Anglais en 1793, d'après des documents inédits* (Paris: Paul Ollendorff, 1898)

Crook, Malcolm, *Toulon in War and Revolution. From the ancien régime to the Restoration. 1750–1820* (Manchester: University Press, 1991)

Fortescue, The Hon. J. W., *A History of the British Army* (13 vols.) (London: Macmillan & Co., 1906)

Hampson, Norman, *A Social History of the French Revolution* (London: Routledge, 1956)

Hampson, Norman, *La Marine de l'An II. Mobilisation de la Flotte de l'Océan. 1793–1794* (Paris: Libraire Marcel Rivière, 1959)

Herbert, John Beresford, *Life and Services of Admiral Sir Thos. Foley, GCB, Rear Admiral of Great Britain* (Cardiff: Daniel Owen, 1884)

Hibbert, Christopher, *The French Revolution* (Harmondsworth: Penguin Books, 1982)

Hood, Dorothy, *The Admirals Hood* (London: Hutchinson, 1941)

Hoste, Lady Harriet, *Memoirs and Letters of Captain Sir Edward Hoste, Bart, RN KCB KMT* (2 vols.) (London: Richard Bentley, 1835)

Hutt, Maurice, *Chouannerie and Counter Revolution: Puisaye, the Princes and the British Government in the 1790s* (2 vols.) (Cambridge: University Press, 1983)

Innes, Mary C., *A Memoir of William Wolseley, Admiral of the Red Squadron* (London: Kegan Paul, Trench, Trübner, 1895)

James, William, *The Naval History of Great Britain* (5 vols.) (London: Richard Bentley, 1822–1824)

Lacour-Gayet, Georges, *La marine militaire de la France sous le règne de Louis XVI* (Paris: Honoré Champion, 1905)

Lavery, Brian, *Nelson's Navy: The Ships, Men and Organisation 1793–1815* (London: Conway Maritime Press, 1989)

Lewis, Michael, *The Navy of Britain: A Historical Portrait* (London: George Allen & Unwin, 1948)

Mahan, Captain Alfred Thayer, *The Influence of Sea Power upon the French Revolution and Empire 1793–1812* (Boston: Little, Brown & Co., 1892)

Maurel, Paul, *Histoire de Toulon* (Toulon: Libraire Edouard Mont Barbon, 1943)

Morriss, Roger, *The Royal Dockyards during the Revolutionary and Napoleonic Wars* (Leicester: University Press, 1983)

Pons, M. Z. (ed.), *Mémoirs pour servir à l'Histoire de la Ville de Toulon en 1793* (Paris: C. J. Trouvé, 1825)

Rose, J. Holland, *Lord Hood and the Defence of Toulon* (Cambridge: University Press, 1922)

Smith, Sir Sidney, *Memoirs of Sir Sidney Smith, KCB, etc* (2 vols.) (London: Richard Bentley, 1839)

Steel, David, *Naval Chronologist of the War: From its commencement in February 1793 to its conclusion in 1801* (Reprint) (London: Cornmarket Press, 1969)

Index